The Andy Clyde
Columbia Comedies

The Andy Clyde Columbia Comedies

JAMES L. NEIBAUR

McFarland & Company, Inc., Publishers
Jefferson, North Carolina

ALSO BY THE AUTHOR AND FROM MCFARLAND

The Hal Roach Comedy Shorts of Thelma Todd, ZaSu Pitts and Patsy Kelly (2018); *The W.C. Fields Films* (2017); *The Jerry Lewis Films: An Analytical Filmography of the Innovative Comic*, by James L. Neibaur and Ted Okuda (1994; paperback 2013); *Chaplin at Essanay: A Film Artist in Transition, 1915–1916* (2008); *Arbuckle and Keaton: Their 14 Film Collaborations* (2007); *The RKO Features: A Complete Filmography of the Feature Films Released or Produced by RKO Radio Pictures, 1929–1960* (1994; paperback 2005); *The Bob Hope Films* (2005)

Frontispiece: **Drawing by James L. Neibaur**

LIBRARY OF CONGRESS CATALOGUING-IN-PUBLICATION DATA

Names: Neibaur, James L., 1958– author.
Title: The Andy Clyde Columbia comedies / James L. Neibaur.
Description: Jefferson, North Carolina : McFarland & Company, Inc., Publishers, 2018 | Includes bibliographical references and index.
Identifiers: LCCN 2018026978 | ISBN 9781476668604 (softcover : acid free paper) ∞
Subjects: LCSH: Clyde, Andy, 1892–1967—Criticism and interpretation.
Classification: LCC PN2287.C N549 2018 | DDC 791.4302/8092—dc23
LC record available at https://lccn.loc.gov/2018026978

BRITISH LIBRARY CATALOGUING DATA ARE AVAILABLE

ISBN (print) 978-1-4766-6860-4
ISBN (ebook) 978-1-4766-3097-7

© 2018 James L. Neibaur. All rights reserved

No part of this book may be reproduced or transmitted in any form or by any means, electronic or mechanical, including photocopying or recording, or by any information storage and retrieval system, without permission in writing from the publisher.

Front cover photograph: Andy Clyde in *Love Comes to Mooneyville*, 1936 (author's collection)

Printed in the United States of America

McFarland & Company, Inc., Publishers
 Box 611, Jefferson, North Carolina 28640
 www.mcfarlandpub.com

For Greg Hilbrich and Rich Finegan.
Thanks, guys.

Acknowledgments

Thanks to Katie Carter who lives each book with me, screening the films and offering valuable insights for each. Her understanding of the cinematic process and appreciation for its performers and filmmakers help elevate every project.

Thanks also to Terri Lynch, my longtime assistant and collaborator, whose contribution continues to be invaluable.

Thanks to those who provided so many important materials that made this book possible: Greg Hilbrich, Richard Finegan, Steve Randisi and my longtime friend and collaborator Ted Okuda.

Special thanks to people and organizations that helped provide materials and information for this book: George Willerman and Rosemary Hanes at the Library of Congress, Rita Belda and Kimberlee Granholm at SONY and Ron Hutchinson of the Vitaphone Project.

Thanks to the late Adrian Booth, who as Lorna Gray co-starred in a film with Andy Clyde and shared her delightful memories with me only months before she passed away at the age of 99. Thank you to Frank Reighter, who arranged this phone interview only days before he passed away. Also thanks to Jon Provost, who worked with Andy Clyde on the *Lassie* TV series and shared his memories. Finally, thanks to the late Emil Sitka, Jules White, Elwood Ullman, Edward Bernds and Russell Hayden for sharing their thoughts about Andy Clyde many years ago; their memories are seeing print for the first time in these pages.

Also thanks to Max Neibaur, Laurie Jacobsen, Leah Smith, Mike Schlesinger, James Zeruk, Jerry Lewis, Kyle J. McElravy, Paul Gierucki, Brent Walker, Kelly Parmelee and Allie Schulz for their contributions, encouragement and support.

Table of Contents

Acknowledgments vi

Preface 1

I. Before Columbia 3

II. The Columbia Comedy Shorts 10

III. Clyde in Feature Films 192

IV. Clyde on Television 194

Notes 197

Bibliography 199

Index 201

Preface

As time progresses and we move further from the early days of cinema, a lot of once-popular individuals in film history become crowded out by time and events. The especially big names whose impact as filmmakers reached a truly extraordinary level (Georges Méliès, Edwin S. Porter, Auguste and Louis Lumière, D.W. Griffith, Mack Sennett, Charlie Chaplin, Buster Keaton *et al.*), are kept alive at least from a scholarly-academic perspective; their most noted works dot university film studies. Some larger cities offer occasional screenings of silent films with live musical accompaniment in a socio-historical manner for those who might want to experience something similar to early movie exhibition. However, it is important to explore past those parameters, to expand one's frame of reference beyond the immediate.

Popular short comedies featuring the Three Stooges and Our Gang (The Little Rascals) are still on television. But history has forgotten a comedian like Andy Clyde, who was a pioneer in the days of silent movies, a top star in short comedies like the Stooges and Rascals had been. His career extended to feature films and television until his passing in 1967. Clyde is known by the comedy film buffs who make an effort to learn about cinema's history, but this is far outside the mainstream.

Sometimes the point of film scholarship is to investigate ideas that have received little attention elsewhere. This book focuses on the most interesting and potentially accessible portion of Clyde's career: his long-running series of comedy two-reelers for Jules White's short subject unit at Columbia Pictures. With Clyde starring in nearly 80 productions, it was the second-longest and second-greatest series for Jules White after the ever-durable Three Stooges.

In fact, it is due to the Stooges that Clyde has any mainstream recognition at all. Sony Home Video released a high-definition DVD box set of the entire Stooges catalogue, from their first Columbia comedy *Woman Haters* (1934), right up to their first feature-length movie for the kiddie market in 1959. An extra disc offered solo work by Stooges Shemp Howard, Joe Besser and Joe DeRita, each of whom starred in his own films before joining the trio. Among these solo shorts are a few Andy Clyde comedies in which Shemp Howard appears. Beautifully restored and enhanced by Shemp's presence, Clyde's comedies emerge as very funny and spotlighted a delightfully appealing star comic.

Clyde's Columbia two-reel comedies constitute a long, creative and consistently enjoyable series that remains amusing and enjoyable in the 21st century. This book aims to make that case by reviewing each production in the series. It will explore each of the Clyde short comedies for Columbia, film by film, examining common themes, Clyde's reaction to the studio's methods and his ability to sustain his character over a long period of time. Opening chapters will offer an overview of Clyde's silent and early sound shorts which led up to his Columbia series. Concluding chapters will summarize Clyde's many feature film appearances, including a recurring role in the popular Hopalong Cassidy westerns, and his work on the TV shows *Lassie* and *The Real McCoys*.

As we take a careful look at Clyde's Columbia comedies, our discoveries will not fall within the realm of lofty cinematic artistry as found in the work of Chaplin or Keaton. Instead the films we examine will be pure entertainment with an appealing, amusing central character from which all points of plot, narrative and conflict will stem. We will look at the Columbia short comedy style, the approaches of different directors and Clyde's own substantial contribution.

Clyde's short comedies for Columbia are, for the most part, well-constructed slapstick vehicles with good writers, good directors a skillful leading comedian with a very likable character, and top-level supporting players. Each film has its own process and that is what we will examine.

I

Before Columbia

Early Life

Andrew Allen Clyde was born on March 25, 1892, in Blairgowrie, Perthshire, Scotland. His father was John Clyde, Scottish actor and owner of the John Clyde Stock Company, a popular outlet for theatrical productions throughout the area. He had six children, and when a child was needed in a particular production, one of his own would invariably be used. Thus, Andy grew up on stage, taking a variety of roles throughout his childhood and teen years, working hard to please his rather stoic father.

At the age of 18, Andy was given a strong role in one of his father's productions and rehearsed carefully. On opening night, he turned in an outstanding performance, and afterward was congratulated backstage by everyone, from cast and crew to various audience members. While accepting the accolades, Andy looked around for his father, as it was his approval he truly sought. Finally, John Clyde made his way through the backstage crowd and gave Andy the unsmiling order to be at rehearsal the next day to go over his lines, and then left the area just as quickly, offering no further reaction to his son's performance. Andy's spirit was crushed. Following the run of this play, he left acting and became a stockbroker. While successful in this position, he often found that he missed the theater. It was in his blood. But whenever he entertained the notion to return to the stage, he reminded himself of the heartbreaking incident with his father and the pain would be enough to overcome his theatrical desires.

It took a few years, but Andy did eventually return to the stage, and not with his father's company. He worked successfully in other stock companies, eventually finding his way to London. Andy's talents were not limited to his wide range and versatility as an actor. He'd also learned about stage makeup while working for his father, and by the time he was 20 he had become something of a creative expert in that field.

Coming to America

Clyde first came to America in 1912 with Graham Moffatt's traveling company for the vaudeville-style play *The Concealed Bed*. He continued to work on various theater projects until 1919, when James Finlayson, a fellow Scotsman with whom he'd appeared in several plays, beckoned for him to come to Los Angeles to act in the movies. Finlayson had been hired the previous year by Mack Sennett and was appearing in comedies for his studio. Finlayson believed that Clyde would be a good fit for the company, and Sennett was ready to see what he had.

Clyde joined the Sennett company in 1920 and made his debut the following year in the comedy *On a Summer Day*. Sennett was impressed with the ease Clyde exhibited when doing slapstick, and would use him often in bit parts to punctuate gags. Eventually, Clyde's prowess with makeup became noted. Andy was acting on location at the docks near

Andy Clyde was unrecognizable without his trademark makeup.

the Los Angeles harbor. After one scene, he snuck behind a pile of lumber and changed his makeup. When he returned, the director did not recognize him until he was told. Andy did this again and again, a total of around six times, during the course of the production, bringing a new character into the scene each time. Since it was an ensemble crowd scene that was almost fully improvised, this helped expand the sequence's scope, improving it discernibly.

Sennett liked performers who had abilities in other areas, and was especially pleased with the fact that Clyde could play several different roles in one film, using different makeup for each. Working in support of such stars as Harry Langdon and Ben Turpin, and being teamed in a few movies with Billy Bevan, Clyde honed his comic skills and enhanced his makeup artistry to the point where he became a presence in many of the studio's most popular productions. In the year 1927 alone, he made appearances in over 20 movies, ranging from starring roles to quick gag bits.

By the mid–1920s, even the critics noticed. In its February 21, 1925, issue, *The Exhibitor's Trade Review* said of Clyde's film *Water Wagons*[1]:

> Needless to say, some laughs are provided, not the least of which is when Captain Andy Clyde, after seeing his daughter plunged into the water, stops to lift her out by her legs. He lifts out two stuffed limbs instead with a sign attached: "Two miles to Jones' department store."

There are many highlights in Andy Clyde's silent screen career. One of the more noted comedies from this time was the two-reeler *Whispering Whiskers* (1926). (It was retitled *The Railroad Stowaways* when it was reduced to one reel and released by Castle Films as an 8mm subject sold in department stores.) Clyde is teamed with Billy Bevan and they were directed by Del Lord, one of Sennett's most talented craftsmen. As two hobos traveling by train, Bevan and Clyde engage in slapstick and perform effectively as a unit. Lord also directed Bevan and Clyde in the very funny *Ice Cold Cocos*, in which they play ice delivery men.

Bevan and Clyde were paired frequently, with Andy often cast as the irate father of a leading star (Madeline Hurlock's father in *Water Wagons*, Ben Turpin's father in *The Prodigal Bridegroom*). But even in these supporting roles, Clyde still registered with viewers.

By the later 1920s, Clyde had created a makeup that he felt was just right for his character. Graying his hair, affixing a large mustache, letting a grizzly stubble grow, and donning eyeglasses, Clyde developed an old man character that continued to make him one of the most popular comedians on the Sennett lot. He dubbed his character Pop Martin, and he became as popular by that name as his own.

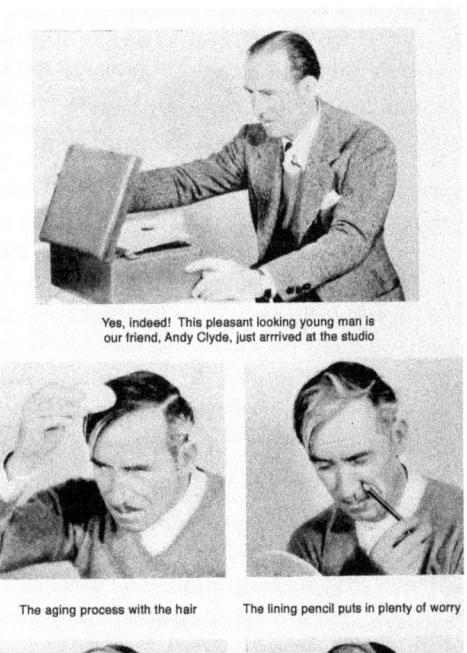

Yes, indeed! This pleasant looking young man is our friend, Andy Clyde, just arrrived at the studio

The aging process with the hair   The lining pencil puts in plenty of worry

Glue comes next   And then the crowning glory

The process of how Andy applied his makeup was of interest to his fans.

From Silent Movies to Sound

Once the silent era ended, Sennett began producing sound comedies to be distributed by Educational Pictures. Clyde's years on stage made him comfortable in speaking roles, so he developed a verbal delivery that fit his old man makeup. Underneath the guise, Clyde was still a relatively young man. For audience members, seeing what seemed to be an old man character do wild pratfalls made the slapstick even more outrageous.

Clyde's comedies continued to register with audiences. *Hello Television* (1930) was an innovative look at a young couple (Nick Stuart and Ann Christy) meeting and falling in love via TV. This short was quite visionary for its time and became one of the more successful Clyde films.

The Bluffer (1930) was another groundbreaking two-reeler because it was filmed in color. Advertisements heavily touted this fact, but critics felt the film was just fine without it. The January 1930 issue of *Screenland* said that *The Bluffer* was "a funny comedy with the aid of color—as if it needed it." In its November 1930 issue, *Film Daily* stated:

> [This is the] first of the Mack Sennett Brevities, one-reelers done in Mack Sennett's Natural Color process. The color is very well handled and looks like a real novelty in the comedy short field., combined with the comedy antics of Andy Clyde. Clyde carries this easily for the comedy and the color peps it up, adding a lot of class to a nifty short.[2]

A salary dispute with Sennett caused Clyde to leave his longtime employer and finish the last two years of his contract working for producers Al Christie and E.H. Allen. The shorts continued to be released by Educational Pictures. Andy's comedies remained popular, and his well-meaning, fidgety Pop Martin character continued to be likable.

Perhaps the most notable Clyde short from this period is *Dora's Dunking Doughnuts* (1933), chiefly because it contains an early appearance by Shirley Temple. The film features Andy as an earnest, befuddled but well-liked schoolteacher whose girlfriend owns a doughnut stand. When she invents "the greatest doughnut" (it soaks up almost an entire cup of coffee when dunked), Andy gathers his talented students and puts together a radio show. The show is a hit and becomes a series.

There are musical bits, slapstick gags and a few fleeting opportunities for Temple to be singled out and work directly with Andy. Some of the humor is absurd. At one point, Andy asks his class to sing a note and hold it until he tells them to stop. A hand-delivered note summons him to the doughnut stand and he forgetfully rushes to Dora, leaving the students holding the note. After he plays an entire scene where Dora shows him her new doughnut

I. Before Columbia

Trade ad for *The Bluffer*, a Mack Sennett comedy in color.

recipe, the kids come marching to the stand from school, still dutifully holding the note until Andy permits them to stop. When Temple became a star in her own right, the film was re-released, giving her top billing. One charming footnote to this comedy was a blurb that appeared in the September 1933 issue of *Photoplay*:

Andy Clyde ate so many doughnuts while making *Dora's Dunking Doughnuts* he had to go on a diet. In one scene he ate four. The scene was shot from four angles and retakes had to be made. Add em up yourself.[3]

One of the aspects of Andy's character in these Educational releases was his ability to become fearlessly aggressive against a larger man (usually Bud Jamison). In *Dora's Dunking Doughnuts*, he attacks Bud and starts choking him, believing he ruined the radio act (in fact it was a success). In *His Weak Moment*, he is intimidated by Bud throughout the film until the end, when he realizes Bud's earlier gun purchase was merely for a lipstick ad. Reacting to the misunderstanding, Andy grabs a rifle and chases Bud down the street, shooting at him.

Andy Clyde and Shirley Temple rest between scenes on the set of *Dora's Dunking Doughnuts* (1933).

Andy Joins Columbia Pictures

In 1934, Clyde considered an opportunity to make short subjects for producer Jules White at Columbia. White was building a comedy stable and wanted Clyde to be among his first hires. Andy had married Elsie Tarron, a former Mack Sennett Bathing Beauty, in 1932 when he was 40 years old. He wanted children, so he sought a grounded series that would sustain his career. Columbia looked like a good place for this, and so he negotiated a contract with White rather easily.

White was first active doing the Mermaid comedies started by his older brother Jack, a comedy writer and director. He supervised short subjects at MGM with his partner Zion Meyers, creating the Dogville Comedies in which trained dogs were dressed and placed in dramatic situations with overdubbed voices. This outrageous novelty was popular; one of the films, *The Dogville Melody* (1930), was such a hit at an Indiana theater that the audience insisted it be run twice! White and Meyers also wrote and directed an MGM Buster Keaton feature, *Sidewalks of New York* (1931).

White was hired by Columbia president Harry Cohn to head a short subject unit at that studio. White got right to work hiring the best comedy stars, directors and writers whom he knew were available. In its June 19, 1934, issue, *Variety* announced, "Columbia has closed deals with Leon Errol, Harry Langdon, Andy Clyde and Walter Catlett. Each will be used in a series of six two-reel comedies." White also hired the Three Stooges, Moe Howard, Larry Fine and Jerome "Curly" Howard, who had left their mentor Ted Healy, and accepted other comedians with proven track records to help build his unit.

Clyde had been enjoying success in comedies for so long, he was already a comfortable fit with a studio that emphasized violent slapstick. White was very aware of Clyde's consistent success in short comedies since the silent era. White told this author, "Andy was one of those comedians who we hired because he already had a career in pictures. He worked for Sennett and came to us with all that experience and talent. We hired him right away."[4] Clyde signed a contract with White under the condition that he was not expected to limit his work to Columbia, and could take on other roles if they did not interfere with this production schedule. White agreed to this, and offered Clyde $500 per short, with the opportunity for salary advancement if the comedies achieved consistent success. Satisfied with all negotiations, Clyde went to work on his first short production for Columbia.

At Columbia, Clyde made what is arguably his best comedy films. However, even with his success, Andy never completely let go of the hurtful experience with his father when he was a young man. According to Emil Sitka, who acted often with Andy Clyde, "We used to ride to work together on the same bus. He didn't really talk much about the weather, sports or anything like that. He was constantly going over his lines. Everything had to be perfect."[5]

II

The Columbia Comedy Shorts

Andy Clyde made nearly 80 two-reel comedies for Columbia, while at the same time appearing in feature films and even occasional shorts at other studios. There will be chapters at the end of this book discussing his feature film appearances and later work in television; the bulk of this text will examine each of the Clyde comedies made for Columbia's short subject department.

Not all of the Andy Clyde shorts for Columbia were truly original. Several of the later ones are remakes of earlier productions. Beginning in the late 1940s, Columbia's comedy shorts' budgets were drastically reduced. In a cost-cutting measure, White would often take films made years earlier, retitle them, replace a few old scenes with newly shot ones, and market it as a new release. This was often done with the Three Stooges. For instance, their film *He Cooked His Goose* (1952) featuring Shemp Howard as the Third Stooge was re-used as *Triple Crossed*, a 1958 subject featuring Joe Besser, who took the Third Stooge role after Shemp passed away. All of the footage in *Triple Crossed* is from *He Cooked His Goose*, except the scenes with Shemp were removed, re-shot with Joe, and edited in. Mary Ainsley, who acted in the former film, was no longer with the studio, so her scenes with Shemp were replaced by a double, Connie Cezan, who keeps her back to the screen and has Ainsley's dialogue dubbed in. This allowed White to stay well under budget as television began making short comedies obsolete.

It was even easier to do this with Andy Clyde comedies. Andy was wearing the same old man makeup in 1934 as he was in 1954. So when he made *Marinated Mariner* (1950), it was really just *The Peppery Salt* (1936) with only a few minutes of new footage. This happened several times in Clyde's filmography toward the end of this Columbia tenure. So the assessments will be more limited on these chapters, other than to acknowledge that the film is a remake, with ample stock footage, and identify the new scenes.

For each entry, credits will be provided. In the remakes, there are cast members only seen in the stock footage. Sometimes this means that an actor who was deceased when the remake was produced will be visible in the older footage. For instance, in the Three Stooges film *Pies and Guys* (1957), a remake of *Half-Wits Holiday* (1946), Symona Boniface is prominent in the older footage seven years after her death.

In the case of Andy Clyde's later remakes, there is the odd situation where Bennie Bartlett appears as a child in the film *Swing You Swingers* (1939) and again, via stock footage, in the remake *Tootin' Tooters* (1954). However, by 1954, a grown-up Bartlett was appearing in the Bowery Boys comedies for Allied Artists. It might have been quite unsettling for his fans to see him so young in an ostensibly new release in 1954.

There is also the occasional situation where supporting players from the older movie will be hired to appear in the later footage. When the Clyde comedy *A Bundle of Bliss* (1940) was remade as *A Blissful Blunder* (1952), the studio went so far as to hire actor Fred Kelsey, who appears in the earlier movie, to repeat his role in the remake's new footage.

Finally, there are a number of comedies for which no copy was available to me. In these cases, it will be noted that the film is inaccessible and we will offer as much information as our research uncovers. In some instances, there are picture and sound negatives housed at the Library of Congress, but no screening print. Sadly, in a few cases, there isn't even any pre-print material available and the film is considered lost. All of these issues will be addressed in the text.

It's the Cats

Directed by Al Ray; *Story and Screenplay:* Andrew Bennison; *Produced by* Jules White; *Cinematography:* Henry Freulich; *Editor:* Al Clark; *Cast:* Andy Clyde, Dorothy Granger, Inez Courtney, Del Henderson, James C. Morton, Sam Lufkin, Kay Hughes, Frances Morris, Ceil Duncan, Mary Foy, William Irving, Raymond Brown; *Shooting Dates:* August 23–28, 1934; *Released on* October 11, 1934; *Columbia Production Number:* 151

Jules White secured the services of Andy Clyde and knew he had hired a true veteran of physical comedy who would fit neatly into the unit he was rapidly building. Therefore, Clyde was given a great deal of creative freedom, and worked closely with the filmmakers on all of his two-reelers.

It's the Cats features Andy as a loyal, hard-working man asked by his boss to attend a meeting of the Homeless Cats Society (the boss' cat-loving

Andy parties with Dorothy Granger and Inez Courtney in *It's the Cat's* (1934).

wife is a member). The boss dislikes cats, but wants to humor his wife. However, since she will not be in attendance, he plans to send Andy instead. Andy is to impersonate the boss, make a donation and give a prepared speech. However, Andy gets sidetracked into a banquet where there's drinking and carousing. He sits with two attractive women and has a few drinks before realizing he is in the wrong place. When he drunkenly stumbles into the correct meeting, he quickly starts giving his speech, but lines like "whose going to rub up against your leg at night" appall the staid cat lovers and he is thrown out by security. Stumbling back into the banquet, he is arrested in a raid under his boss' name and the publicity causes his boss' wife to leave him. But the boss is not angry with Andy; he comes to his house to thank him for this freedom.

Clyde had already established his niche as a flustered old man who finds himself in embarrassing situations, so with his first Columbia short, he utilizes that same structure. What sets it apart is producer Jules White's vision, which emphasizes physical comedy over situational. Clyde's Keystone training made him fully equipped to handle this sort of knockabout humor, while at the same time getting humor from the situations.

II. The Columbia Comedy Shorts 13

It's the Cats opens with Andy's boss (Del Henderson), on the phone with his wife, angrily agreeing to donate to, and appear at, the cat society meeting. When he calls for Andy, his secretary indicates that Andy has not yet arrived at work. The boss snarls, "He's never been late in 20 years, so he's either here somewhere or dead!" In fact, Andy's watch has stopped for the first time in 20 years, so he is indeed late. He hurries out the door, muttering to himself, but while running to catch a cab, his umbrella opens and the wind draws him backwards. The umbrella gag is a good example of the physical humor that fills *It's the Cats*, and gives it the Columbia stamp. It is slapstick, but not the sort of aggressive type of physical-violent humor of the Three Stooges.

Clyde makes great use of facial expressions and hesitant gestures around his boss to further show that this is an innocent character in over his head, immediately endearing him to the audience. There is one delightful moment when he laughs at his boss' snide remark about his wife going to live in a home for cats, but his boss glares at him instead of laughing with him. Andy's facial expression in reaction to this is wonderful comic nuance that is far better seen than described.

Another amusing visual bit is rather subtle. Andy finally has a chance to wear his best suit, and pulls it out of the closet. It is wrapped in newspaper with headlines that announce a war in Spain. When the papers are removed, the suit is infested with moths. Andy tries to brush it, and it disintegrates into tatters.

The situations allow Andy to put himself in embarrassing predicaments. But because he is drinking at the banquet, he does not respond with embarrassment. Instead, he rather boldly and confidently starts to give his prepared pro-cat speech. It is especially amusing when he does so in the correct venue, because his drunkenly blurting out phrases that are innocent but can be taken otherwise cause a delightfully funny reaction from the women.

Andy also gets to have some fun in the banquet scenes where he starts drinking. He is seated with two pretty girls, and has the sort of "whoopee," "hot ziggety" reaction that an oldtimer would in such a situation. The young women believe him to be an important businessman and humor him. Andy responds as if they are, indeed, interested in him. The situations allow for the humor in this scene, and it is one of the more amusing ones in the short.

There are a few minor touches that add to the amusement of each scene. For instance, when Andy hurries to work, he has several papers in his hands. These are not identified, but it stands to reason that they have some importance to his business. When he finally arrives at work, after the tumult of being late, the papers have been reduced to several wads and are thrown upon his desk. Another quick slapstick bit has Andy preparing to leave for the meeting, tying a scarf around his neck but unwittingly fastening it to the bureau behind him. When he takes a step forward, the bureau falls on top of him, knocking him to the floor.

There is one unrelated tangent. As Andy heads to the meeting, he is stopped by two acquaintances who are putting in a plate glass window. Andy is asked to hold the glass in place while they get some necessary tools. He does so, but is accosted by a dog who playfully starts chewing and pulling on the cuff of his pants. It is a funny scene, but does not fit in the context of the rest of the movie, and seems like a distraction.

The concluding confrontation with Andy's boss wraps up the movie nicely. The boss thanks him for his actions resulting in his wife leaving "with her ten cats" and freeing him from his situation. Andy tells the boss about the girls he met at the banquet, and the boss playfully shoves him, but it is a bit too forceful, and Andy goes out the window. Hanging on to keep from falling to the ground, Andy shouts, "If I don't fall, remember the blonde is mine!" This bit of funny dialogue neatly caps Andy Clyde's first Columbia two-reeler.

Notably, the existing script for *It's the Cats* includes notes that offer another possible ending. In the alternate ending, which was not used, Andy is sitting in a chair at home, and has rigged a shotgun by tying it with a string to an open door. When somebody shuts the door, the gun will go off. The boss then phones and thanks Andy for saving his life by ending his marriage, giving him both a raise and a promotion. Andy prepares to head down to the office and grabs his hat. When he bumps the door, the gun goes off and shoots him in the backside.

It's the Cats is a far better Columbia debut than the Three Stooges had with the confusing yet interesting musical vehicle *Woman Haters*, released five months earlier. Whereas the Stooges spent a few shorts finding themselves, having split from their leading comic Ted Healy and now figuring out how to function as a separate unit, Andy's character was fully established from the beginning.

The *It's the Cats* screenwriter is Andrew Bennison, who in his short life did some interesting work in films. He penned such popular Stooges comedies as *A Ducking They Did Go* and *Oily to Bed, Oily to Rise* (both 1939) and died in 1942. When he wrote *It's the Cats*, he had already co-directed (with John Ford) 1930's *Born Reckless*, a film featuring a young John Wayne. Director Al Ray helmed over 75 movies during the silent and early sound era, but he never created a real vision or established a style. For *It's the Cats*, his contribution is keeping the action within the frame and offering some effective establishing shots.

But the real vision for *It's the Cats* belongs to Andy Clyde. While Jules

White had his own ideas about slapstick comedy, a veteran like Clyde gave the producer some comfort as to how things would go. Throughout the entire process, Clyde came up with various ideas to enhance each scene, adding nuance to his character while effectively maintaining the slapstick pace.

Motion Picture Daily, one of the few trades that offered reviews of short subjects, stated in its October 22, 1934, issue, "Clyde's antics provide several good chuckles."[1] *It's the Cats* works nicely as his debut at a new studio.

In the Dog House

Directed by Arthur Ripley; *Story and Screenplay:* Richard Smith, Arthur Ripley; *Produced by* Jules White; *Cinematography:* Henry Freulich; *Editor:*

Vivien Oakland has put Delmar Watson and Andy Clyde *In the Dog House* (1934).

William A. Lyon; *Cast:* Andy Clyde, Vivien Oakland, Delmar Watson, Chuck Callahan; *Shooting Dates:* October 17–22, 1934; *Released* December 1, 1934; *Columbia Production Number:* 155

For his second Columbia comedy, Andy Clyde settles into a domestic setting, which would serve him well throughout his tenure at the studio. However, *In the Dog House* features conflicts that are a bit shaky as to how effectively they work as comedy.

The plot is simple enough. Andy is married to his second wife (Vivien Oakland) and has custody of his grandson. The wife does not like the grandson or the grandson's dog. At one point, she plans to send the child's dog to the pound and send the child to an orphanage, simply because she finds the two of them intrusive. She is then told that Andy's grandson put her dog's license on his own dog, causing her pet to be picked up by the dog catcher for being unlicensed. They all race to save it from being gassed at the pound. On the way home, the wife apologizes and promises to be more accepting.

In the Dog House has a potentially amusing premise, but it is not as strong a comedy as *It's the Cats*. First, Vivien Oakland has nothing comical about her. This is unlike Oakland's usual roles in comedies, as she had a long career playing nagging wives opposite many of the top comedians (Edgar Kennedy, Leon Errol, Oliver Hardy, et al.) and always had comic flair. Andy requested her services often throughout his time at Columbia, and they worked very well together. In this film, however, she comes off as angry and dislikable without the inherent comic sensibility underlying these character traits. She is mean to Andy, and even meaner to his grandson. The grandson is never shown as troublesome or bratty, so there is no justification for her ire.

There are some scattered funny bits strewn throughout. Andy's fidgety expression when asked to investigate a strange noise coming from the kitchen exhibits a cowardice that helps explain his submissive response to his shrewish wife. A pie gets stuck to the ceiling and falls onto Vivien's face when Andy bends her over to kiss her. The grandson throws punches in his sleep while having a nightmare, and knocks Andy out of the bed. Vivien gets soap in her eyes and the water she is given is filled with small frogs that Andy and the grandson planned to use as bait for fishing.

The film concludes with Andy, the wife and the grandson racing through the streets to get to the pound on time. Director Arthur Ripley does an excellent job, using both actual outdoor footage and indoor process screen shots, including close-ups of Andy's reactions as he races through traffic. This fast-paced scene is the comic highlight of the film. The car is out of control when it reaches the pound, and bursts through its gas chamber where several dogs are being put down. The auto comes out, still running, and containing all of the dogs that had been in the chamber.

While Ripley is responsible for the effectiveness of the car scene, his screenplay is the reason for Vivien's dislikable character. Ripley wrote many of Harry Langdon's silents, and Harry often was beset by angry, shrewish wives. But this worked out better with his character, a childlike innocent. In this Clyde comedy, most of Vivien's anger is taken out on the child, whose innocent actions do not deserve that sort of treatment. The main conflict seemed to be the wife vs. the grandson, with the meek Andy struggling to please both. And while he appears intimidated by her at the beginning, he does sort of stand up to her at the end, so there's that element of character growth which is commendable.

Oakland does her best with the material she is given. It is difficult to find even a trace of comic potential in the character as written, and Oakland really has no way of expanding the role's parameters so that she could come off less disagreeable.

Thus, *In the Dog House* is one of the weaker Andy Clyde Columbia comedies.

The film was successful upon its release. *Motion Picture Herald* indicated "there is an abundance of comedy in this two-reeler which Andy Clyde sustains."[2] *Film Daily*, however, noticed some unevenness:

> This one is played for sentiment as well as the humor that Andy Clyde can always deliver. Andy is as funny as ever, but mixing the material of comedy with the sympathy stuff for the kid seems to have cramped his opportunities.[3]

In a section of *Motion Picture Herald*, where theater owners indicated how well movies played in their venues, an Alabama theater owner opined, "Another good Columbia comedy. They sure have improved with the new product. We haven't received a bad one yet. This one has plenty of laughs."

One thing that can be considered an opportunity with *In the Dog House* is allowing Andy Clyde to work with a youngster. Clyde's comedy responded well to children, and he would invariably play a kindly old man who loved kids, or an old grump who disliked them but was won over in the end. For his next film, *I'm a Father*, Andy Clyde explores both perspectives.

I'm a Father

Directed by James Horne; *Story and Screenplay:* Jack White (billed as Preston Black); *Produced by* Jules White; *Cinematography:* Benjamin H. Kline; *Editor:* James Sweeney; *Cast:* Andy Clyde, Lillian Elliot, Geneva Mitchell,

Andy is relieved the baby is not his in *I'm a Father* (1935). Left to right: Grace Goodall, Beulah Hutton, Andy Clyde and Lillian Elliot.

Phil Dunham, Ferdinand Munier, Inez Courtney, Robert Allen, Allyn Drake, Mary Gordon, Grace Goodall, Louise Carver, Charles Dorety, Bess Flowers, Billy Engle, Frank Yaconelli, William Irving, Don Roberts, Bobby Burns; *Shooting Dates:* December 14–19, 1934; *Released* February 7, 1935; *Columbia Production Number:* 151; *Remade in* 1944 as *Oh Baby* with Hugh Herbert

Clyde works the limits of his screen persona in *I'm a Father*, his third Columbia comedy and an improvement over the first two. He is cast as an old grump who dislikes children. His wife, however, is kind-hearted and has purchased an entire trunk of diapers and baby clothing for a neighbor lady who is expecting. When Andy comes home and finds the trunk, he believes his wife is going to have a baby, and his demeanor completely changes to one of happy giddiness.

I'm a Father is fascinating for giving Andy the opportunity to draw from each of his various character perspectives. His grouchy character is established in the opening scene, which takes place at the office. One of the young workers is passing out cigars in anticipation of becoming a father. All gather to congratulate him except Andy. The expectant father offers Andy a cigar, and Andy grumpily refuses, stating that it is foolish to bring a child into the world during the economic crisis as the country was experiencing at the time.

Andy's character is contrasted with his kindly wife, played by Lillian Elliot. Her response to a neighbor's pregnancy is to offer her the trunk filled with baby clothes. Despite the economic woes of the time, the frugal Andy is financially quite comfortable, so it is easy for his wife to help out a neighbor who has fallen on hard times.

The movie becomes something of a *tour de force* for Andy when he discovers the trunk filled with baby items. Suddenly his grumpiness turns to giggly elation as he tickles his wife's chin and insists on doing her chores, including preparing dinner. His ineptitude (the male stereotyping of being helpless in the kitchen being the framework) results in an explosion. Andy, still unperturbed, decides to simply warm up a couple cans of beans. When he goes to the kitchen with the dirty dishes, the swinging door hits him and we hear the plates crash to the floor. "The dishes are done!" he calls from behind the closed door.

I'm a Father extends beyond the household parameters and returns Andy to the office, where his complete change of demeanor astonishes and delights his co-workers. He has flowers for the women and cigars for the men. He even joins his boss in weeping happy tears over his impending fatherhood. Since the viewer is fully aware that Andy is not going to be a father, and this is all a misunderstanding, these scenes with him reacting with delight are even more amusing.

When Andy returns from the office, he is told by a neighbor lady that his wife has gone to the hospital with her friend. Of course this is the friend who is having the baby, and Mrs. Clyde is going along to help. But Andy concludes it is his wife having the baby and the friend is about to help. Andy yells to the neighbor, "Why didn't anyone call me? I'm the father!" which causes the woman to scream and run away in one of the film's funniest scenes.

Some of the movie's other big laughs occur in the hospital waiting room where several expectant fathers are stationed, including Andy and his neighbor's husband, neither realizing the misunderstanding. One man receives a message from the nurse and bursts into tears. When asked what is wrong, he states, "I've been waiting for three days in the wrong hospital."

Andy's wife's friend ends up giving birth to triplets, causing Andy to faint when concluding they belong to him. When he is revived, he is told he's been wrong all along. The film concludes with him adopting multiple children, a closing gag he would revisit a few years later in another film.

Director James Horne, who had been directing since the silent era, worked often with comedians (including Charley Chase and Laurel and Hardy) at the Hal Roach Studios, where he did most of his work during the 1930s. Horne was good at collaborating with the lead comedian, which allowed Clyde more input. Horne's own veteran skills are evident in the way he presents the contrast between Andy and his wife in the establishing scenes. First, Andy at the office. Then the wife at home with the neighbor. This cuts quickly to Andy arriving home and chasing screaming children from his yard. They get even by turning on the hose as he stands near it.

Variety would occasionally review short subjects in its pages. They reviewed this Clyde comedy, stating:

> Full quota of laughs in this situation comedy, with Andy Clyde clicking notably. Andy Clyde, who's been around the comedy scene for years, shows how effective his clowning can be when in the hands of a capable director. Director James Horne has realized on Clyde's comic potentialities.[4]

Motion Picture Daily concurred: "Andy Clyde hands out laughs right and left in this comedy. The final scenes, shot in a hospital waiting room, are packed with laughs. Should have audiences howling."[5]

In an interview conducted by James Curtis, Jules White called *I'm a Father* "[o]ne of the funniest I ever made with Andy Clyde. This could have been a full-length feature."[6] In the same interview, he also addressed the absurdity of Clyde, playing an old man, becoming a first-time father. White stated that Clyde's popularity was such that they could investigate a lot of possibilities with his character:

> [Audiences] were acquainted with Andy Clyde's character because he had worked at Sennett. He was the old man with the big moustache. He was sort of a very lovable kind of a character, sort of a foxy grandpa type of guy. And yet we played him also as a youngish man with younger women—romantic type of things.

In only his third Columbia comedy, Clyde had established himself as a funny, clever, creative addition to the studio's growing short subject roster. His past work, though quite vast, was a successful growth period that led to the work he was now doing at Columbia. Clyde's films would improve greatly beginning with his next release, *Old Sawbones*, due to Jules White hiring veteran comedy director Del Lord.

Old Sawbones

Directed by Del Lord; *Story and Screenplay:* Jack White (billed as Preston Black); *Produced by* Jules White; *Cinematography:* John Stumar; *Editor:* Bur-

II. The Columbia Comedy Shorts

Andy is a doctor who prefers old-fashioned ways in *Old Sawbones* (1935).

ton Kramer; *Cast:* Andy Clyde, Lucille Ward, James C. Morton, Phyllis Crane, Helen Dickson, Bud Jamison, Marie Wells, Lou Archer, Billy Franey, George Ovey, Cal Harris, Si Jenks, Ford West, Marvin Loback, John Rand, Hubert Diltz, Charles Dorety, Harry Semels, Johnny Kascier, Wes Warner, Rudolph Chavers; *Shooting Dates:* March 5–9, 1935; *Released* April 11, 1935; *Columbia Production Number:* 164

The significance of *Old Sawbones* has to do with the fact that it was directed by Del Lord, who had known and worked with Andy Clyde quite frequently during the silent era.

Lord directed many comedies for Mack Sennett, and was especially adept at creating, choreographing, and filming some really elaborate gag sequences, especially car chases. He was a master at keeping action within the frame and sustaining gag sequences with quick edits. He was one of the top directors for Mack Sennett comedies during the early '20s, and remained with Sennett during the early sound period. However, by 1933 when Sennett began curtailing production, Lord freelanced sporadically for different studios. He had to take a job selling used cars to maintain a more steady income. Jules White recalled for Ted Okuda and Edward Watz in their book *The Columbia Comedy Shorts* that writer-director Arthur Ripley "came to me one day and said, 'Do you know who's selling used cars on Ventura Boulevard? Del Lord!' So I got in contact with Del and told him, 'We've got a comedy starting tomorrow, and I want you to come in and direct it.'"[7]

Lord continued directing Columbia comedies for many years, including some of the best work of Andy Clyde, Harry Langdon, Charley Chase and the Three Stooges. He is considered the best director the Columbia shorts had. In fact, the Three Stooges films got a real boost in creativity once Lord began directing them, and it is he who was most instrumental in their films becoming the classics they are known as today.

Clyde was especially pleased to have Lord with Columbia, as he was not only aware of Lord's mastery at filming slapstick comedy, he also knew that this was a director who welcomed creative input from the comedian. Since Clyde and Lord had a similar vision, this resulted in a great working relationship. For all of this mastery at visual comedy, Lord was not particularly adept at verbal humor. Clyde had comfortably mastered dialogue and was able to help each film's structural progress in that area.

Old Sawbones features Andy as a country doctor hoping for a county position that would increase his pay and improve his standing in the community. Dr. Oak E. Doak is vying for the same position. When the county board cannot decided which doctor to hire, it is decided that whichever one treats the most patients during the next week will be hired. Both doctors tie at 104 patients and race to be the first to examine one more.

Perhaps contemporary political correctness would find fault with this film's opening gag. A woman is waiting to see Dr. Andy along with a man whom she believes to be an expectant father. Andy comes out and proudly announces, "Four babies, and one of them is black!" The woman can't believe it. "One of them black?" she wonders aloud. It is then that Andy comes out with a basket filled with puppies, one of which is indeed black. In the context of its day, such a gag is not malicious, but seems unsettling in our more enlightened times.

The conflict between Andy and Dr. Doak is interesting in its immediate dynamic. Andy is presented as being old and out-of-date, behind the times in his lifestyle as well as his work. He still drives a horse and carriage and agrees to deliver puppies as well as babies, despite not being a veterinarian. Andy doesn't balk when a patient can't pay. His equipment is equally old-fashioned (but still effective). More of a hotshot, Doak lives in a fancy house, drives a fancy car and is up-to-date on all technology. Oddly, though, Doak is not played by a young man, but by actor James C. Morton, eight years older than Andy Clyde. It shows how Andy was always playing a much older man than his age. Morton, already past 50 when he filmed this movie, is likely playing a slightly younger character.

II. The Columbia Comedy Shorts

While the chief conflict is between Dr. Andy and Dr. Doak, the film's opening establishes a problem between Andy and his wife. Andy is a doctor, but also agrees to look after the townspeople's pets. When they are unable to pay, Andy forgoes the bill. His wife angrily confronts him: "We owe the butcher, we owe the grocer...." Her forceful approach causes Andy to step backwards into an electric fan, which tears off the seat of his pants. "And now," his wife continues, "we'll owe the tailor!"

The action comes to a head when Andy and Doak compete to treat the final patient and win the county position. Andy races through the streets in his horse-drawn carriage while Doak travels in his roadster. Andy weaves in front of Doak, keeping him from passing. He takes a shortcut through a wooded area where a car would not get through. While Doak's racing results in engine trouble and a flat tire, Andy's carriage falls apart from under him as he bounces through his journey. Lord's expertise at staging and filming such scenes makes this conclusion the highlight of the movie. To top it off, the final patient is actually Doak's wife, who is delivering their child (although she ends up having septuplets!).

There are other funny bits, some of them contributions by Clyde. When Dr. Andy makes a house call, the script had him run up to the door. Clyde suggested to Lord that he instead try to hop the picket fence where the gate is, and have the gate open, causing Andy to fall on the ground. Lord liked the idea, and it is one of the funnier quick gags in the short.

One slapstick sequence might be the result of Lord working on a few films for Hal Roach just before joining Columbia. Although Lord did not direct Laurel and Hardy, there is a bit in *Old Sawbones* that is similar to their style of humor. Andy and Doak are fighting over a patient. A passerby intrudes and is punched by Doak. Another passerby is punched by that one. Soon, the melee escalates as others join the fray, and a group of men are punching and kicking each other. The prospective patient ends up with his clothes torn off. This scene concludes with him running away in his underwear, pursued by both Andy and Doak.

Laurel and Hardy mastered the idea of a small conflict growing into a larger donnybrook. They had used it extensively in silent comedies (*The Battle of the Century, Should Married Men Go Home, You're Darn Tootin,' Big Business*). It even extended to Roach productions without them, such as *A Pair of Tights* with Anita Garvin, Marion Byron, Edgar Kennedy and Stuart Erwin. While the *Old Sawbones* sequence does not have the same slow, methodical pace as the Roach examples, it does have the same structure, albeit with a rapid and more violent presentation as fitting the Columbia style.

Critics at the time enjoyed this Andy Clyde comedy with *Motion Picture Daily* stating in its May 5, 1935, issue, "This short has the always reliably funny Andy Clyde going through his paces as a small town doctor. The situations are amusing."[8] According to the May 11, 1935, *Motion Picture Herald*, "Andy Clyde is always an entertaining comedian when the story is right, and here he has a reasonably good story. Things move at a fast and furious pace."[9] Theater owners, reporting to the trades, indicated that moviegoers were even more impressed than the critics: It's seldom that we report on a short, but this comedy gave our audience more laughs than I have heard in a theater for a year. Typical slapstick comedy that had the house in an uproar. Let's have more of the same.

Because Clyde had established himself as a short subject star before arriving at Columbia, he quickly became one of the most popular comedians in the Columbia unit after only his fourth effort there. Jules White was very pleased with the critical and audience reaction to the Clyde comedies and, for a time, these films were securing better bookings than any other Columbia short subjects. The Three Stooges shorts would become the unit's most popular films, but Clyde's popularity continued to be strong, especially in rural areas where his old man character engendered laughter as well as affection for his folksy charm.

An amusing bit of trivia regarding *Old Sawbones*. While it was shooting in March 1935, Andy's son John (named for Andy's father) was born. In the March 15 *Film Daily*, a columnist stated,

> Mrs. Andy Clyde and the new baby, John Allan, have returned home from the Mount Sano Hospital. Andy Clyde, who has been working every day since the baby's arrival, in a Jules White comedy at Columbia, dashed home in makeup to greet them.[10]

Tramp Tramp Tramp

Directed by Charles Lamont; *Screenplay:* Ewart Adamson; *Produced by* Jules White; *Cinematography:* John Stumar; *Editor:* Charles Hochberg; *Cast:* Andy Clyde, Dot Farley, Bobby Barber, Al Thompson, Charles Dorety, Lew Davis, Charles Sullivan, Heinie Conklin, Eddie Gribbon, Bobby Burns; *Shooting Dates:* April 8–12, 1935; *Released* May 22, 1935; *Columbia Production Number:* 169; *Working title: Helping Handout*

Tramp Tramp Tramp continues the Andy Clyde series on a high note, this time confronting the Depression and using these difficult circumstances for comedy. Andy's wife wants to help people affected by the severity of the current economic times. Andy supports her charitable work. When she invites

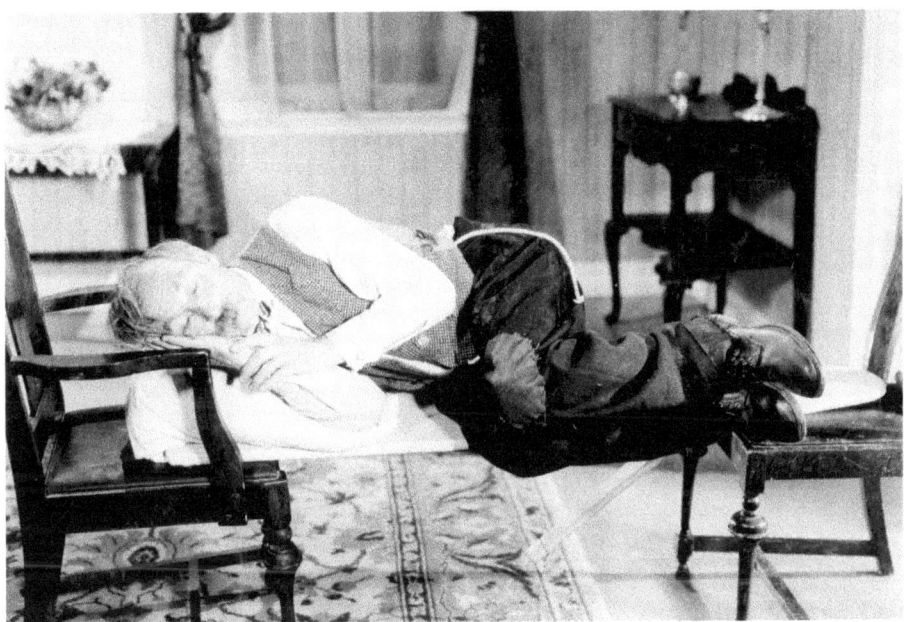

When his wife opens up their house to the downtrodden, Andy can't find a good place to sleep in *Tramp Tramp Tramp* **(1935).**

a large group of hobos to eat and sleep at their house, they completely take over, causing a lot of problems for Andy. To combat this, Andy responds with his own charitable cause: He chooses to open up the Clyde home to stray animals.

Comedies would often address the Depression, but sometimes it was difficult to find humor in something that was adversely affecting a lot of unfortunate Americans. But in *Tramp Tramp Tramp*, Clyde offers a very funny comedy that makes great use of the situation without ever having the potential of being offensive.

The scenes involving the hobos taking over the Clyde household feature a lot of fun situations. Andy comes home to find a beautiful turkey dinner his wife prepared, assuming there will be enough for everyone. However, when Andy sits at the very full table, he finds only the carcass of the turkey remains by the time it's passed to him. Eventually so many hobos crowd the table that Andy is pushed off his chair onto the floor. When he complains to his wife, another hobo, not realizing Andy is the man of the house and believing him to be one of the other bums, throws him out the window. Andy gets even by putting toy blasting caps in the food, causing it to explode when bitten into or jabbed with a fork.

The laughs continue when the hobos bunk down for the night. Andy can't find a place to sleep because the hobos occupy every surface of the house, and it is virtually impossible to wake any of them despite his attempts. The resourceful Andy lays a board across two chairs to sleep on. However, in the seconds it takes him to turn around and grab a blanket, one of the hobos climbs onto the makeshift bed and falls asleep. It is important to here that the hobos are generally good-natured, and Andy's problems stem from the quantity, not the quality of people in the house. This helps to make the humor inoffensive to the plight of the Depression downtrodden. Meanwhile, Andy's masterful double-take reactions to the proceedings are hilarious.

Andy's choice to go on a charitable crusade of his own is less about altruism and more about vigilantism. Dedicated to saving all the stray animals, Andy fills his home with everything from puppies and kittens to a full-sized bull that takes over his bed. What finally gets rid of the hobos is the family of skunks he unleashes in the house. The skunks not only force out the bums, but also Andy and his wife, who must spend the night in a tent pitched in the yard.

While slapstick is the key comic element, as usual, *Tramp Tramp Tramp* also has some fun with dialogue. In one exchange, a society lady visits the Clydes and talks Mrs. Clyde into contributing to aid homeless people:

Society woman: This Depression is so terrible. Just the other day I saw a man on my front lawn eating the grass.
Mrs. Clyde: Oh, my, what did you do?
Andy (interrupting): She told him to go out back because the grass was longer there!

This joke gets a good laugh out of Andy's wife, but the visitor is not amused.

It was Andy's idea to cast Dot Farley, an old friend from the Sennett comedies, as his wife. Farley was currently working steadily at RKO in the Edgar Kennedy shorts as his fussbudget mother-in-law. She works very well within the framework of this short, exhibiting patient benevolence to the hobos while maintaining her devotion to her husband, despite his misgivings. Her comic reactions to the animals are very funny. It's unfortunate that she did not work with Clyde more frequently

Clyde is also comfortably surrounded by other silent screen veterans such as Heinie Conklin, Eddie Gribbon and Bobby Burns. Filling out the supporting cast with men whose comedy careers dated back even further than Clyde's made it easier for director Charles Lamont to stage slapstick sequences.

Lamont was another old hand; before Columbia, Andy had worked with him on some early 1930s Educational releases for Sennett. Lamont didn't have quite the directorial vision or creative prowess that Del Lord had, but he knew how to work with comedians like Clyde and gave him the freedom to contribute his own ideas. For instance, when Andy is thrown out the window by one of the hobos, he is confronted by a little boy. Some caps fall out of the boy's toy gun, and when Andy stands up, he steps on several, causing a series of blasts that cause a frightened, dancing reaction. It is a funny little addition to the scene, and Lamont shoots it so that Andy's entire flailing body is on camera.

Another relentlessly funny comedy, *Tramp Tramp Tramp* again presented Clyde as one of the top comedians in short subjects. With each new production, more theaters requested Andy Clyde short comedies to enhance their programs, reading in the trades how well they were going over with audiences. Jules White remained pleased, noticing that screenwriter Ewart Adamson and directors Lamont and Del Lord were able to work with Clyde to achieve good results.

Clyde was a hard-working comedian who always wanted to achieve an optimal level of humor with his work, known to constantly go over lines and come up with gag ideas. White knew that it was necessary for Clyde to continue working with writers and directors who understood his style and were willing to collaborate with him.

Alimony Aches

Directed by Charles Lamont; *Story and Screenplay:* Ewart Adamson; *Produced by* Jules White; *Cinematography:* George Meehan; *Editor:* Charles Hochberg; *Cast:* Andy Clyde, Jan Duggan, Vivien Oakland, Bud Jamison, Tommy Bond, Ray Turner, Lon Poff, Bobby Barber; *Shooting Dates:* May 10–14, 1935; *Released* June 29, 1935; *Columbia Production Number:* 171

Andy Clyde engages in marital comedy in *Alimony Aches*, one of his most raucous vehicles. He marries for the second time, and while on his honeymoon he is visited by his ex-wife demanding $1000 in back alimony. She brings along her bratty son from another of her multiple previous marriages, and insists on staying with Andy and his new wife until she is paid off. Since she threatens to turn Andy over to the police if they do not accede to her demands (presenting a newspaper article indicating that errant husbands are being put on chain gangs), they allow her to stay. Little do they realize, his ex-wife has remarried and is not entitled to any money.

There is a lot of good outrageous slapstick during scenes where Andy believes he has the measles after a bottle of mercurochrome sprays in his face. As both wives intend to care for him, it becomes a competition. There is a lot of violent knockabout as hot water and mustard plasters are clumsily affixed, his feet are forced alternately into a bucket of ice and a tub of hot water, etc. When the bratty son mixes a medicinal concoction that includes liniment, Andy's body starts uncontrollably flipping. As *Variety* opined, "This is done mechanically, somehow, but it's very funny, turning him over so fast it looks like an invisible explosion might have caught him."[11]

The short gets even more outrageous when Andy smears iodine on his chest and fires a pistol to fake his own death. When he shoots the gun in the air, it hits a chandelier that comes down on Andy's head, knocking him out. The ex-wife is ready to believe he is dead, shifting her focus to the possibility of his insurance money paying the back alimony. His new wife weeps and loudly laments, "My first husband died on the first day of my first honeymoon!"

More slapstick ensues when a flower delivery man believes Andy is a ghost, and when undertakers show up to take the body away. Andy's body is strapped to a gurney that rolls down the street, narrowly missing traffic, the women and undertakers in pursuit. The film concludes with the bratty son revealing the ex-wife's marriage.

Alimony Aches is the first Columbia-Clyde comedy to feature the sort of slapstick that the studio was best known for doing. It is his roughest and most violent Columbia short thus far. And it perfectly illustrates how effectively Andy's low-key persona works within those parameters. His performance never becomes blatant or loud. He character is central to the situations and anchors each one of them with his nuanced reactions. For instance, when his feet are being alternately forced into a tub of ice, then a tub of hot water, he alternates between shivering and yelling in pain. It is all done quickly, is perfectly timed, and very funny. The slapstick routines effectively escalate as the film progresses. A simple argument with the ex-wife quickly becomes a series of outrageous events and misunderstandings. The pace never slows, and each occurrence leads into the next in a way that makes sense.

Vivien Oakland shines as the shrewish ex-wife. When compared to her dislikable character from *In the Dog House*, we can see how a similar role can be played with enough comic effect to become amusing. She is calculating, unscrupulous, but still quite funny as she makes every effort to help heal Andy with her only motivation the money she hopes to collect.

Jan Duggan, playing Andy's new wife, made her screen debut in the W.C. Fields feature *The Old Fashioned Way* a year earlier. In the Fields film, she is a rich dowager who fancies herself a singer, but her histrionics are unbearable.

Fields, wanting her to finance his show, promises her a part with one line, and she earnestly rehearses that line backstage. Of course it was all a ruse to get her money. She never has the chance to go on. Duggan plays a very similar character here. She sings as badly, but Andy loves her and therefore likes her singing. She is every bit as shrill, her mannerism every bit as affected as her character in the Fields movie, but here they are championed by Andy, who cares for her, while Fields was merely using her for her money. In fact, she plays a wealthy woman in this movie also, but her wealth is not so much a plot point other than to serve as the catalyst for Vivien to attempt to extort the thousand dollars. The contrast between those two characters is striking. They have good chemistry playing women whose connection to Andy is the only thing they have in common.

Vivien's bratty son is played by Tommy Bond, who later played the bully Butch in Hal Roach's Our Gang comedies. It would be the role for which he'd be best remembered, and he extended that role to other characters he played outside the Gang in movies with Laurel and Hardy, et al. Although Bond was already appearing with Our Gang when he did this Clyde comedy, it was in general roles, not significant ones. This Clyde comedy is something of a blueprint for the sort of characteristics Butch would later have. It would not be the first time Bond played a brat, as he essayed such a character in a Charley Chase short, *I'll Take Vanilla*, a year earlier. It would also not be the last time Bond played a brat in a Clyde film for Columbia.

Alimony Aches was among the best received of the Andy Clyde comedies. According to *Variety*, "This is nothing but slapstick, but it is played so fast it computes to a rather high total of laughs. It also has a few tricks of the gagman's mind that are new. It should bring no audience pains unless from the big laughs drawn."[12] Theater owners reported to the trades that *Alimony Aches* was a hit for any program, one stating: "This is one of the best comedies we have ever had the privilege to play."

The most interesting aspect of *Alimony Aches* is how effectively Clyde's character fits into the more blatant slapstick Columbia style. His character's lifting of an eyebrow, comical shudder and muttered asides settle comfortably amidst some typically wild Columbia slapstick. Charles Lamont once again offered solid direction. But his days at Columbia were numbered. While Lamont enjoyed doing the comedies and working for Jules White, he had an intense hatred for studio head Harry Cohn (many did) and left the studio.

Clyde continued to show White that acquiring his services for the studio's short subject unit was resulting in consistent success. White renewed Andy's contract with the unit by picking up his option and raising his salary from the standard $500 to $850.

It Always Happens

Directed by Del Lord; *Story and Screenplay:* Ewart Adamson; *Produced by* Jules White; *Cinematography:* George Meehan; *Editor:* James Sweeney; *Cast:* Andy Clyde, Esther Howard, Geneva Mitchell, Bud Jamison, Esther Muir, Arthur Housman, Robert McKenzie, Sam Lufkin; *Shooting Dates:* July 30–August 2, 1935; *Released* September 15, 1935; *Columbia Production Number:* 202; A partial remake of Clyde's Mack Sennett short *Taxi Troubles* (1931). *Remade by* Andy Clyde as *His Tale Is Told* (1944); *Remade by* Bert Wheeler as *Innocently Guilty* (1950)

It Always Happens brings back Del Lord as director and is another of the funniest Andy Clyde comedies for Columbia. This story of suspected marital infidelity is fairly typical, but it is structured to utilize a lot of layered situations which are accented by slapstick gags. It also gives director Lord a chance to utilize his prowess for wild street scenes.

Salesman Andy travels to nearby Los Angeles to secure a deal with a tractor company run by Mr. Smith. Smith leaves a message at Andy's hotel that their scheduled meeting has to be changed to the following morning. Meanwhile, Andy's trusting wife has a suspicious sister who believes Andy is just going to LA to hook up with "some blonde." This premise is already amusing. The idea that innocent, befuddled Andy could possibly be a womanizer is outrageous, and presents his sister-in-law as so highly suspicious, she even suspects someone like him.

Andy gets mixed up with an obnoxious drunk and is taken to dry out overnight in jail by a cop who suspects both men. Meanwhile, Andy's wife and her sister have been in his room all night, wondering why he never came home. When he does return, a woman living across the hall, looking for the janitor, pleads with him to help her turn off her bathtub faucet, as it is flooding her bathroom.

The situations compile here. The drunk (played by Arthur Housman, who specialized in such roles in the 1930s) hangs on Andy and causes him to get stuck in a revolving door, and Andy ends up striking a cop. That is what causes his overnight jail stay. His absence from his room helps confirm the suspicions of his sister-in-law. His innocently attempting to help the woman turn off her tub water results in his doing a pratfall on the slippery tiled floor, getting wet, and emerging from her place barefoot and wearing her robe. Of course the wife and sister-in-law run into him, and will not accept an explanation. Andy eventually makes up with his wife, who does accept his innocence, much to her sister's chagrin.

The idea of Andy as a womanizer is revisited when he finally has his appointment with Mr. Smith, who is ready to turn down his services because a younger, more vibrant man is desired. He then notices lipstick on Andy's collar (from his making up with his wife) and concludes that Andy is a rascal with the ladies. Andy uses this to secure the sales rights, and starts boasting about his exploits, even to the extent of flirting with Smith's pretty young secretary (who gives him a boot in the behind).

Once again, the incongruity of Andy suspected as a womanizer is part of the humor, but it is further established in this film's second half, when Smith jumps to that conclusion and Andy finds it necessary to play along. Andy leaves the office having secured the deal, and once again runs into the woman whom he helped with the bathroom. She wants to apologize, but he wants to get away from her, so he hurries into his car, closes it on her dress, and starts to drive off. This tears off her clothes, so she jumps into his back seat. He takes the torn dress and plans to get it fixed at a nearby tailor, but runs into Smith while at the same time seeing his wife and sister-in-law coming up the street. He grabs Smith and drags him into the car, but the woman in the back seat writes a note telling Andy that Smith is, in fact, her husband. Smith is a large, imposing man who revealed to Andy in the office that he is violently jealous.

This gives Del Lord the opportunity to engage in one of his car chase sequence specialties. Distracted Andy is behind the wheel and narrowly missing oncoming traffic. Smith asks if Andy has been drinking. Andy sees another opportunity and starts acting drunk, purposely weaving in and out of traffic, so Smith doesn't realize his wife is hiding in the back seat in her underwear. Smith insists on being dropped off. Andy then drives to Mrs. Smith's apartment, is given a key, and plans to get her something to wear so she can leave the car. While Andy is in the apartment, Smith comes home so Andy rushes into the bathroom and turns on the bath water. Andy's wife and sister-in-law come over and reveal that they saw Andy and a woman coming out of this apartment. Smith believes the worst, and plans to crash into the bathroom, just as his wife enters, her underwear-clad body covered with a trash barrel surrounding her. As he prepares to break down the bathroom door, Andy opens it and Smith goes crashing into the filled tub. Andy runs out of the apartment and hides in a nearby baby buggy. When Smith comes out, the buggy gets bumped and goes flying out the door and into traffic. Smith pursues it, firing a pistol.

The situational layers that sustain the plot of *It Always Happens* never become convoluted or confusing, but it does result in a lot of loose ends at the conclusion. When Smith busts into the bathroom and Andy runs off, the wife and sister-in-law have suddenly disappeared from the scene. They had been waiting outside the bathroom also, but are nowhere to be found once Andy comes running out and ends up in the baby buggy.

The baby buggy idea is truly bizarre. Andy switches places with a baby and somehow scrunches his body into the buggy, puts on a bonnet and hides quietly. As the buggy starts to roll down the hallway, we see the baby smiling and reacting (revealing to the viewer that the child would not have been injured or in danger, which would kill the gag).

This would not be the last time that an Andy Clyde two-reeler had enough plot elements and various character conflicts to fill a complete feature, but somehow the material is contained and keeps in pace within the parameters of a short subject. The Columbia players are well represented, with big Bud Jamison as Smith, Geneva Mitchell as his pretty wife, Esther Howard as Andy's wife and Esther Muir as her suspicious sister. Although he has very little to do, Robert McKenzie gets a big laugh as an elusive, giggling janitor. McKenzie would be given much more to do in future Clyde films where he plays the comedian's adversary for the hand of a woman (again Esther Howard).

Once again, the critics made note of the fact that Clyde's comedies were using typical conflicts, but offering new twists on standard material, including some clever slapstick gags. Clyde emphasizes each piece of knockabout. When he is kicked by the secretary, he flies into a nearby wall. When he slips on the bathroom floor, his entire body flails as he hits the floor.

Clyde's more subtle nuance is also notable. His general level of earnest befuddlement is evident throughout. Even a simple ad lib like absent-mindedly trying to fold his hat and place it in his shirt pocket adds to the consistent level of humor throughout the film. And when the woman in the back seat of the car holds up a sign stating that Smith is her husband; we, the audience, see it before Andy does, which makes his reaction funnier. While most of the Columbia comedies were slapstick vehicles with little plot exposition, Clyde's comedies added subtle nuance and more layered plot structures while still retaining the slapstick for which the studio's short subject unit was noted. *Variety* stated:

> *It Always Happens* is one of the strongest Andy Clyde comedies ... and offers a real progression in both plot structure and slapstick style. Clyde would continue to do some of his best work, while exploring new and clever ways to present standard ideas, making them seem fresh and original.[13]

Hot Paprika

Directed by Jack White (as Preston Black); *Story and Screenplay:* Harry McCoy; *Produced by* Jules White; *Cinematography:* Benjamin H. Kline; *Editor:* Charles Hochberg; *Cast:* Andy Clyde, Helene Martinez, Julian Rivero, Bud

Carefree Andy dances with Helen Martinez in *Hot Paprika* (1935).

Jamison, Ethelreda Leopold, Phyllis Crane, Harry Semels, Bobby Barber, A.R. Haysel, June Gittelson, Johnny Kascier, Al Haskell; *Shooting Dates:* October 15–18, 1935; *Released* December 12, 1935; *Columbia Production Number:* 209

Hot Paprika continues Clyde's streak of successful Columbia comedies. This series already surpassed anything he'd done elsewhere and continued to maintain its positive momentum.

In this one, Andy is told by his doctor that he has only three months to live. The doctor did this only to scare him out of his hiccups. He plans to wait until the following day to reveal the truth "to make sure his hiccups are gone." A despondent Andy decides to throw caution to the wind and spend his savings by taking a trip around the world and living it up. He gets as far the Latin American country Paprika. While enjoying a good time at a cantina, he stumbles into a revolution.

This premise is quite standard, even being used by Jerry Lewis nearly 35 years later in the feature *Hook, Line and Sinker* (also a Columbia release). Andy plays it beautifully within the context of his established character. He goes from his usual harmless, befuddled self into one who is bold enough to take opportunities he'd only dreamed about up to now. Returning to work, Andy passionately kisses a pretty office girl, pours ink over the books of a stuffy accountant and flips his boss' toupee inside out.

Once Andy is having a good old time at the Paprika cantina, the film shifts to spotlight his carefree exuberance. Andy drinks, makes friends and even flirtatiously dances with a pretty senorita. When fascist military forces start trouble, he flees with his new friends, who happen to be insurrectionists attempting to overthrow a tyrannical government. They convince Andy that the military men are "bandits."

The two rebels are impressed with Andy's cleverness and ingenuity when he shows them how to put together a makeshift cannon that appears to be firing (but it is only Andy throwing mud balls at the enemy). Andy then marches behind a wall, holding up part of a picket fence, giving the military the illusion of several soldiers with bayonets.

It is interesting that Andy's carefree nature has also resulted in a certain bravery that sparks his ingenuity. While he does run from the suppressive military forces and their blasting guns, believing them to be bandits, he also chooses to fight back, even though they have an entire army and he just has his two new friends. He is convinced he is dying anyway, so he battles the army. Because he is confident and resourceful, he is also successful.

Fooled by Andy's gag with the picket fence, and believing they are outnumbered, the army decides to attack from the rear. They then discover Andy's ruse. He is captured and put before a firing squad. Now he receives a telegram revealing that his heart is fine and he is not dying. Andy's friends, in the bushes, shoot at the firing squad's belts, causing their pants to come down. One of them throws his gun in the air and it hits Andy in the head. In the film's slapstick highlight, Andy falls into the fence behind him, breaks down a door and goes sliding downhill. He knocks into a soldier, and a machine-gun ends up in his lap. After a long slide, he crashes into the cantina just as the army is battling with the revolutionaries. Andy loses control of the machine-gun and blasts his way to victory, Having defeated the tyrannical army, he is a rebel hero.

Hot Paprika is funny throughout, and does a good job of allowing Andy to explore areas incongruous to his established character. It is funny to see stammering, befuddled Andy transforming into an arrogant womanizer who is cleverly heroic in battle. Once he realizes he is not dying, he returns to the character traits we identify with Andy, and he is soon plummeting down a hill on a door and losing control of a machine-gun. He triumphs by accident instead of due to his cleverness in battle.

Screenwriter Harry McCoy was a real veteran of comedy, having been an actor at the Keystone studios supporting Charlie Chaplin, Mabel Normand, Fatty Arbuckle *et al*. He began writing for Mack Sennett in the 1920s, and worked often with Andy Clyde, who was able to offer ideas for this short as well. McCoy was just establishing himself as a writer for Columbia shorts, bringing his vast frame of reference to this unit's slapstick comedies. He died in 1937.

At this time, director Jack White was billing himself as Preston Black. He was going through a pretty contentious divorce and wanted to hide his success, and his income, from his estranged wife. Jack White's direction responds nicely to McCoy's script, using the budget allowed for outdoor scenes, some stock footage as establishing shots, and with a nice, vastness to his shots in the cantina, with several extras filling the negative space. There's a rather impressively quirky transition when the camera closes in on a spinning globe, and the setting shifts from the U.S. to Paprika.

There is a great deal of visual humor, including a very funny dance routine in the cantina where Andy sprays the other dancers with a champagne bottle clumsily stuck in his pocket, and concludes by sitting on a cactus plant.

There are a lot of ideas in *Hot Paprika* that had been, and would be, used by other comedians. The uncontrolled machine-gun was used by Stan Laurel in the Laurel and Hardy feature comedy *Pardon Us* (1931). The sliding down the hill on a piece of wood was used a year later by Our Gang in *Divot Diggers* (1936). This shows how standard the ingredients for *Hot Paprika* were. But in the hands of Andy Clyde, his supporting cast and the filmmakers, everything comes off as fresh and original. *Film Daily* stated: "Good Andy Clyde technique in a yarn that has plenty of action and excitement...."[14]

Edward Bernds, the sound man on this short, recalled in his autobiography that while working on a Del Lord film was a good experience, working on one helmed by Jack White was not. "When he headed Educational Pictures, Jack White was Jules White' boss," Bernds wrote. "Now Jules was Jack's boss. The brothers quarreled and production slowed down." Bernds shared pages from a diary he kept during his movie days, which included the following:

> October 15: Start Jack White Andy Clyde comedy. Unpleasant going. Brothers White argue every set-up. Time wasted. Should have been an easy day. October 18: More

quarrelling, sinful waste of time. Work until past midnight, then they decide we can't finish. Home about one a.m.[15]

Despite these off-screen situations, Andy Clyde had hit his stride at Columbia and his comedies continued to work well within the unit's slapstick parameters while exploring what they could do with plot and character.

Caught in the Act

Directed by Del Lord; *Screenplay:* Al Ray, Arthur A. Greenlaw; *Story:* Al Ray; *Produced by* Jules White; *Cinematography:* George Meehan; *Editor:* Charles Hochberg; *Cast:* Andy Clyde, Anne O'Neal, John T. Murray, Bud Jamison, William Irving, Al Thompson; *Shooting Dates:* January 20–25, 1936; *Released* March 5, 1936; *Columbia Production Number:* 222; *Released by* Columbia in the early 1960s as a silent, abridged short for 8mm projectors

The incongruity of Andy Clyde being a ladies man started to become a recurring theme in his comedies. Throughout his Columbia tenure, many of his short films featured the unlikely scenario of an old man caught in compromising positions with attractive younger women, causing wives and jealous boyfriends to jump to the wrong conclusions.

Caught in the Act has Andy being mistaken for a notorious kissing bandit known as Jack the Kisser, played with comic flourish by John T. Murray. Wrapped in a sheet, Jack accosts women by kissing them and then running away. Because of these assaults, Jack is sought by the police.

Andy is, yet again, a clean-living sort, this time all set to marry his love. (The girl is played with a flourish by Anne O'Neal, who was new to movies at this time, but became known for such roles as her career continued. Anne had just come off playing a similar dowager part in the Three Stooges short *Ants in the Pantry*.)

When Andy attempts to propose, he is first bothered by her dog, causing him to say "Go away you mutt" in the middle of his proposal. He then gets tongue-tied, asking, "Will you bribe my bee, bub my bree, er, will you marry me?" His intended has to make sure Andy is right for her, asking, "You don't snore, do you?" "Well," Andy replies thoughtfully, "I never stayed awake all night to see if I did." She and Andy make excellent comic counterparts. When they decide to turn on the radio and dance in celebration of their impending nuptials, they hear a news bulletin about Jack the Kisser.

Later in the film, Andy hears the doorbell while taking a bath. He grabs a nearby sheet to conceal himself, goes to the door, comes out to retrieve a bottle of milk, and is locked out of his house. His indecent exposure results

Cop Andy rescues fiancée Anne O'Neal from the clutches of John T. Murray in *Caught in the Act* (1936).

in him being accused of being Jack the Kisser and he is taken to the police station. An energetic dog pulls away his sheet, so he is given a police uniform to wear to the station.

The remainder of the film involves mistaken identities and wrongheaded situations. Andy runs into the actual Jack the Kisser, who helps him escape police custody by handcuffing himself to Andy. Since Andy is in a police uniform, it simply appears as though an officer has a man in custody. Once safely away, Jack suggests they place their handcuff chain on railroad tracks and allow a train to run over it, thus breaking the chain and allowing them to separate. Andy agrees but as the train approaches, he realizes he is about to be hit and jumps off the tracks. A key is found in the police uniform Andy is wearing, so Jack the Kisser frees himself and runs off.

Andy's fiancée is waiting impatiently with the wedding party. She decides to go look for Andy herself, and runs into Jack the Kisser, but is rescued by Andy. After a wild chase through the streets on a bicycle, with Andy balanced on the handlebars, Jack is put in custody and Andy makes it to his wedding.

Writer Al Ray previously penned Clyde's first Columbia short *It's the Cats*. Once again, the story for *Caught in the Act* relies chiefly on situations. But with Del Lord as director, these situations are continually punctuated with slapstick. Falling out of windows, banging into doors, picture frames that fall onto someone's head when a door is slammed, and one of the director's signature wild street chases make the standard plot that much funnier. These situations also lead into each other nicely, getting increasingly crazier as the film progresses.

Once again Andy is delightfully befuddled throughout. There is a lot of stuttering wordplay after the aforementioned proposal scene. When taken into police custody, Andy is expected to say Rubber Buggy Bumpers several times to prove he isn't drunk. After a few false starts, and the demonstration that none of the cops can handle the tongue-twister either, Andy says it ten times perfectly. His triumph is brief, as the police chief states, "He's drunk, lock him up." Later, when Andy catches Jack accosting his fiancée, he states, "I'll kiss that killer—er—I mean I'll kill that kisser!"

Andy's romantic expression to his fiancée is also quite amusing, especially due to the visual dynamic presented. She is quite a homely woman, with the studio makeup department accenting her various facial flaws, but Andy calls her his "sweetsy-weetsy" and "tootsie-wootsie" while referring to himself as her "Andy-dandy." His sloppy romantic nature is, however, limited by the woman, who says, "Wait 'til we're married," when Andy attempts to move past a few tentative kisses.

Caught in the Act closes with a gag. Andy and his fiancée are married and as Andy goes to kiss the bride, his embrace causes the loose handcuffs still on his wrist to swing up and hit him in the face.

Clyde's short comedies continued to present a lot of layered situations and in this one they are effectively wrapped up. *Caught in the Act* is briskly paced, offers funny situations, provides some wild slapstick, and is amusing throughout. The budgets on the Columbia comedies allowed for some location and outdoor scenes that expand the scope of the film and enhance its production values.

The Clyde comedies continued to be very popular with moviegoers, and theater owners clamored for more. In the two years since Jules White began producing short comedies for Columbia, the Clyde series, along with the simultaneously produced Three Stooges shorts, made Columbia Hollywood's

#1 short subject unit. Of the comedians Jules White hired when first building his unit, by 1936 Walter Catlett was appearing only sporadically, Leon Errol had already left for RKO, and Harry Langdon made his last Columbia short in 1935 and wouldn't return to make another until 1938. Clyde and the Stooges continued to consistently produce eagerly sought product for the studio. As a result, the trio, and Andy Clyde, asked that they be given a pay raise. Clyde's salary per short went from $850 to $1000. The popularity of his comedies showed that he was worth that salary.

Share the Wealth

Directed by Del Lord; *Story and Screenplay:* Jack White (Preston Black); *Produced by* Jules White; *Cinematography:* Benjamin H. Kline; *Editor:* William Lyon; *Cast:* Andy Clyde, Mary Gordon, Vernon Dent, James C. Morton, Blackie Whiteford, Al Thompson, Bobby Barber, Tom Dempsey, William Irving, Bud Jamison, Fay Holderness, Bobby Burns, Charles Dorety, Johnny Kascier, Lew

Vernon Dent and Andy Clyde dated back to the Sennett comedies. They appeared together for the first of many times at Columbia in *Share the Wealth* (1936).

Davis, Heinie Conklin, Robert Barry, Bobby Dunn; *Shooting Dates:* February 4–14, 1936; *Released* March 16, 1936; *Columbia Production Number:* 215

Andy Clyde runs a shoe repair shop and is kept busy, but his customers never pay their bills. As a result, Andy is nearly a year behind on his rent, and his landlord happens to be the mayor. Andy goes to see his landlord to avoid eviction just as gangsters are in the mayor's office threatening him because they believe they got him elected and he should come through on a few "promises." In a desperate attempt to get more time to pay up, Andy tells the mayor there should be a program where people share their income. The gangsters like the idea and decide to back Andy for election. Andy ends up winning just as he inherits $50,000. He must now come up with a way to avoid sharing his windfall.

With Jack White (again billed as Preston Black) providing the scenario, and Del Lord as director, *Share the Wealth* is one of the most relentlessly funny Clyde comedies. The amusing premise is punctuated by a series of clever visual gags every few minutes.

Some of the best moments occur when Andy and his wife decide to skip town to avoid sharing the $50,000. Andy tells his wife they are returning to Scotland (a charming little in-joke, as both Clyde and co-star Mary Gordon were born there). Andy packs their things and they try to sneak away, but they are stopped by the gangsters who are backing Andy's mayoral run, and who are quite interested in receiving a share of the inheritance. The suitcase pops open and clothes fall to the floor. Andy states, "See? We aren't leaving, we're all unpacked." The gangsters are watching the house, so Andy and his wife attempt escaping up the chimney. All they succeed in doing is falling back down, covered with soot.

Once Andy wins the mayoral race, the townspeople respond to his "share the wealth" platform and start helping themselves to anything and everything, including all the shoes in Andy's shop. This results in a fistfight among the townspeople, who end up on the sidewalk in front of the shop. The governor calls for reinforcements, and there are shots of tanks and airplanes headed to the town to restore peace.

Lord's direction is quite brilliant here. He crosscuts between long shots and medium shots to show the many people fighting over the wares in Andy's shop. Customers in the closer shots are grabbing items, and then pulling at each other's holdings. The longer shot reveals all of the various people going through Andy's things and claiming items as their own. One customer hits another, then another one gets involved, and soon it extends outside onto the sidewalk, Lord neatly dovetailing the action from one setting to the next, and cutting back to show the violent activity involving more and more people.

The film concludes with a broken and dejected Andy sitting on the floor of his shop, surrounded by empty boxes that once contained shoes. He phones the president and manages to get through by insisting, "It's important!" Andy states that the Share the Wealth idea is "a bust" because "we just tried it." He hangs up, and then picks up the receiver once again to instruct the operator to "reverse the charges."

Share the Wealth is a somewhat topical short in that its original idea comes from populist presidential candidate Huey Long, who was campaigning with that slogan and planned to implement that very idea if elected. Long, who was the governor of Louisiana from 1928 to 1932, came up with the idea in 1934, in an attempt to combat the Depression that was sweeping America. He planned to run for president in the 1936 election, but was shot to death in 1935. Still, his idea remained of some interest in political circles as his Share the Wealth clubs had nearly eight million members. Jack White used this piece of the current culture as the basis for his movie's plot. *Film Daily* referred to the title as being "based on a slogan that repeatedly hits the daily newspapers."[16]

This is Clyde's first Columbia comedy with old friend Vernon Dent, whom he had known since the Sennett days. In Bill Cassara's book *Vernon Dent: Stooge Heavy*, film historian Edward Watz recalls being told by Dent's widow Eunice that Andy Clyde was a family friend who frequently came to their house to watch baseball, as the Dents owned one of the first televisions in the late 1940s.[17] Dent appeared frequently in Andy's Columbia shorts.

Share the Wealth appears to present the best context for Clyde's comedy: Put him in an amusing situation and season it with the sort of slapstick gags that Clyde had no trouble performing. *Share the Wealth* is different because it does not rely on a stock situation like being caught in the company of a pretty young girl by his wife, or the now-standard one where Andy is mistaken for a ladies man. This short has him comfortably married to another older Scottish person, and it ventures into the political realm in a way that is unlike Andy's regime-battling situations in *Hot Paprika*. It isn't exactly political satire, but there's still a message that not everything that sounds good is good in practice.

The Peppery Salt

Directed by Del Lord; *Story and Screenplay:* Al Ray; *Produced by* Jules White; *Cinematography:* Benjamin H. Kline; *Editor:* William Lyon; *Cast:* Andy Clyde, Mary Lou Dix, Warner Richmond, Blackie Whiteford, Sam Lufkin, Fred (Snowflake) Toones, Bert Young, John Ince, Harry Keaton, Bobby Burns, Jack Kenney, Al Thompson, Heinie Conklin, Idalyn Dupre, Ethelreda

Andy comes to the rescue of Mary Lou Dix in *The Peppery Salt* (1936).

Leopold, Tom Dempsey, Sidney Kilbrick, Charles Phillips, Antrim Short, Valerie Hall, Chuck Colean, Sidney Kibrick; *Shooting Dates:* March 9–13, 1936; *Released* May 15, 1936; *Columbia Production Number:* 212; *Remade by* Andy Clyde as *Marinated Mariner* (1950)

In another of his strongest comedies, Andy is a landlubber who works at a shipyard and enjoys telling children tall tales about his adventures at sea. Andy then gets word that he has inherited "The Admiral Dewey," which is to be found at Pier 67. He believes he now has his own ship, and excitedly goes to a clothing store and buys an admiral's uniform. When he discovers his "ship" is actually a lunch wagon stationed on the dock, he makes the best of it and serves customers wearing his admiral uniform. When his old boss' pretty daughter is kidnapped, he ends up rescuing her and becoming a hero.

The Peppery Salt is not only very funny, it also boasts some impressive production values. There are a few big scenes that would require a larger budget to successfully film, and there is a nice musical score backing up the action.

One of the big scenes features Andy in the lunch wagon, serving customers. He decides to nail up a sign which identifies him as the proprietor. When he nails the wooden sign, the nails go through the wall and into a ship docked next to the lunch wagon. When the ship takes off, the lunch wagon is fastened to it. When Andy's customers leave, they fall into the ocean. So does Andy, after which the lunch wagon becomes unfastened and falls into the ocean on top of him. Shot on location and with the use of a rather large ship as one of the scene's props, this gag indicates what Columbia's short subject department could do in 1936. That would not be the case in the 1940s.

This scene also allows the movie to transition to the plot of the kidnapped girl. After falling in the ocean and having his diner destroyed, Andy paddles to safety, ending up on the ship where the kidnappers are holding the girl for ransom. When Andy discovers the girl, he attempts to find a way to help her escape, resulting in a series of mishaps including run-in with a monkey on board the ship, as well as placing a lit kerosene lamp on an upright nail, poking a hole in it and causing the kerosene to ignite. The crooks believe Andy to be an actual admiral and they surrender, believing the U.S. Navy has surrounded their ship. However, another crook recognizes Andy as "the guy who runs the lunch wagon," and soon they are in pursuit of both him and the girl. Andy doubles back, sneaks behind the kidnappers and knocks each of them out, fleeing to safety with the girl.

Andy's befuddled manner and the continuous progression of the plot makes *The Peppery Salt* almost seem like a condensed feature film rather than a two-reel comedy. The stock music, composed by W. Franke Harling, further broadens the scope of this film, adding a layer of technical substance not found in the usual short comedy. And even though his intentions are good, almost all of Andy's heroics are accidental, which makes it funnier. Notable is Andy's expression when the crooks mistake him for an admiral: brief confusion followed by bravado as he takes advantage of the situation.

Director Del Lord's choreographing of Andy's antics on the ship are impressively funny. For instance, Andy throws a rope ladder from below deck, and it lands around the neck of a man on the upper deck, anchoring it enough for Andy to climb it. Andy lights a candle to see what he is doing, then puts it down, not realizing he is placing it on the back of a turtle. The turtle walks on, and Andy can't find his candle. When the kidnappers are sneaking along the deck looking for Andy, he doubles back with the girl, each of them holding a club, and conk the crooks one by one.

The Peppery Salt also does a good job examining the trajectory of Andy Clyde's screen character. He boasts to the kids, but in an amusing, endearing manner, not as an off-putting braggart. When the telegraph about "The Admiral Dewey" is delivered, the delivery man suggests it might be a nomination for president of the Liar's Club. But Andy is looked upon by his boss as a distracted and less productive. Andy is not necessarily disliked, but he is also not respected. Clyde works within these character parameters effectively, such as his delightfully amusing double take when he first sees himself in the mirror wearing the admiral's uniform.

And yet he approaches his lunch wagon duties earnestly, he cleverly finds a way to rescue the girl, and he is successful as the movie concludes. Our rooting interest in Andy's success allows for audience gratification. *Film Daily* stated:

> Produced in a light vein and studded with frequent humor, this is a mirthful little picture with Andy Clyde cavorting through a series of nonsensical experiences. It is sound, run-of-the-crop comedy that the average audience will find diverting.[18]

Motion Picture Daily was somewhat less enthusiastic, dismissing *The Peppery Salt* as "a fair comedy with few laughs."

Audiences enjoyed *The Peppery Salt* very much, and it is one of the Clyde Columbia comedies that holds up well today. Although there was a decidedly larger budget for this short, it was not a harbinger of things to come for the Clyde comedies. Subsequent movies would not be incorporating musical backgrounds or other such luxuries. It is unknown why *The Peppery Salt* receives deluxe treatment.

Mister Smarty

Directed by Jack White (as Preston Black); *Screenplay:* John Grey; *Story:* George Crone; *Produced by* Jules White; *Cinematography:* Benjamin H. Kline; *Editor:* William Lyon; *Cast:* Andy Clyde, Leora Thatcher, Bud Jamison, Tommy Bond, Bobby Barber, William Irving, Jack "Tiny" Lipson, Henry Manna, Billy Engle, Harry Tenbrook, William J. O'Brien, Frank Mills, John Rand, Robert McKenzie, Lew Davis; *Shooting Dates:* May 25–29, 1936; *Released* July 15, 1936; *Columbia Production Number:* 220; *Remade by* Andy Clyde as *Sunk in the Sink* (1950)

Mr. Smarty is gag-oriented, but also allows Andy Clyde to investigate male and female stereotypes, challenging them for comedic results.

Andy comes home and happily enters his house, only to stumble over a bunch of debris his wife has left in the living room. His wife is in the middle of a massive spring cleaning project, and Andy balks not only at the clutter, but also at what he believes is his wife's lack of efficiency. He doesn't like that his fishing gear and hunting rifles are being moved to the garage, even though the reason is because he hasn't built shelves on which to put them. The wife wants to hire carpenters to complete this task, but Andy insists he can save

When Andy takes over the household chores, he is in over his head in *Mister Smarty* (1936).

money by doing the job himself. He also believes he is more efficient and can clean up the house in a more timely manner than his wife. She decides to let him prove it and leaves the house.

The opening scene offers a perfect set-up. A happy, whistling Andy comes home looking forward to the evening because it is chicken and dumplings night. He wipes his feet on the porch's floor mat, unlocks the door, walks in and tumbles over the various debris the wife has laying around during cleaning. The rhythm of this opening is very effective. Andy's relaxed happiness is abruptly interrupted by his pratfall upon entering his home. Using all of his slapstick skills, Clyde makes this fall really count. He flails, stumbles, tumbles and slams to the ground.

Once he is put in charge of the cleaning, he hires all manner of helpers, including floor polishers, chimney sweeps and painters. He has them scheduled to come at different times but they all show up at once, getting in each other's way. Director Jack White nicely films the scene with the workers all converging on the living room, trying to accomplish their tasks. The action is framed in a medium shot that shows all of the workers, each moving in a different direction, causing a shaking pandemonium that results in a lot of disruption and little achievement.

Meanwhile, Andy plans to build the shelves for the upstairs closet. He orders only enough wood for this project, but enough wood to build an entire shed is inadvertently delivered. The wood pieces are large and long. Just the act of bringing a board into the house causes Andy to knock things over, and catch a nail on a chair's fabric and rip it open. Even simple things like leaning the boards against the wall causes them to tip over onto Andy's head. For all his bragging, Andy is inept at the task. When he finally balances the wood so that a shelf will stay up, Andy can't close the closet door. He pounds the wood in more, it goes through the wall and damages the other side in another room, causing more work for the painter and more money for Andy to pay.

So far *Mister Smarty* is a series of slapstick set pieces responding to mounting frustration. This extends to Andy locking himself in his own closet while the workmen downstairs discover beer in the refrigerator. While they're in the kitchen drinking, Andy's two young sons, who've been out of everyone's way up to now, come home and are attracted to the workers' various machines. They turn on a machine meant to vacuum out the chimney and fireplace, and they connect it to a chair Andy has ripped open, causing the feathered stuffing to come rising out of Andy's chimney.

Once Andy extricates himself from the closet, he gives his sons permission to sell some old stuff from the garage to a traveling junk dealer. The kids mistake some items for discards and sell them at a cheap price to the junk man (Andy's fishing poles and hunting rifles, his wife's fur coat, etc.). One point that was presented as the wife left the house was that Andy was to be especially careful of her china cabinet and the priceless china it contains. Of course, in the course of events, the china is destroyed.

Mister Smarty concludes with the wife coming home and finding the house a worse shambles than when she left, and a crowd of men in her living room drinking beer and drunkenly singing "The Music Goes Round and Round," a hit at the time. Meanwhile Andy is commiserating with his neighbor, who just painted his new car. The neighbor notices the feathers rising from Andy's chimney and laughs about it until he sees that they are sticking to his freshly painted car. He angrily gets out a rifle just as Andy's wife approaches. She says to the neighbor, "Don't shoot him, do you want to go to jail?" and then takes the rifle and starts shooting at Andy herself, as he runs away.

Mister Smarty is a movie where everything seems to go wrong, but rather than responding with some level of resourcefulness such as he does in other films, Andy responds to the frustration by seeking but never attaining control. Clyde's character grows more desperate as things get worse, and he's willing to do almost anything to fix things before his wife gets home. It seems less like he's desperate to prove her wrong, as the beginning of the film would indicate, and more like he's scared of her reaction. His response to the frustrations is his usual determined-yet-befuddled manner, and it works nicely within this context.

Much of the footage centers on Andy's attempts to build the shelves: wrestling with the long pieces of wood, desperately attempting to balance the materials, sawing through the wood and everything beneath it, being hit by falling boards, etc. This culminates in his inadvertently locking himself in his own closet while the workmen drink up his beer, and his sons cause an even greater mess. On top of all this, the writers decided that the Andy character's last name would be Bowser, resulting in a running gag with various people calling him the wrong name (Mouser, Boozer, et al.).

Mr. Smarty is very funny in Columbia's inimitable slapstick style, but what is most interesting about it is how it explores territory that was offbeat for Andy Clyde comedies. It also shows that Clyde, within the parameters of his short comedy series, could play essentially the same character but in a variety of contexts and with subtle variations. He can be a sheepish, henpecked husband, or a demanding chauvinist. He can be a cranky old man who dislikes children, or a family man who has kids of his own. And in each case he brightens every scene and nicely performs every slapstick set piece.

Motion Picture Herald called *Mister Smarty* "[a] comedy replete with funny situations and with Andy Clyde grunting and groaning in his well known style." A theater owner in that same issue reported, "Everyone made so much noise laughing you could hardly hear a word."[19]

Clyde's comedy series was maintaining its popularity and high level of quality as Clyde explored different ideas. *Mister Smarty* does a nice job challenging male and female stereotypes. Instead of trivializing housework, aka "woman's work," it shows just how difficult it can be, and in a comedic manner. Clyde does a great job with the idea. *Mister Smarty* is yet another of his funniest Columbia comedies.

Am I Having Fun!

Directed by Jack White (as Preston Black); *Story and Screenplay:* Al Ray, Arthur Ripley; *Produced by* Jules White; *Cinematography:* Benjamin H. Kline; *Editor:* Charles Hochberg; *Cast:* Andy Clyde, Leora Thatcher, Arthur Housman, Bud Jamison, Harry Semels, Jack "Tiny" Lipson, Lew Davis, Charles Dorety, Bobby Barber, Gail Arnold, Helen Martinez, Johnny Kascier, Bobby Burns, Al Thompson, Bert Young, Chuck Callahan, William Irving, Ethelreda

A drunken Arthur Housman takes cab driver Andy on a complicated journey in *Am I Having Fun!* (1936).

Leopold, C.L. Sherwood, Sam Lufkin; *Shooting Dates:* August 4–10, 1936; *Released* September 18, 1936; *Columbia Production Number:* 253; *Remade by* Billy Gilbert as *Crazy Like a Fox* (1944)

Having hit his stride several films ago, Clyde continued to offer consistently amusing two-reel comedies with *Am I Having Fun* also among his best from this period. Cinematically, its structure is disjointed. But on a purely visceral level, from which Columbia two-reelers invariably operate, it is another wildly funny farce.

Classic movie drunk Arthur Housman plays a drunken press agent who is helping publicize a visiting maharajah. He goes on a three-day bender, paying cab driver Andy to accompany him. The agent then promises Andy $200 if he can get him to the hotel to meet the maharajah by Wednesday. While Andy calls his shrewish wife to let her know what's going on, the press agent finds out from a passerby that it *is* Wednesday (he and Andy have lost track of time). He steals Andy's car and drives to the hotel. Andy, whose wife gives him the ultimatum to come home with that $200 or else, follows his cab on foot and ends up at the hotel. The maharajah, tired of waiting for the press agent, has angrily left, so Andy must take his place in disguise, otherwise he won't get the $200. Andy's wife comes to the hotel, bringing along her overbearing brother, and the two of them go after Andy. When the real maharajah returns to the hotel, he and Andy are mistaken for each other and a chase through the hotel ensues.

Mistaken identity, embarrassing situations, Andy's comical befuddlement and large doses of slapstick are the ingredients for this fast-paced, outrageous two-reeler. The dynamic between Clyde and Arthur Housman is particularly amusing in its comic incongruity. Andy is forever sober and conservative and tries to avoid any trouble while fulfilling his duties. Housman is the drunken bad influence whose status as a paying customer forces Andy into situations he prefers to avoid.

Housman spent most of his career playing drunks, and had just come from doing a great cameo in the Laurel and Hardy feature *Our Relations*. He had worked at Columbia before, most notably as the ringside attendant in the Three Stooges comedy *Punch Drunks* a couple of years earlier. Previous studies have claimed that Housman had an actual drinking problem off screen. Housman remained married to one woman from 1919 until his death in 1942 and worked steadily right to the end of his days,

Am I Having Fun features Housman at his very best, and as the perfect counterpart for Andy's sober befuddlement. While Andy refuses to drink with the press agent, he is willing to drive him around and collect the massive fare. He is okay with securing an extra $200 for helping with the press agent's ruse.

Andy seemed most comfortable in roles where his character was socially rather conservative—not one to drink, carouse or investigate anything outside the norm. To him, these elements remained on the faraway fringe. When they entered his immediate world, he was at a loss as to how to confront them. Thus, the dynamic between Andy and a drunken press agent whom he must satisfy is that much funnier. Housman's drunk is not dangerous or out of control, but he is an influence on the hapless cabbie, whose own story, as is presented in the movie, includes a nagging wife and a hovering mother-in-law. The two actors play off of each other perfectly while offering characters that they had honed to perfection.

The structure of this two-reeler is uneven. It opens with a road chase: The drunken press agent fools Andy into thinking he has a flat tire, and then takes off with his vehicle once Andy steps out to inspect the wheels. Andy follows on foot, jumps onto the back, and must now deal with the drunk's dangerous weaving in and out of traffic, even going head-on toward an approaching streetcar. It is fun slapstick action, but initially introduces a tempo that is not sustained or built upon. After this scene, the film settles into its narrative plot, slowing down the rhythm and re-establishing the film's narrative progression.

There are several amusing moments with a made-up Andy posing as the maharajah, complete with harem girls and a bevy of reporters. He is clearly out of his element, but knows he must earn the necessary $200, so he does his best to pull off the ruse, reacting to the proceedings in a manner that he believes best represents royalty. Clyde designed the makeup for this character. When Andy's wife and brother-in-law arrive on the scene, Andy must deny knowing them, causing a slapstick chase that soon involves the returning maharajah. The action that takes place is similar to what we saw in the earliest portion of the film. Thus, the movie opens with an action scene, settles into its narrative, then moves to another action scene.

Leora Thatcher had played Andy's wife in *Mister Smarty* and is even more shrewish here. Big, imposing Bud Jamison is her brother. There is a great deal of violence in this short, from Bud beating up the maharajah, believing him to be Andy in disguise, and Andy's wife pummeling her hapless husband as the movie concludes.

Critics called *Am I Having Fun* one of Clyde's better comedies. *Motion Picture Daily* stated that it had "fast moving action and comic excitement which will satisfy the comedian's following."[20] This is quite accurate, as theater owners reported that patrons laughed from start to finish.

Just as the popular Three Stooges were sustaining a strong series of Columbia comedies, Clyde continued to offer some of his best work, with one popular and successful comedy after another. This was at a time when budgets for short films were generally good, and location shots around Los Angeles, especially near the studio on Sunset Boulevard and Gower, were plentiful.

Love Comes to Mooneyville

Directed by Jack White (as Preston Black); *Story and Screenplay:* Ewart Adamson; *Produced by* Jules White; *Cinematography:* Benjamin H. Kline; *Editor:* Charles Hochberg; *Cast:* Andy Clyde, Esther Howard, Robert McKenzie, Lew Davis, Sam Lufkin, Robert McClung, George Gray; *Shooting Dates:* September 28–October 1, 1936; *Released* November 14, 1936; *Columbia Production Number:* 256; *Semi-remade by* Andy Clyde as *Scratch Scratch Scratch* (1955)

By the time he made *Love Comes to Mooneyville*, Andy Clyde was well

Sheriff Andy plots with deputy Bob McClung in *Love Comes to Mooneyville* (1936).

settled into his Columbia surroundings, drawing from elements of his established screen character in any manner the script dictated. In his next short, would he be a doting henpecked husband, or a crotchety old loner? Would he delight in the company of children, or was a cranky old goat who hated kids? Each Clyde comedy offered a different dynamic. But Andy was always befuddled, always challenged, usually clever enough to come out on top at the end, but sometimes defeated by the odds. And he was always funny and well received by moviegoers.

This time, Andy is the sheriff and Cy Ruggles (Robert McKenzie) the fire chief in the small town of Mooneyville. Both are smitten by the widow Ivy Flowers and engage in a series of slapstick battles to win her hand. *Love Comes to Mooneyville* is consistently funny, nicely paced, and has gag situations that build upon each other. Clyde and McKenzie work well together, engaging in bouts of reciprocal destruction.

The set-up has Andy initially exhibiting disdain for women and relationships. But once Ivy removes a speck from his eye, her kind, gentle nature attracts him and he quickly becomes smitten. But she has already attracted

Cy, so the two men vie for her attention. This is what leads to the slapstick give and take.

At one point, Andy is at Ivy's house courting her when he hears a police whistle, not realizing it is merely Cy, trying to trick Andy into leaving. Running out, Andy is met by a giggling Cy, who runs into the house. Andy responds by pulling a fire alarm, causing Cy to run out while Andy hurries back in. This situation is further enhanced by Cy, and then Andy, putting a sawhorse in front of the door, so either man trips over it as he frantically leaves for what he believes is a call of duty.

Another highlight is when both men are at Ivy's house for tea. Ivy brags about her baking skills and admits she is attracted to men with strong appetites. Andy puts shaving cream in Bob's cake, but Bob sees him from an adjacent room, and switches pieces of cake. The camera closes in a poor suffering Andy's expression as he consumes the tainted cake slice to impress the widow with his appetite, and not reveal he had sabotaged Bob's cake.

Andy's next ploy is an attempt to make Ivy jealous. He hires an attractive woman to pose as his date at a barn dance. The two of them are a delight on the dance floor and Ivy does become jealous as planned. The fire alarm rings, but fire chief Cy thinks it's another set-up until he discovers his own feed store is aflame. As Cy tends to the fire, it is revealed to Ivy that Andy's date is merely an imposter to make Ivy jealous. She realizes Andy is indeed the man for her. Andy concludes the film by teasingly saying to Ivy, "Do you think there's still a bit of dust in my eye?"

The relationship between Andy and Robert McKenzie works nicely. McKenzie's Cy Ruggles character comes off as more aggressive, and he punctuates each gag that he pulls on Andy with an increasingly louder cackle laugh. Andy is more grounded, but is easily driven to defending his honor with violence, never once backing down from the bigger man. The short is sustained by their slapstick battles and attempts at one-upmanship. But when the comedy evolves into Andy's ploy to make Ivy jealous and distract her from Cy, it takes on another dynamic. Andy keeps company with a ditzy blonde who fully understands the situation. Their dance bit at the party is a nice tangential sequence (comic dancing had been done in earlier Clyde shorts, including *Hot Paprika*).

Period reviewers didn't pay much attention to *Love Comes to Mooneyville* as slapstick was considered lowbrow entertainment. Movie theaters, however, were very happy with this short, one of them advising others: "[B]reak your arm to show this one."[21]

Producer Jules White must have felt this set-up was especially effective, because the same structure was used for two more Clyde shorts within the next several months. While not necessarily sequels in the most traditional sense, two other comedies featured Andy and McKenzie in the same roles. In *Stuck in the Sticks*, they once again contend for a character played by Esther Howard again using Ivy Flowers as her name. However, in that film, there is no reference to this one. Ivy is still someone with whom both Andy and Cy are smitten but, despite a similar character name, she plays a different person. Then Clyde and McKenzie's characters were used once more in *He Done His Duty*, only their object of affection is an attractive younger woman passing through town.

It was not unusual for Jules White to re-use ideas that he felt had worked before, but sequels were out of the ordinary for him.

Knee Action

Directed by Charles Lamont; *Screenplay:* Al Giebler, Elwood Ullman; *Story:* Al Giebler; *Produced by* Jules White; *Cinematography:* Benjamin H.

Andy's marriage is complicated by his bride's son, Tommy Bond, in *Knee Action* (1937).

Kline; *Editor:* Charles Hochberg; *Cast:* Andy Clyde, Vivien Oakland, Tommy Bond, Bud Jamison, Frank Mills, James C. Morton, Robert McKenzie, Eva McKenzie, Helen Dickson, William Irving, Lew Davis, George Gray, Lew Kelly; *Shooting Dates:* October 14–23, 1936; *Released* January 9, 1937; *Columbia Production Number:* 261; *Remade with* Joe DeRita as *The Good Bad Egg* (1947).

Andy Clyde was not above recycling past ideas, and Columbia was practically famous for doing so. In the case of *Knee Action*, Clyde once again investigated the dynamic of having a shrewish wife, a bratty kid and nobody in whom to confide. Andy is trapped by his situation and milks it for comic possibilities.

The film is structured a bit differently. It starts out with Andy, nervous and jittery, trying to rest in the country. When eggs are brought up early one morning, Andy asks that eggs and chickens never be mentioned to him again. When asked why, Andy explains and we are shown, in flashback, how he got to this point. The egg is a symbolic catalyst. Andy ends up marrying a woman who advertises for a husband by writing advertisements on egg shells. She comes as part of a package, with a bratty kid who accompanies them on their honeymoon and continues his disruptive presence as they set up housekeeping. The mother nags Andy and dotes on her son, never seeing any of his actions as negative. Andy must put up with both situations.

Clyde's screen persona worked well as a crabby man who disliked children or a happy man who loved them. Here he balances between aspects of both. He is ambushed with the information that he now has a stepson (he is told in the car as they leave the wedding), but plans to make the best of it. The child's behavior changes his position. He and the kid are adversarial through most of the movie.

Tommy Bond registers perfectly as the bratty kid, a precursor to the Butch character he would play in the Our Gang comedies at Roach at about the same time. Bond had earlier appeared with Our Gang in some nondescript roles, but by the time he did this movie, he was freelancing in features and shorts at the various studios. Bond had appeared with Clyde before, most notably as the similarly bratty child of Andy's ex-wife in *Alimony Aches*. Here he is given the spotlight and rises to the occasion in several scenes with the angry, frustrated and eternally befuddled Andy.

The child calls Andy "Featherpuss," shoots arrows at his picture on the wall and continues his disruptions to the point where Andy finally blows up and breaks the boy's bow and arrow. His enabling mother insists Andy pay for the ruined toy. Andy reluctantly pulls some money out of his wallet, and the bratty kid grabs the entire wad and runs away. His mother's reaction: "Oh, isn't he cute?"

Vivien Oakland, who had appeared with Clyde before, was, like Tommy Bond, on the verge of a pretty consistent gig, hers at RKO in comedies with Edgar Kennedy and Leon Errol. Oakland does a great job alternating between the angry shrewish wife and the indulgent, enabling parent. It keeps the comedy rolling at a fast pace, and allows Andy to react to the situations in a most amusing manner.

The film shifts gears slightly as it concentrates on a dishwashing machine invention Andy has created. He believes his high-powered concept will make dishwashing more efficient. When a potential backer comes over to see the invention, the brat has tampered with it and the high power results in destroying the dishes, turning them into sand. Andy attempts to rework it into a clothes washing machine, with similar results.

This comedy is a continuous series of overwhelming frustrations for Andy, but they are played in a comic fashion, and offer the perfect situation for his established character to react with anger and befuddlement. His anger is a natural reaction to the proceedings. His befuddlement is just what he can do about it. The problems are so extreme, the opening scene with his having escaped to the country after this awful ordeal, makes perfect contextual sense. As Andy's story concludes, the film shifts back to real time. The sympathetic listener who has heard all of Andy's troubles, with the catalyst having been an egg, joins Andy in shooting and killing all of the chickens on the farm, in one of the most outrageous conclusions of any Columbia short comedy.

While there is a fair-sized supporting cast in *Knee Action*, the comedy centers on the relationship between Andy, the child and his mother, whom Andy has hastily married. Clyde's ability to brilliantly play the kindly old man who likes kids, or the angry old goat who dislikes them, is on display here, as he has to straddle both aspects of his character's persona. Andy's initial delight in the prospect of becoming a father, and having a ready-made family, is quickly dampened by the child's behavior. And since Tommy Bond has since become virtually iconic for his role as bully Butch in the Our Gang comedies, *Knee Action* has even greater appeal in the 21st century. A couple of films later, he debuted his Butch character in the Our Gang short *Glove Taps*, and he continued playing the character until 1940. He would also play a similar character in other films, most notably *Block-Heads* (1938) featuring Laurel and Hardy.

Knee Action is another of Clyde's funniest films. Jules While was especially pleased with this and his Three Stooges series especially, expanding his short subject unit to include other silent movie comedy veterans like Harry Langdon and Charley Chase.

Stuck in the Sticks

Directed by Jack White (as Preston Black); *Screenplay:* Ewart Adamson; *Produced by* Jules White; *Cinematography:* Andre Barlatier; *Editor:* Charles Hochberg; *Cast:* Andy Clyde, Esther Howard, Bob McKenzie, Jack Evans, Robert Burns, Tom Dempsey, Eva McKenzie, Jack Hendricks, Bud Jamison, Ethelreda Leopold; *Shooting Dates:* January 22–25, 1937; *Released* March 26, 1937; *Columbia Production Number:* 265; *Released by* Columbia in the early 1960s as a silent, abridged short for 8mm projectors.

Stuck in the Sticks is sometimes called a sequel to *Love Comes to Mooneyville*, because it features some of the same characters and a similar structure. However, it can be argued that the redefinition of the female character keeps this from being a proper sequel and is merely another idea utilizing the same characters. Sheriff Andy and Fire Chief Ruggles (Bob McKenzie) are once again rivals for the attention of town widow Ivy Flowers (Esther Howard), but this time this situation goes in another direction and offers a neat twist.

The film initially re-establishes the rivalry, at all levels, that exists between Andy and Ruggles. It opens at a party where the two men are bobbing

Sheriff Andy tells Esther Howard to get out of town in *Stuck in the Sticks* (1937).

for apples, bumping heads in their zealous attempt to best the other. When a blindfolded man playing Pin the Tail on the Donkey gets sidetracked and jabs Andy in the backside, Andy bites hard into an apple and pulls it out of the bucket, winning the match.

Later, Ruggles and Andy play horseshoes, a game Andy is especially good at. However, Ruggles replaces his own horseshoes with magnets, thus ensuring ringers. There is some fun effects-driven comedy when Ruggles clearly misses his target, but the magnification causes the horseshoe to glide from its faraway spot and find its way to the post. Andy is undaunted: "You think you outfoxed me with magnetic horseshoes, but I will outfox you with my magnetic personality!"

The body of the film features Ruggles printing flyers that indicate that Ivy is actually a swindler known throughout the nation for marrying men and stealing their money. Sheriff Andy must uphold the law so, despite his misgivings, he goes to a confused Ivy's home and gives her one hour to get out of town so that he doesn't have to throw her in jail. He then goes to tell Ruggles of her misdeeds, feeling it is the right thing to do, Andy's integrity contrasting with Ruggles' unscrupulousness.

While Andy is looking for him, Ruggles sneaks over to Ivy's house, marries her and gives her $1000 in cash which she has requested. Ruggles eventually tells Andy about the wanted poster ruse and that he has now married Ivy. Andy, of course, is furious at having been duped, and a fight breaks out between them. A cop comes along and distracts the boys, and then indicates Ivy actually is a swindler and he is seeking to arrest her. Believing that this is another part of the ruse, Andy hits the cop, who does not arrest him because he is a fellow lawman. However, when they all go to Ivy's house, they discover she has indeed fled, leaving behind a note for Ruggles indicating that she has run out on him with his $1000 and referring to him as "You dumb cluck!" The chubby Ruggles faints and, as he falls, he lands on Andy.

This is all very funny situational humor, punctuated by slapstick gags. Andy works nicely in this context, as his rural old codger fluctuates effectively from explosive anger to bewildered befuddlement. He has the courage to strike a policeman whom he believes is a phony, and stammers a fumbling apology upon discovering he actually did hit a law enforcement officer. Watch Andy's masterful double takes as he reacts to Ruggles' magnetic horseshoes.

And the rivalry between Andy and Ruggles continues to be cheerfully funny. Bob McKenzie's giggling mischievousness comes off as amusing, even though the viewer automatically supports central figure Andy. The twist of having Ivy an actual swindler is a fun development that helps make *Stuck in the Sticks* arguably funnier and breezier than *Love Comes to Mooneyville*.

Clyde and McKenzie revisited this setting, and these characters, in *He Done His Duty*.

Sequels were not the norm with Columbia comedies, so one wonders why Jules White chose to make three of the same type of movie with the same setting. Perhaps he was considering a series with these characters. Or maybe he simply liked the team dynamic that Clyde and McKenzie offered.

My Little Feller

Directed by Charles Lamont; *Screenplay:* Ewart Adamson; *Produced by* Jules White; *Cinematography:* Benjamin H. Kline; *Editor:* Charles Hochberg; *Cast:* Andy Clyde, Doodles Weaver, Beatrice Curtis, Leora Thatcher, James C. Morton, Robert Rousch, Cy Schindell; *Shooting Dates:* March 12–17, 1937; *Released* May 21, 1937; *Columbia Production Number:* 272

A remake of *Ten Baby Fingers* (1934) with George Sidney and Charley Murray

Doodles Weaver and Andy take care of an abandoned baby in *My Little Feller* (1937).

Apparently Jules White liked the set-up where the leading male comedian had to take care of a difficult child. Andy already dealt with bratty children in a few films, and here he must care for a baby. *My Little Feller* is also interesting in that White apparently was continuing to experiment with Clyde in a team dynamic, this time with Winstead "Doodles" Weaver, who plays opposite him in a manner as if the two were a comic duo.

There isn't much substance to *My Little Feller*, its idea being very standard, and the ensuing gags are too often mechanical with only a few moments of real cleverness. The previous Clyde comedies take a much more creative approach to their comedy than a series of fairly predictable gags.

Andy and Doodles find an abandoned baby on their doorstep. They have no idea how to respond to the situation, so they choose to care for the child, believing it is the right thing to do. Unbeknownst to them, the baby was left there by kidnappers who had abducted the infant. As a result, Andy and Doodles are accused of having kidnapped the baby.

A lot of the humor comes from typical antics with a befuddled Andy and his dimwitted partner attempting to feed the baby, change it, and other such domestic activities in which they have no experience. It is a dynamic that would continually be used in television and more modern feature films like *Three Men and a Baby* (1987).

However, a lot of the gags here are mechanical. Andy puts a milk bottle on the stove to heat it up, forgets about it, and the glass shatters, the oven explodes and milk spills all over Doodles. There are a few instances where the baby almost falls, and either Andy or Doodles has to lunge toward the child and catch him, injuring themselves in the process.

At the same time, there are a few amusingly clever sequences. Andy runs down the street to find milk for the baby, sees a milk bottle on a doorstep and plans to steal it. When he looks around to see if anyone's watching, a man comes out of the house, grabs the milk bottle, and replaces it with an empty one. Andy reaches back, grabs the bottle and runs off, doing a whopping double take when he sees he has an empty bottle. At one point, Andy pokes holes in the fingertips of a rubber glove, fills it with milk, and allows the baby to suck milk from the glove's fingers, creating a makeshift nipple.

The kidnappers return to reclaim the baby and Andy and Doodles, having read about the situation in the newspaper, work to keep the child from the criminals as well as clear their own names. Andy chases the kidnappers' car on a bicycle with the kidnappers in pursuit, and drags a "DETOUR" sign across the road to throw them off. The car goes over a bump, the baby flies into the air, and Andy catches the giggling infant. The film concludes with

Andy getting ahold of one of the kidnappers' guns during a tussle, and keeping them at bay until help arrives. The baby is returned to its parents.

Clyde responded personally well to this structure, having become a father himself only a few years earlier. He is one of the few comedians who believed he worked particularly well with children, no matter how effortlessly their very presence could steal a scene. In *My Little Feller*, the baby is an especially fun presence, enhancing the proceedings nicely. The Three Stooges would use ideas similar to this film for their comedies *Mutts to You* (1938) and *Sock a Bye Baby* (1942).

While *My Little Feller* is a milder effort in Clyde's Columbia filmography, it was an important venture for movie newcomer Doodles Weaver. A former star on stage, Weaver had broken into movies in small parts only a year before *My Little Feller*. He touted his appearance in an interview: "In the picture I dance, sing, and do my best to play a good stooge. The preview was well accepted, and I am very evident all through it, on account of there being only two in the cast outside of a little baby."[22] Weaver was exaggerating that he and Andy were the only ones in the cast, but they are the central characters and command most of the footage. He shares the screen with the movie's star, and gets roughly the same amount of screen time. That is quite a big role for a newcomer, and Weaver rises to the occasion. Weaver also appeared with Clyde in his next film.

Lodge Night

Directed by Jack White (as Preston Black); *Screenplay:* Ewart Adamson; *Produced by* Jules White; *Cinematography:* Benjamin H. Kline; *Editor:* Charles Hochberg; *Cast:* Andy Clyde, Joan Woodbury, Doodles Weaver, Nick Copeland, Bonita Weber, Louise Carver, William McCall, Sammy Blum, Antrim Short, Eva McKenzie, Penny Parker, Georgia O'Dell; *Shooting Dates:* March 25–31, 1937; *Released* June 11, 1937; *Columbia Production Number:* 270; *Remade by* Andy Clyde as *Blonde Atom Bomb* (1951)

Another very funny Clyde comedy, and one that is a bit more complex, with a lot of mistaken identity twists and turns.

Back in the 1930s (and until the 1960s), one of the standard comedy conflicts in marital situations was the man's distraction by his own social activities. Often men are shown as being a part of a lodge—a fraternal organization that allows some level of escape from the drudgery of their working lives and the limited parameters imposed upon them in their home life. In *Lodge Night*, Andy's wife believes he is spending too much time away from home. Her

Andy waters showgirl Joan Woodbury along with the plants in *Lodge Night* (1937).

gossipy friend warns her that Andy could be engaged in dalliances with other women when he claims to be attending lodge meetings. Andy is once again playing a button-down conservative family man who would never consider straying, thus making such a suspicion absurdly funny in and of itself.

Adding to the complexity of the situation is Andy's nephew Jimmy, played by Doodles Weaver in the second of his two appearances in Clyde comedies. Jimmy is a carefree womanizer who often gets into trouble, resulting in Andy having to bail him out. Andy confronts Jimmy about the young man's current plans to meet up with Lola, a nightclub singer. Jimmy ignores Andy's advice and sneaks off. Andy discovers this via an address that has been left behind, and follows him.

When Andy's wife sees the note with the address of the club, she believes it is Andy who is going out on the town. Influenced by her gossipy friend, she goes after him. Jimmy is backstage with Lola while her jealous boyfriend is on stage doing his act. After being distracted by running into a family friend, Andy manages to get backstage. Jimmy is alerted that Andy is looking for him, so he sneaks away. Andy enters Lola's room and pulls out some money, asking how much she wants to stay away from Jimmy. Seeing he has money, Lola puts on an act as if she is interested in Andy. He resists, but she manages to take his money. Andy attempts to retrieve his money just as the jealous boyfriend enters the room.

While all of this is going on, Andy's wife arrives at the club, sees the friend and is told that Andy is backstage in the female singer's room. Andy's angry wife pulls the leg off a chair and heads backstage, ready to cause whatever mayhem she deems necessary.

From this point, the film becomes a long chase that breaks off into slapstick tangents. Andy must avoid his wife as well as evade the jealous boyfriend while also trying to retrieve his money. He dons a stage costume and mask similar to the one the boyfriend wears for his act, which is enough to fool Lola into believing Andy is her boyfriend, so she gives him the money. Once he has his money, Andy is ready to sneak off and go home, but his wife catches up with him, hits him over the head and drags him away.

The tangential slapstick bits that occur within the chase offer some interesting and creative ideas. First, Andy and the boyfriend, wearing similar costume and makeup, confront each other in what they both believe is a mirror. They do a mirror bit similar to the one seen in the Marx Brothers' Paramount feature *Duck Soup* (1933). Each man moves exactly as the other, mirroring each other until Andy accidentally lifts the wrong arm and blows his cover.

Another tangential bit also recalls a Marx Brothers movie, this time their MGM feature *A Night at the Opera* (1935). As a haughty singer is bleating what is supposed to be an operatic number, the tussles Andy and the boyfriend are having backstage cause various canvases to fall behind her. At one point Andy swings across the stage on a rope. These gags are similar to when the Marx Brothers do what they can to stall a stage production of an opera in their feature.

Although central to the narrative conflict, Doodles Weaver is really given little to do. He had essentially co-starred with Andy in the previous *My Little Feller*, but with *Lodge Night* he is decidedly peripheral to the action. Weaver would never appear in another Clyde comedy, but his career continued with Spike Jones' band, on several TV shows (including his own TV shorts in the '60s, *A Day with Doodles*) and working in the films of everyone from Jerry Lewis to Alfred Hitchcock. Joan Woodbury, who plays Lola, went on to become a veritable queen of B movies, appearing in the Charlie Chan and Boston Blackie series and a Brenda Starr serial, as well as movies with the Marx Brothers and Joe E. Brown.

At around this time, Columbia Harry Cohn's former secretary Hugh McCollum began producing some of the short subjects, alleviating the load on Jules White. One of the studio's recent acquisitions was veteran comedian Charley Chase who, like Andy Clyde, had been in films since the silent era and had recently moved on from his previous studio (Hal Roach). Chase was starring in his own films at Columbia, but also producing, directing and writing the films of others. Chase and McCollum produced Andy's next Columbia short comedy.

Gracie at the Bat

Directed by Del Lord; *Screenplay:* Al Giebler, Elwood Ullman; *Story:* Del Lord; *Produced by* Charley Chase, Hugh McCollum; *Cinematography:* André Barlatier; *Editor:* Arthur Seid; *Cast:* Andy Clyde, Leora Thatcher, Vernon Dent, Eddie Fetherston, Bud Jamison, Louise Stanley, Ann Doran, Bess Flowers, William Irving, Frances Bowling, Beatrice Curtis; *Shooting Dates:* August 25–30, 1937; *Released* October 29, 1937; *Columbia Production Number:* 407; *Working title: Slide Nellie Slide*

Gracie at the Bat is a comedy that uses the popular sport of baseball as its backdrop. And considering how important baseball was in 1937 America,

Lobby card for *Gracie at the Bat*.

it is surprising that so few slapstick short comedies used it for comedy. Even the Three Stooges, active at the same studio, did no baseball comedies (they did comedies about football, boxing, even wrestling). Perhaps the closest Columbia came to another baseball comedy is Charley Chase's *The Heckler*, made in 1940 and remade with Shemp Howard six years later as *Mr. Noisy*. However, this was about an obnoxious fan, not about the game of baseball.

In 1937, baseball was an extremely significant part of American culture. It featured the transition from veteran Babe Ruth to newcomer Joe DiMaggio, who broke into the major leagues the year before and would lead the New York Yankees to three consecutive World Series wins (1936, 1937, 1938). Lou Gehrig enjoyed his final great season before his numbers began to plummet the following year, due to an illness that would not only take his life, but would thereafter be represented by his name.

Another offshoot of baseball: the women's leagues that had been active for some years by this time. (This is before the era as depicted in Penny Marshall's film *A League of Their Own*. That period was during World War II, when male ballplayers joined the service, and the female teams were able to help keep the game alive, amidst much publicity.) In 1937, women's baseball was more of a novelty, buoyed by such events as a 1931 exhibition game when female pitcher Jackie Mitchell managed to strike out both Lou Gehrig and Babe Ruth.

Thus, *Gracie at the Bat* responds to this popularity with Andy playing an old veteran of baseball who is now a stadium groundskeeper. Long retired from playing, Andy simply wants to keep close to the game. However, he always complains loudly when having to clean up the stadium after a women's game. For humorous purposes, Andy is seen having to clean up powder puffs, discarded lipstick tubes and other such female items. His complaints, including such lines as "They oughta be home darning socks," annoy the park owner to the point where Andy is fired.

At home, out of work, Andy is contacted by an old teammate, now an executive, for a position as a baseball coach out of town. He is thrilled with the prospect of using his veteran savvy for a new team and hurries to the offices, only to find that he will be coaching a female team.

In one of the film's highlights, Andy is in the offices having just accepted the coaching job, not yet realizing it is for a women's team. The management discusses how to round up the players during the off season, mentioning such things as "Mayberry is with the ballet" and "Wayne is working in a beauty parlor," causing Andy to react each time. When they finally mention, "and Callahan became the mother of triplets," Andy faints.

Clyde is a master at flustered reactive comedy, and his background in silent film had honed his ability to react non-verbally in a comic manner. At first he registers a puzzled bemusement, wondering why ballplayers would be active in the ballet or working in a beauty parlor, but such things would still be, at least, feasible. This is the buildup to his swooning reaction to the "mother of triplets" revelation. It is one of the funniest scenes in the film.

The film delves into some level of stereotyping, not just Andy's sexist attitude toward female players, but the actions of the players themselves. After Andy has accepted the job and is making the best of the situation, he is confronted with the stereotypical cattiness of the female players. A conflict between the pitcher and the catcher ("I won't play if she plays") is being ironed out in Andy's office when his wife stops in for a surprise visit. In the lobby, she overhears Andy and the woman talking, with the woman asking, "Make up your mind, which one of us do you want?" Andy responds, "I can't see why I can't have both of you!" His wife believes the worst.. Andy comes out of his office, delightedly surprised to see his wife, and is completely baffled when she slaps him and storms out.

All of these scenes build up to the climactic game where Andy confronts the usual problems, including a neat slapstick bit where a catcher's chest protector has blown up with too much air and floats away. Andy climbs through the audience, stepping on patrons, in order to retrieve it, and it ultimately blows up.

Pro athletes will invariably become thick-skinned to the catcalls of audiences members during a game, but the comic stereotyping goes in another direction with female players. Their star pitcher angrily leaves the game due to being heckled, putting Andy in a bad position as he has no backup. Andy's wife, listening to the game on the radio, realizes that Andy is coaching girls, is innocent of her initial conclusions, and hurries to the ballpark. She grabs a uniform and says, "Put me in, Pa, we have a game to win," allowing us to realize, for the first time, that she herself is a former star baseball player. Andy is delighted. When a heckler speaks negatively about his wife's age, Andy goes into the stands and punches him.

The film then settles upon comic effects to show how Andy's team wins the game with his wife's help. She throws fastballs that ignite and start on fire due to the momentum. Balls whiz past players and cause their hair to blow back. When the wife hits a ball, her long slide into home plate knocks everyone down in her path. Along with providing an amusing, triumphant conclusion, the wife's prowess balances the stereotyped presentation of the other women.

Another very good Clyde comedy, *Gracie at the Bat* was warmly received by audiences. Theater owners, writing in the trades, called this one of the

Andy and his all-girl baseball team in *Gracie at the Bat* (1937).

comedian's best shorts, indicating how it would have even greater appeal to baseball fans. It's worth noting his character's arc in response to the female ballplayers. His initial sexism is very off-putting, but by the end of the film, after spending more time around them and watching his wife play, he has undergone a complete reversal. It's nice to see how invested he is in cheering on his wife.

But *Gracie at the Bat* also has some significant differences from his previous efforts. Switching from Jules White to Charley Chase and Hugh McCollum as his producers, Andy is now working with a more developed story and subtler humor than the gag-after-gag slapstick outings to which he'd become accustomed. While White's more aggressive slapstick style is an art unto itself, the more subtle approach that Chase and McCollum employ offers another perspective that is equally effective.

Clyde's usual screen persona of stammering befuddlement, old-fashioned kindness alternating with crotchety anger, and a clever ingenuity for coming out on top in the end, are all evident in this context. His character seems more layered, and it is given more to do than perform and react to slapstick gags. Clyde had great range as an actor. He had continued appearing in different roles at other studios while doing his Columbia comedies, including the rustic drama *The Barrier*, released by Paramount about a month after *Gracie at the Bat*. So when he had to alter his comic character to fit comfortably within a subtler, more situational comic approach, he was able to rise to the occasion.

Thus, from here on, Andy Clyde's comedies would respond differently depending on which producer was working on them. White continued to utilize wild slapstick situations, while Chase and McCollum would allow for greater depth of character and a more layered narrative. White recalled in an interview with James Curtis:

> It was too big a load for me to carry all these shorts and keep making them. And so we split the department and let McCollum make half and hire the directors, and I made my half. We just cut the program in half and we each took half. This way I could direct everybody and make some of each, which is what I wanted to do. Then, of course, we got to the point where we cut down the number of films we were making and it was no longer feasible to have two producing units. McCollum was out and I continued to make them.[23]

One of Andy's co-stars in *Gracie at the Bat* is Ann Doran, who would work often in Columbia comedies, including those starring Charley Chase, the Three Stooges and Harry Langdon. In a *Filmfax* interview conducted by Steve Randisi, Doran remembered Clyde as "the funniest man who ever lived."[24]

He Done His Duty

Directed by Charles Lamont; *Screenplay:* Ewart Adamson; *Produced by* Jules White; *Cinematography:* Allen Siegler; *Editor:* Charles Nelson; *Cast:* Andy Clyde, Bob McKenzie, Dorothy Granger, Lester Dorr, Hank Bell, Bud Jamison, Robert McClung, Ray Bourbon, William Lally, James Leong, Betty Mack; *Shooting Dates:* September 13–17, 1937; *Released* December 10, 1937; *Columbia Production Number:* 411

This was the third and final Andy Clyde comedy in which he plays the sheriff and Robert McKenzie portrays fire chief Cy Ruggles in the town of Mooneyville. The object of their affection, Ivy Flowers, swindled Ruggles and left town in the previous film *Stuck in the Sticks*, so in this one there are new conflicts. First, Cy decides to run for sheriff against Andy. Then Kitty, a younger, prettier female swindler, stops in town posing as a federal investigator. Andy and Cy's rivalry for a woman is again rekindled—and Cy is swindled out of another $1000.

In some ways, going through the same routine with the same setting and conflicts would seem a bit tiresome, but *He Done His Duty* is actually the funniest of the three films that utilize this plot.

Robert McKenzie laughs as Andy breaks the windows of his own store in *He Done His Duty* (1937).

McKenzie, as Cy, is once again a giggling delight as he plasters his own campaign posters all over Andy's store. When an irate Andy starts impulsively smashing the windows containing the posters, Cy reminds they are his own shop's windows. Andy's double take reaction is typically masterful. In another fun sequence, Cy prepares to buy a box of candy from Andy's store. He decides to "test" the candy before purchasing the box by biting into several pieces. Deciding he doesn't want to buy the candy, he leaves the store, having effectively ruined the merchandise. Andy once again fumes.

Attention is paid to the rustic setting of the small rural town, extending to the peripheral characters. Robert McClung as Andy's young store helper, for instance, was just beginning to establish himself in movies as an amiable small town bumpkin. Betty Mack, who makes a rather brief appearance, was already a veteran of short comedies, having worked in several of the Hal Roach-produced comedies featuring Charley Chase.

The film focuses on naive Andy and Cy being easily fooled by the wily, city-bred Kitty. Cy, having more money, is more attractive to Kitty. Cy gets his comeuppance when he finds that he's been swindled out of the same amount of money Ivy had absconded with in the previous film. They do make reference to Ivy Flowers having swindled Cy in the previous movie (Cy blames Andy).

The slapstick in this one is faster and more aggressive, with a good car chase as the film's centerpiece. Kitty causes several accidents as she barrels down the country paths in her car, attempting to throw off Andy and Cy who are racing behind her. Watermelon wagons and laundry trucks are among her casualties. This time they do retrieve Cy's money after the chase ends in a crash right into a man's bedroom. The film concludes with the two rivals becoming friends.

Motion Picture Daily made note of the "thrilling automobile chase" and stated that the film has "plenty of vivid slapstick comedy, the type that audiences find highly amusing."[25] *Film Daily* was less enthusiastic, dismissing the film as having "too much slapstick," and stating, "It gets rather monotonous as the rough comedy is piled on to the screeching point."[76] Nevertheless, *He Done His Duty* was another big hit with moviegoers.

Andy would once again explore a rustic setting with his next film *The Old Raid Mule*.

The Old Raid Mule

Directed by Charley Chase; *Story and Screenplay:* John Bell Clayton; *Produced by* Charley Chase, Hugh McCollum; *Cinematography:* André Barlatier; *Editor:* Arthur Seid; *Cast:* Andy Clyde, Olin Howland, Ann Doran, Dorothy Appleby, Vernon Dent, Robert McKenzie, Bud Jamison, Eddie Laughton, Sam Lufkin; *Shooting Dates:* November 2–6, 1937; *Released* March 4, 1938; *Columbia Production Number:* 417

The Old Raid Mule was adapted from a short story by John Bell Clayton, based on the rural adventures of an old hillbilly who keeps getting swindled by a neighbor. Hugh McCollum felt it could make a good comedy for Andy Clyde, whose forte was playing the very type of old codger depicted in the story. Charley Chase, McCollum's co-producer, responded well when McCollum alerted him to the story. Chase had made several rural comedies of his own, including *The Real McCoy* (1930), *One of the Smiths* (1931) and *Southern Exposure* (1935), and his familiarity with the concept made it more attractive to him. He chose to direct the movie himself.

As part of the deal, Clayton wanted screenplay credit, but it was actually

Vernon Dent looks on as Andy, Eddie Laughton and Bud Jamison check out a grandfather clock in *The Old Raid Mule* **(1938).**

Chase himself who adapted the story. Clayton might have offered a treatment for filming, but Chase is the one who had experience with writing screenplays.

For all its potential, *The Old Raid Mule* is one of the weaker Clyde comedies from this period. Its rural setting works, Andy is amusing in the role, he has a good supporting cast, and Chase has an eye for cinematic detail unlike most of the others who helmed Columbia comedy shorts. But *The Old Raid Mule* is slow, plodding and not particularly funny. Understandably, the slow pace is conducive to the laid-back hillbilly concept that director Chase is trying to convey, but this doesn't save *The Old Raid Mule* from being a humdrum effort.

Andy plays a crotchety oldtimer whose naiveté results in his being continually swindled by a cagey acquaintance named Ben Cole. First, Andy trades his mule for a car that quickly breaks down. Then he trades his gun for a grandfather clock that stops. Andy becomes more frustrated and plans to shoot Ben. However, when Andy traded his gun, he forgot to remove a cork from it (placed there to keep the buckshot in). So when Ben sees Andy approaching angrily approaching his house, he pulls out the gun to shoot Andy, the weapon blows up in his face and causes his entire house to collapse around him. Satisfied with the karma, Andy turns and heads home.

Film Daily was called it "an amusing short" and opined that Olin Howland, who plays Ben Cole, "contributes good support." *Motion Picture Daily* was equally enthusiastic, pointing out it was "a different type of Andy Clyde comedy... The hillbilly atmosphere will keep the audience smiling constantly." In a trade paper, a theater owner called it "another fine Andy Clyde comedy. Andy Clyde and the Three Stooges never fail to please our audience."

There are some impressive shots in the film. Charley Chase had a good understanding of shot composition, so during a scene where Andy is in a drug store where other hillbillies are lazily hanging around, Chase first shows Clyde in a medium shot beginning his story, then switches to a long shot where all of the hillbillies seated about are in the frame at the foreground, with Clyde in the background telling his story. Even though Clyde is in the back, Chase manages to make him the focal point of the shot, while the foreground with the others is the negative space in which he is framed. This is just one example of Chase's directorial vision, as he makes great use of the backgrounds, which were shot on sets used by Columbia for its westerns.

Olin Howland and Andy Clyde worked together as semi-regular featured players on the TV series *The Real McCoys* years later. Actress Ann Doran, who enjoyed working with Clyde, told *Filmfax* interviewer Steve Randisi that Andy requested her for the role she played in *The Old Raid Mule*.

Clyde's Columbia comedies had been pretty consistently good for some time, so it is not unusual for a weaker entry to come along. *The Old Raid Mule* is that weaker entry.

Jump, Chump, Jump

Directed by Del Lord; *Produced by* Jules White; *Cast:* Andy Clyde, Gertrude Sutton, Bud Jamison, George Ovey, Fred "Snowflake" Toones; *Shooting Dates:* December 14–18, 1937; *Released* April 15, 1938; *Columbia Production Number:* 403

Andy wants an explanation from Gertrude Sutton in *Jump, Chump, Jump* (1938).

Jump Chump Jump is the first film in this study for which a copy print was not available. The sound and picture negatives are confirmed to be housed in the Library of Congress, but no screening print exists in their archives. The information on this film is culled from research.

After the offbeat *The Old Raid Mule*, Clyde appears to have returned to the more aggressive slapstick approach that producer Jules White favored, and with the formidable Del Lord as director. *Jump Chump Jump* puts Andy in typical situations to which his character can react, and punctuates the narrative with physical comedy. Andy discovers political corruption right under his nose and gets a schoolteacher friend to help him expose the criminals.

One of the aspects of Clyde's screen character was a nosy and suspicious nature, which usually ended up with him having incorrectly assessed the situation. However, in *Jump Chump Jump* his intuition is accurate and once he convinces the teacher that the situation is serious, she agrees to assist him.

Gertrude Sutton, who plays the teacher, had been taking small parts in feature films since the dawn of talking pictures. As with many small-time actors in feature-length movies, Sutton sought more footage, and opportunity, in short subjects. However, her roles in short films with everyone from Laurel and Hardy to Our Gang were still too small to give her much opportunity to investigate what she could do with a solid comedy role. In *Jump Chump Jump*, she plays opposite Andy and has more time to exhibit her innate comic talents. Clyde was noted for working well with anyone who had even a marginal flair for comedy. Since Sutton had good comic instincts, she plays off of Clyde nicely. He would request her services again.

Jump Chump Jump relies on Andy's fluttery response to trouble, his determination to do what is right, and his chemistry with co-star Sutton. In the July 2, 1938, *Motion Picture World*, an exhibitor reported that it "brought the house down. ...[T]hese Andy Clydes are all good." Jules White recalled for James Curtis: "With Andy we had everything, but a lot of farcical situations. Always we tried to find a farcical situation, and then we would gag it up accordingly."[27]

Ankles Away

Story and Screenplay, Director: Charley Chase; *Produced by* Charley Chase, Hugh McCollum; *Cinematography:* André Barlatier; *Editor:* Arthur

Vernon Dent is about to clobber Gene Morgan as Andy looks on in *Ankles Away* **(1938).**

Seid; *Cast:* Andy Clyde, Ann Doran, Gene Morgan, Gino Corrado, Grace Goodall, Bess Flowers, Vernon Dent, John T. Murray, Symona Boniface, Beatrice Curtis, Claire Rochelle; *Shooting Dates:* January 11–13, 1938; *Released* May 13, 1938; *Columbia Production Number:* 421

Ankles Away is one of the more interesting Clyde comedies, mostly due to its history. Charley Chase, acting as producer, writer and director, reconstructed one of his old ideas for Clyde. In this one, Andy is duped into believing that his fiancée has a wooden leg, and he therefore balks at the prospect of marrying her. Exhibitors reported that it "brought the house down" and called it one of Andy's best. However, in his 1970 book *The Great Movie Shorts,* Leonard Maltin stated:

> *Ankles Away* is a remake of Chase's *His Wooden Wedding,* about a bridegroom who is told by a rival, just before the wedding, that his wife-to-be has a wooden leg. In the Chase silent, it was hilarious material, but somehow, in the remake, it seemed oddly tasteless and unfunny.[28]

While Maltin is a bit harsh in his reaction to *Ankles Away,* he does point out that some concepts do not work in different contexts.

The idea of *Ankles Away* gives Andy a chance to react in his inimitable manner, and to respond once again to a situational narrative rather than a bare-bones plot and a string of slapstick gags. And Chase, as director, remains adept at utilizing impressive establishing shots for each scene, and offering a visual composition that helps frame each gag nicely. But *Ankles Away,* while perhaps not a total misfire, is more interesting than it is funny.

Chase first investigated this idea in his 1925 silent *Fighting Fluid.* Charley plays a heavy drinker who sees two men moving a mannequin in a shop. Since the mannequin is wearing the same type of dress his fiancée wore earlier that day, Charley's blurred vision makes him think two men are accosting his girl. He chases them away, and in the commotion, the mannequin's leg falls off. Charley picks it up, believes his fiancée has a prosthetic limb, and tosses away his engagement ring, not wanting to marry a one-legged woman. Politically incorrect in the 21st century, it was just a funny gag over 90 years ago.

Later that year, Chase made *His Wooden Wedding,* the film that features the same plot as this Clyde subject. The idea can still be seen as edgy, but not completely unacceptable within the parameters that this is an outrageous slapstick comedy. And Chase's vision was subtler than Jules White's and he was more interested in establishing a narrative that fit in two reels. That Chase was the veritable auteur of this short makes *Ankles Away* an unusual effort, with more story and situations than slapstick gags.

Chase was not the only comedian who utilized this idea. In the Harry Langdon silent *Picking Peaches,* which predates the Chase silents by a full year, Harry is a shoe salesman whose customer, while he is distracted, puts a mannequin leg under her skirt to see how the shoe it is wearing might look for her. Harry lifts the leg higher than it should go, and is shocked to find that it appears disconnected. And in the same year that *Ankles Away* was released, Laurel and Hardy's feature *Blockheads* has Hardy, when he sees Stan sitting with his leg tucked underneath him, mistakenly believes that Laurel has lost a leg in combat. One of the screenwriters of *Blockheads* was Harry Langdon.

The Soul of a Heel

Directed by Del Lord; *Screenplay:* Ewart Adamson; *Produced by* Jules White; *Cinematography:* Allen Siegler; *Editor:* Charles Nelson; *Cast:* Andy Clyde, Gertrude Sutton, Bud Jamison, Eve McKenzie, James C. Morton, Cy Schindell, Frank Mann; *Shooting Dates:* January 28–February 1, 1938; *Released* June 4, 1938; *Columbia Production Number:* 424

The Soul of a Heel is another Clyde comedy that is inaccessible. As with many of the elusive films in this study, the sound and picture negatives are housed in the Library of Congress, but no screening print. Clyde stars as a gold prospector who has been engaged to Miranda, the sheriff's daughter, for 15 years. Andy doesn't want to marry Miranda until he has acquired enough gold for them to live comfortably forever. The sheriff, tired of waiting, arranges for Miranda to marry his deputy. These plans are temporarily thwarted when Andy comes home with gold. However, upon further examination, his "gold" turns out to be worthless buckshot, so the sheriff angrily demands that his daughter dump Andy and marry the deputy. Reacting, Andy becomes disruptive and is jailed.

Andy's cellmate turns out to be a tramp he had met while prospecting and it is soon discovered that this tramp stole his gold and replaced it with

Andy and his girlfriend Gertrude Sutton in *Soul of a Heel* (1938).

buckshot. The tramp forces Andy to break out of jail and help rob a bank. Andy, with the help of his mule, subdues the criminal, gets his gold back and ends up marrying Miranda.

Andy asked for Gertrude Sutton to play Miranda, having been pleased with her work in *Jump Chump Jump*. It's unfortunate that no print is available of either film in which Sutton appeared with Clyde. (She did later have a small role in the Clyde short *Gold Is Where You Lose It*.)

Del Lord's contribution as director was to punctuate what was largely a situational comedy and offer the sort of rollicking pace and slapstick gags that helped define the Columbia unit. While Clyde was able to work cohesively with all of his directors and writers, he felt most comfortable with his more frequent collaborators. Lord's history with Clyde, and his openness to Clyde's contributions, resulted in a camaraderie that extended beyond the parameters he enjoyed with other filmmakers.

At about the time *The Soul of a Heel* was released, Clyde helped organize the first annual Lakeside Motion Picture golf tournament. As chairman of the tournament committee, Andy offered a trophy for the first low net score (determined by subtracting the player's handicap from the number of strokes actually taken). Andy and his wife were both among the best golfers in the film colony. Andy shot in the low seventies while Mrs. Clyde shot in the eighties.

Meanwhile, *Film Daily* reported:

> Columbia Studios is now in an uproar. What with the Three Stooges running wild on one set and Andy Clyde cutting up capers on an adjoining stage, the place is beginning to show signs of wear and tear.[29]

Not Guilty Enough

Directed by Del Lord; *Produced by* Jules White; *Cast:* Andy Clyde, Kathryn Bates, Shemp Howard, Bud Jamison, John Tyrrell; *Shooting Dates:* July 29-August 2, 1938; *Released* September 30, 1938; *Columbia Production Number:* 432. A remake of Educational Pictures' Andy Clyde comedy *Half Baked Relations* (1934).

Not Guilty Enough has a special interest in that it is the first of a handful of films in which Shemp Howard appears opposite Andy Clyde. No known materials exist on *Not Guilty Enough*.

It's based on an earlier Andy Clyde comedy, *Half Baked Relations* (1934), which was his last for Educational before joining Columbia. It also has similarities in structure to a much later Three Stooges short, *Idiots Deluxe* (1946).

II. The Columbia Comedy Shorts 77

Andy and Shemp Howard engage in dangerous activity in *Not Guilty Enough* (1938).

The film opens with Andy on trial for beating up his obnoxious brother-in-law (Shemp). Clearly guilty, Andy asks to be allowed to tell just what led him to this mayhem.

    Andy's flashback recalls when he was talked into getting back to the soil and turning his backyard into a nice lot with flowers, tree, and a vegetable garden. He fills his truck with dirt, fertilizer, hay and other items and brings it home to start work. Looking forward to the bliss of enjoying this project, Andy's tranquility is disrupted by his noisy, obnoxious brother-in-law who is similarly attracted to the project and wants to join in. The film then becomes a series of wild slapstick gags involving everything from a broken water pipe to dynamite to a runaway tractor. Once Andy concludes his story to the judge, he is found not guilty and allowed to go back after his brother-in-law, who flees the courtroom in comic terror.

Shemp Howard had been, with brother Moe Howard and Larry Fine, along with Ted Healy, on stage as Ted Healy and His Stooges, and this group made one film for Fox, *Soup to Nuts* (1930). Not interested in continuing with this act due to Healy's angry drinking binges, Shemp went off on his own as a solo performer, and that is when Moe recruited younger brother Jerome Howard, who shaved his head and was nicknamed Curly. After a few film appearances with Healy at MGM, the Stooges went off on their own as a trio and began making shorts at Columbia in 1934.

By 1938, Shemp had appeared as a solo comic in some features and several short films, mostly for Warner Brothers' Vitaphone unit, including a stint as Knobby Walsh in a Joe Palooka series based on the popular comic strip. The character Shemp was playing at the time was a very obnoxious, abrasive type who caused disruptions in the lives of those around him.

Shemp soon established himself in his own comedy series, where he sometimes played the obnoxious meddler, and other times an amiable man with a gruff exterior. When younger brother Curly was forced to leave the Stooges due to illness, Shemp took his place, and that is the work for which he is best remembered. But the three accessible films in which Shemp appeared with Andy Clyde are also among his best work, so it is frustrating that we can't see this first effort in which the two appeared together.

Based on research, the chemistry between Andy and Shemp appears to be discernible in this film. Their comic conflict in screen personalities seems to work nicely with Andy's frustrated befuddlement playing off of Shemp's noisy obnoxiousness. Columbia comic heavy Bud Jamison joins the fracas as a cop whose presence is the result of neighbors complaining.

According to the script, Clyde's mounting frustration in dealing with Shemp's constant disruptions rises to the level where he becomes a raving maniac bent on destroying his adversary. The fact that a judge forgives him and allows him to continue the mayhem is a nice conclusion. The Three Stooges' similarly structured short, the aforementioned *Idiot's Deluxe*, ends the same way.

Andy's wife in the film was played by Kathryn Bates, who was doing bits at Columbia during the late '30s in everything from the Stooges' *Tassles in the Air* (1938) to Frank Capra's feature classic *Mr. Smith Goes to Washington* (1939). Bates plays a supportive wife who enables obnoxious brother Shemp, which forces Andy to put up with his frustrating antics. There is great comic potential in the fact that Andy's frustration develops to the point where he blows up and reacts with enough violence to be put on trial.

Jules White liked the dynamic that Shemp provided with Andy. This is likely why more films were planned for the two of them as Shemp's own solo series was being readied. White's various attempts to put Clyde within the parameters of a comedy team dynamic was consistent, but still occasional, as he realized Andy also worked well as a henpecked husband. But his films with Shemp presented them as adversaries. This conflict was further explored in Clyde's next film.

Home on the Rage

Directed by Del Lord; *Story and Screenplay:* James W. Horne; *Produced by* Jules White; *Cinematography:* Lucien Ballard; *Editor:* Charles Nelson; *Cast:* Andy Clyde, Shemp Howard, Lela Bliss, Gene Morgan, Vernon Dent, John Tyrrell, Robin Raymond, Ace the Wonder Dog; *Shooting Dates:* August 15–18, 1938; *Released* December 9, 1938; *Columbia Production Number:* 436

When producer Jules White saw a formula that worked, he would tend to revisit it a few times. This happened with the relationship between characters played by Andy Clyde and Robert McKenzie vying for the same

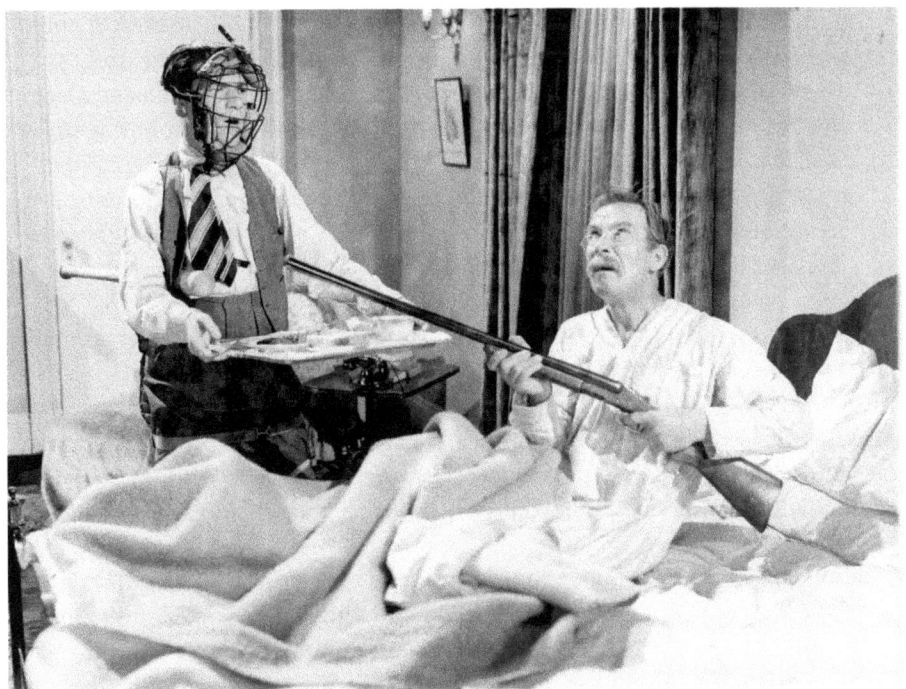

Shemp is taking no chances with a gun-toting, bedridden Andy in *Home on the Rage* (1938).

woman, which was the foundation of three previously filmed shorts. Now it was the conflict between the quietly befuddled Andy and the noisy and abrasive Shemp Howard character. It worked well in *Not Guilty Enough*, so the idea was revisited in *Home on the Rage*.

Andy is a married businessman with a nice home, a supportive wife and a loyal German Shepard dog, but money has been tight due to his gradual recovery from the Depression. He is still a comparatively wealthy man, and his problems are at a much higher level: He had to lay off his servants and his wife has become weary of having to keep up their large home. Andy is excitedly arranging a big real estate deal which will put his finances back in order.

Once this situation has been established, Andy's brother-in-law Shemp bursts through the door for an uninvited visit. From what our research tells us about the previous *Not Guilty Enough*, Shemp makes the same sort of disruption his similar character had made in other movie. This time Shemp is a newly appointed insurance man boisterously attempting to get Andy to become his client. He descends upon Andy's office just as the big real estate deal is about to go through, bullies the client into the waiting area, and gets Andy to sign over an insurance policy (Andy complies to simply get rid of Shemp). However, the disruption evolves to the point where Andy throws an ink bottle at Shemp, who ducks. The ink bottle hits the important client, destroying the deal.

Vernon Dent, as the client, is a very sober, no-nonsense businessman who realizes what a good deal the real estate project is, and has already decided he is going to accept, even before Andy begins his pitch. The brother-in-law noisily descending upon and interrupting this situation is comically jarring and frustrating. Shemp tickles the secretary, who slaps him. He throws the client out and demands Andy's attention. Andy throwing the ink bottle at Shemp and hitting Vernon is given even greater comic punch in that Vernon is dressed in a white suit. The ink destroys it, and even splatters on the hapless secretary.

At this point, the relationships have been fully established: Andy the successful businessman forced to cut corners at home due to the economy, his wife is privileged and has gotten used to servants doing her work, and brother-in-law Shemp is brutally obnoxious and dislikable, a schemer who feels entitled despite a lack of accomplishment. Andy's wife exhibits loyalty to Andy but support to her brother, despite his flaws. Andy must put up with both.

Now the film goes in another direction. Andy's dog, while kind to him, is hostile towards the brother-in-law and even nips at Andy's wife. Shemp and Mrs. Clyde discuss their intention to put the dog down, but without Andy knowing about it. Andy comes home late from work soaking wet from the pouring rain. Shemp, seeing an opportunity to collect insurance on his new client, opens the door so more cold wind will blow in. Andy develops a bad cold, is put to bed, and is attended to by a doctor. While recovering, he hears Shemp and Mrs. Clyde discussing how they can do away with the dog. Andy thinks they are talking about him, believing they plan to collect on the insurance policy once he is dead.

This narrative point allows Andy to draw from his character's mistrust and worry. He conveniently misses the part of the conversations that identifies the dog, and only hears such things as "he's getting old and doesn't get along with people as well. It is time for him to be put down." Andy responds by telling his lawyer, who comes over to protect his client from the murderous plot. He also overhears enough of the conversation to be convinced that Andy is telling the truth.

A telegram arrives indicating that the real estate deal went through after all, so a delighted Mrs. Clyde goes upstairs to tell Andy. He is very happy about the news, but says it doesn't change the fact that she was trying to kill him. When she reveals it was about the dog, he is relieved. But he still instructs the dog to attack Shemp, who runs away with the dog in pursuit. The last shot is the dog walking up with Shemp's ripped pants in his mouth.

There are a lot of good points in *Home on the Rage*. Andy's performance is delightful, lying in bed with a rifle ready to shoot whoever comes into his room, his overhearing about his supposed planned murder causing him to reach this level of paranoia. Shemp is at his loud, blustery best. Vernon Dent, John Tyrrell as the doctor and Gene Morgan as Andy's lawyer contribute to the humorous situations. And the gags show the usual knockabout slapstick and violence that already defined Columbia short subjects.

Writer James Horne had been writing and directing since the silent era. The previous year, he had helmed Laurel and Hardy's classic *Way Out West* (although it can certainly be argued that any Laurel and Hardy movie was Stan Laurel's directorial vision, especially one he produced). Horne certainly understood the dynamic between a boisterous, overbearing personality and a comparatively peaceful one, and this conflict sustains the comedy of *Home on the Rage*. Andy is not merely put-upon, though. He is feisty and willing to fight back.

Swing, You Swingers

Directed by Jules White; *Screenplay:* Ewart Adamson; *Story:* Clyde Bruckman; *Produced by* Jules White; *Cast:* Andy Clyde, Benny Bartlett, Lola Jensen, Elaine Waters, Beatrice Blinn, Blanche Payson, Fredrick Spencer, Lynton

Andy gives music lessons to Lola Jensen, Elaine Waters and Beatrice Blinn in *Swing, You Swingers!* **(1939).**

Brent, Richard Nichols, Dee Dodd; *Shooting Dates:* October 8–13, 1938; *Released* January 29, 1939; *Columbia Production Number:* 434; *Remade as Tootin' Tooters* (1954)

Swing You Swingers is an offbeat Clyde comedy that not only works, it is one of the strongest films from this period. Jules White directed, and while his method usually favored violent slapstick, *Swing You Swingers* is more layered. Andy works with children in this short, a situation that worked well for him. The musical numbers, performed by the kids, are upbeat and fun, perfectly representing the era.

Andrew Beethoven Clyde (Andy), a descendant of Beethoven, runs a music store, but wants it understood that while he has great appreciation for classical music, he detests swing, the big band jazz then enjoying mainstream popularity. Andy's store deals with instrument sales and rental, recordings and music lessons. He enjoys teaching classical music to an assortment of attractive women, but whenever one of them even mentions swing music, he becomes angry and starts yelling about his hatred for the "infernal noise."

The idea of a crotchety old man having contempt for an exuberant form of modern popular music is a fascinating portent to the rock 'n' roll revolution that hit the cultural mainstream a couple of decades later. This is extended to another dimension of Clyde's character when his two orphaned nephews are temporarily placed with him by the welfare department. He discovers that the oldest boy is a musician and has his own band. Andy acts as their conductor, putting them through deadly versions of classical movements. When he leaves the room, the boys engage in swing jazz, exhibiting formidable talent.

Clyde is already noted for enjoying working with children, even babies, unlike many other comedians. However, in this movie, Andy's character has a general dislike of kids, which fits neatly into the realm of one who avoids children and the tumultuous modern music at this level of pop culture. Bennie Bartlett, who plays the older of the two children, was an actual jazz trumpeter whose skills were formidable even at a young age. Clyde had no problem stepping aside and allowing Jules White to spotlight the kids doing a rollicking jazz number in order to exhibit their talents.

The way this is presented also fits neatly in the comedy mode. When Andy is conducting the young band, he is putting them through a dull version of Chopin's "Death March." The youngsters are playing well, but their faces show no enthusiasm, as they are going through the motions without connecting to the music. The drummer is sitting idly with nothing to do, as there is no drum in the piece. The only percussion is a triangle that punctuates each stanza, and is hit by a sleepy-eyed African American boy who actually does fall asleep during the number. Andy angrily storms off wondering why he bothered giving the kids a chance. As soon as he goes, the youngsters perk up and deliver a rocking swing number.

The relationship between Andy and the younger child offers more boisterous comedy. The child makes a mess of himself and Andy must bathe him in the sink. Set down on the floor, the child finds a hammer and starts pounding it on the floor, eventually hitting Andy's toe. His mischief ruins a couple of possible big sales. When he wanders off, Andy must go out looking for him. Andy is so happy to find the child, he doesn't even bother getting angry.

Andy gets home, walks in on the kids' jazz session and finds himself dancing to the music with the younger child in his arms. While doing so, a radio representative comes by, hears the music and offers the boys a chance to go on the air. Andy decides that he now does like swing music, *and* children.

In the April 29, 1939, *Showmen's Trade Review*, their critic called *Swing You Swingers* "[v]ery funny with plenty of slapstick and good swing music. It has Andy Clyde and Benny Bartlett, what more could you as of a short subject?" They also suggested some promotional ideas:

Tie-up with music stores should be easy on this one as the setting is right in one Give Andy Clyde a big plug in your marquee, in your lobby, programs, and newspaper ads. Contests on classical music vs. swing would call attention to the subject.[30]

Audiences enjoyed it as well, having already embraced Andy Clyde's comedy, and enjoying the swing band on another level.

Jules White worked well with Andy and while his shooting of the gag sequences were in his wheelhouse, White also exhibits impressive vision when spotlighting the boys' swing band, alternating between medium shots and close-ups of the various band members. The number they are doing is brisk, so White keeps the edits quick, responding to the music's rhythm. It is really quite impressive.

Boom Goes the Groom

Directed by Charley Chase; *Story:* Churchill Ross; *Produced by* Charley Chase, Hugh McCollum; *Cinematography:* André Barlatier; *Editor:* Arthur Seid; *Cast:* Andy Clyde, Vivien Oakland, Monty Collins, Dick Curtis, Payne Johnson; *Shooting Dates:* November 8–11, 1938; *Released* March 24, 1939; *Columbia Production Number:* 440

Boom Goes the Groom is yet another film for which the sound and picture negatives are housed at the Library of Congress, but no screening print exists in their archives.

In this one, Andy thrives on "get rich quick" schemes and has recently sunk a lot of money into a gold mine, much to the chagrin of his fiancée and others. Just as their wedding is about to take place, Andy is told that his gold mine is indeed just that—it is worth a fortune. Andy now has misgivings about getting married to his intended, but doesn't want to reveal why. Most of the film deals with Andy trying different ways to artfully get out of the marriage.

Clyde once again works with Charley Chase, who responds better to characters, situations and story construction than he does to the isolated slapstick gags preferred by Jules White. Clyde was a good enough actor to tone down the more bombastic aspects of his personality when he worked with Chase. Furthermore, Chase's approach to the material seems to respond well to Clyde's method of doing things, even if the more blatant aspects of Andy's screen character are diluted. The conflict with Vivien Oakland's character, who goes from haughty to coyly accepting when she realizes her admonishing Andy for "wasting money" on the gold mine was wrong, is central to the comedy.

As he typically relied more on character and conflict, Chase continued

II. The Columbia Comedy Shorts

Dick Curtis and Monty Collins are not letting Andy get away in *Boom Goes the Groom* (1939).

to impress with his establishing shots and the fluidity of his camera movement. Clyde is great when conflicted by his sudden wealth. This allows him a comeuppance against all the naysayers, but he is also able to lord it over his fiancée. He wonders if his wealth could net him a younger, prettier bride.

At the time *Boom Goes the Groom* was released, an exhibitor in Paris, Arkansas, sent a note to the *Motion Picture Herald* referring to Will Hays, president of the Motion Picture Producers and Distributors of America. The exhibitor wrote:

Mr. Hays is being quoted in the papers as saying that audiences are growing up and don't go for comedies. Mr. Hays gets a big salary but he is utterly ignorant of the small town theater's needs. The shorts offered today to take the place of comedies are tragedy and driving away all kinds of business. Mr. Hays, nor anyone else, ever saw a walkout while a good comedy was on the screen. No, Mr. Hays isn't right.[31]

By 1939, few comedies were being made. MGM still had the Our Gang series and more sophisticated fare like Robert Benchley. But they had mostly left comedy and were releasing musicals and dramas, along with James Fitz-Patrick's *Travel Talks*. RKO was still doing comedies, but Paramount and Warner Brothers were concentrating more on cartoons.

While studio heads and other high-level decision-makers might have felt comedies were less important, moviegoers continued to welcome them. *Boom Goes the Groom* was met with the usual enthusiasm for an Andy Clyde short.

Now It Can Be Sold

Directed by Del Lord; *Screenplay:* Charley Chase; *Produced by* Hugh McCollum, Charley Chase; *Cast:* Andy Clyde, Tommy Bond, Anita Garvin, Dick Curtis, Bud Jamison, Fred Toones; *Shooting Dates:* January 9–12, 1939; *Released* June 2, 1939; *Columbia Production Number:* 448; *Working title: Away with Women*

No material exists on *Now It Can Be Sold*. Based on what research reveals, this appears to be a particularly strong Andy Clyde comedy.

The filming of *Now It Can Be Sold* must have felt like something of a reunion for co-producer Charley Chase. Two of his co-stars from his long tenure with Hal Roach productions, Anita Garvin and Tommy Bond, appear. Bond had last appeared with Andy in *Knee Action* and soon was cast as the bully Butch in the Our Gang comedies. By the time of this film, Roach had sold that series to MGM and Bond's tenure was winding down (the last Our Gang comedy featuring him was released in 1940). The child actor began freelancing, and Andy requested his services for this film. Chase, who had famously worked with Bond in the Hal Roach production *I'll Take Vanilla*, was happy to oblige.

The central portion of this film's narrative features Andy teaming up with bratty Tommy to solve a crime. Tommy considers himself a Junior G-Man, having been influenced by the current wave in popular culture. Melvin Purvis left the FBI and in 1936 started hosting *Junior G-Men*, a radio show about kids solving crimes. It became quite popular in the late 1930s up until

II. The Columbia Comedy Shorts

Andy and Clarence Muse are having trouble with a stubborn mule in *Now It Can Be Sold* (1939).

America got involved in World War II, when all attention focused on the war effort. However, during the time *Now It Can Be Sold* was filmed, FBI men were heroes and young men wanted to also engage in the war on crime. The radio show's listeners were invited to join Junior G-Men clubs, with various items being sold through the mail such as badges, manuals and other secret agent materials. These clubs soon were formed throughout the United States as a counterpart to the Boy Scouts. Their slogan was "It's easier to build boys than to mend men."

Initially Tommy's interest becomes obtrusive to Andy's attempt to run his swap shop. Tommy is consistently suspicious of everyone who enters the shop, getting in the way of Andy's deals. However, when an actual crime is committed, Andy teams with Tommy, who shows his formidable skills at crime-solving. Dick Curtis, usually cast as a bad guy, plays a detective who ends up following Tommy's lead.

While less bombastic, as per Charley Chase's usual approach, Andy still has ample opportunity to exhibit his double-take reactions, punctuating each scene with comedy. Very popular by this time, including with youngsters, the connection to the popular Junior G-Man clubs made this effort especially attractive to youngsters. Del Lord's direction was uniformly sound, and he continued to consult with Andy as to the process, which producers Chase and McCollum encouraged.

Now It Can Be Sold was yet another popular Clyde comedy, utilizing a topical situation in a short that appealed to kids as well as grownups. The April 8, 1939, issue of *Showman's Trade Review* stated:

> Andy Clyde, one of the screen's oldest comedians, can still draw a good laugh from an audience, judging from this comedy. It is a real howl. More comedies of this kind wouldn't be amiss on many programs, but there are fewer and fewer being made these days.

It is unknown whether the anonymous reviewer, in referencing Andy as "one of the screen's oldest comedians," was referring to his veteran status in movies, or if the critic was actually fooled into thinking the comedian was the age of the character he played (Andy was only in his 40s when this film was released). The same reviewer also offered marketing suggestions: "A good gag on this one would be to set up a swap shop in your lobby. If handled right, this can be a great stunt. Put Andy Clyde on your marquee. He is well worth plugging."

Trouble Finds Andy Clyde

Produced and Directed by Jules White; *Cast:* Andy Clyde, Ann Doran, Al Thompson, Beatrice Blinn, Dick Curtis, Cy Schindell, James Craig, Beatrice Cutis, Charles Dorety, Ethelreda Leopold, Lela Bliss; *Shooting Dates:* January 14–18, 1939; *Released* July 28, 1939; Remade as *A Blunderful Time;* Columbia Production Number: 442

Another film where the sound and picture negatives are housed in the Library of Congress, but no screening print exists in their archives, *Trouble Finds Andy Clyde* appears to have been inspired by the 1936 Laurel and Hardy feature *Our Relations*. In that feature, Stan and Ollie's twin brothers come to town and the two sets manage to confuse and anger wives, girlfriends, etc. However, in the Laurel and Hardy movie, the duo played themselves and

Lela Bliss is a bit confused by Andy's twin brother Al Thompson in *Trouble Finds Andy Clyde* (1939).

their brothers. In *Trouble Finds Andy Clyde*, Andy plays himself and Al Thompson plays his twin brother. Because Clyde hid his actual face with a lot of makeup, a big mustache, glasses, etc., it was not difficult for the comedian to apply the same face to Thompson.

Trouble Finds Andy Clyde, although directed by Jules White, appears to be a bit disjointed. The first half concentrates on Andy getting into trouble with his wife due to his twin brother's exploits, and then the film apparently shifts gears to where Andy runs off, joins the service and becomes a hero. Based on reviews and exhibitor reaction, the results are not as consistently funny, especially considering that White is at the helm. According to *Showman's Trade Review* stated,

> The comedy is full of slapstick situations that will cause a number of hearty laughs, but on the other hand there are long stretches which, although supposed to be funny, cause not a ripple in the audience.[32]

The film's publicity played up the twin factor with the line "Andy chases himself in a dual role that makes him twice as funny as ever." But it wasn't a dual role, the twin being played by another actor.

There appear to be a lot of problems with *Trouble Finds Andy Clyde*. First, the twin brother mistaken identity is just a backdrop to allow for a lot of mechanical gags that don't seem particularly inspired. Next, the shifting to Andy's military exploits doesn't seem to flow organically from the established narrative. Finally, since Andy is a master at reaction comedy, he needs something to which he can react. This film appears to offer little of that. Of course, we are limited by not being able to screen the film for specifics. Reports and reviews from the time of its release offer just so many details. We are unable to determine specifically how effectively the idea of doubling Andy in a comedy with a twin brother dynamic was executed.

All American Blondes

Directed by Del Lord; *Screenplay:* Elwood Ullman; *Produced by* Hugh McCollum, Del Lord; *Cast:* Andy Clyde, Helen Servis, Dick Curtis, Mabel Smaney, Monty Collins, Maxine Conrad, Linda Winters, Vernon Dent, Richard Fiske; *Shooting Dates:* August 22–25, 1939; *Released* October 20, 1939; *Columbia Production Number:* 460

Lobby card for *All American Blondes* (1939).

The success, both aesthetic and financial, of the Andy Clyde comedy *Gracie at the Bat*, in which he reluctantly coaches a girls' baseball team, is what likely inspired *All American Blondes*. Here Andy is coaching a girls' basketball team and with similarly amusing results. It is unfortunate that this is another film where the sound and picture negatives are housed in the Library of Congress, but no screening print exists in their archives.

The set-up is the same as in *Gracie at the Bat*. Andy is hired to coach a team, and is surprised to discover it is all girls. However in this film, things become more complicated when gangsters bet on the opposing team, and threaten to kill Andy if his team wins.

Andy is comically conflicted. As a coach, his competitive spirit makes him want to win the game, while at the same time he fears what will happen if the gangsters end up losing their bet. However, when his star player is injured due to the actions of the other team, Andy believes they will simply lose naturally and he has nothing to fear. He replaces the star with a bumbling player (Helen Servis) who usually warms the bench. She not only surprises everyone by winning the game, but she also manages to fight off the gamblers and deliver them to the police.

Tall and skinny, Servis had a comical appearance that was usually used to punctuate blackout gags. For instance, in the Three Stooges comedy *Spook Louder* (1943). the trio is going door to door selling weight-reducing machine. She comes to the door, very tall and very slim; hardly in need of a machine that would help a person lose weight. In *All American Blondes*, Helen towers over the others, but has poor coordination. Played for laughs, her coming in and ending up winning the game is a delightful surprise, but Andy is upset because it means he could be killed. That she manages to overpower the crooks makes her character as triumphant as it is amusing.

Andy has ample opportunity to utilize his penchant for displaying the perfect double take, as well as reacting with flustered fear as he pretends to cheer on his team while secretly hoping they lose. The action on the court is punctuated by director Del Lord's cutaways to Andy's reactions.

There is a bit of marketing prowess to *All American Blondes*. It was released on October 20, opening day for the pro basketball season. Thus, a comedy about basketball began making its rounds in theaters as Americans were responding to a new season of the sport.

The screenplay was written by Elwood Ullman, who'd written other Clyde comedies. A member of the Columbia shorts unit since 1936, Ullman told Ted Okuda and Ed Watz for their book *The Columbia Comedy Shorts*:

> Many's the time I paced up and down the lot, striving to come up with ideas. Miraculously, I kept coming up with them. I'd submit my ideas to Jules White or Hugh

McCollum both verbally and written down on paper. If they liked the idea, they'd give me an okay to elaborate and expand upon it. But the director is the one who fills out the gags; it's up to him to decide how they're going to look on film.³³

The director of *All American Blondes*, Del Lord, worked exceptionally well with Clyde, so the ideas Ullman's script provided were filmed effectively.

Andy Clyde Gets Spring Chicken

Produced and Directed by Jules White; *Story and Screenplay:* Felix Adler, Clyde Bruckman; *Cinematography:* Harry Davis; *Editor:* Arthur Seid; *Cast:* Andy Clyde, Lorna Gray, Eve McKenzie, Beatrice Blinn, Richard Fiske, Kay Vallon, Ethelreda Leopold, Don Beddoe, John Tyrrell, Dorothy Appleby; *Shooting Dates:* August 29-September 2, 1939; *Released* December 15, 1939; *Columbia Production Number:* 463; *Remade as Love's a Poppin'* (1953)

Fay McKenzie does not seem to approve of Andy flirting with Dorothy Appleby and the other girls (actresses unidentified) in *Andy Clyde Gets Spring Chicken* **(1939).**

II. The Columbia Comedy Shorts 93

In the late 1930s, one of the most popular film series was MGM's Andy Hardy movies. Their depiction of small town life, with an ensemble cast headed by Mickey Rooney as Andy, really captured the interest of moviegoers, especially in the heartland where Andy Clyde comedies were also especially popular. In July 1939, MGM released the latest Hardy feature, *Andy Hardy Gets Spring Fever*. When Clyde's latest film started production, the Hardy feature had become among the year's top box office attractions. Since the Clyde short featured the comedian's thoughts on the spring season, Jules White titled it *Andy Clyde Gets Spring Chicken*.

White enjoyed doing plays on words with his movie titles. For instance, the Three Stooges did a 1941 comedy entitled *So Long Mr. Chumps*, with a title based on *Goodbye Mr. Chips*. When Paramount did a movie version of the novel *Valiant Is the Word for Carrie*, the Stooges made a film called *Violent is the Word for Curly*. *Andy Clyde Gets Spring Chicken* is another example of Jules White having some fun with titles.

The title fits the narrative. Andy is a wealthy old widower who shares his luxurious home with his daughter and son-in-law. Every year when the weather gets warmer, Andy gets spring fever, kicks up his heels and proposes to every woman he meets. It is then up to his daughter and her husband to annul the marriage and extricate Andy once he settles down and comes to his senses.

Andy notices a pool party next door and wants to find a way to go over and meet the pretty young girls there. He throws his hat in order to simulate it having blown there by the wind, but he succeeds in knocking an older woman into the pool. He runs over to help her, and gets pulled in himself. Realizing his wealth, the woman invites him to join the party. White's penchant for outrageous slapstick is evident quickly, with pratfalls into the pool occurring three times. Along with the first two, Andy states that he will change into a swimsuit by taking a shortcut, and steps right into the pool again.

For the next several minutes, Andy busily proposes to nearly every girl at the party, getting sympathetic refusals. He remains undaunted, simply going on to the next girl. The one acceptance he gets is a tall, strong girl with a deep husky voice (dubbed by male actor Richard Fiske), and she pursues him throughout the grounds. When the woman who owns the house indicates that Andy is a millionaire, all of the girls to whom he has proposed suddenly become interested in marrying him. But the woman wants Andy to marry her daughter June so that she can benefit from his wealth.

It is interesting how White's direction alternates between his usual penchant for slapstick and a more subtle approach. For instance, when Andy prepares for a return to an evening party, there is a very quaint scene where he has hired an instructor to quickly teach him the latest dance steps, as well as a sloppily funny sequence where Andy takes a bath and proceeds to splash water all over the floor as he washes, causing the moisture to make the roof cave in on a staid bridge game occurring downstairs. The dance instructions are a portent to a scene at the party where Andy dances with June. In an interview for this project during her 99th year, Lorna Gray, who played June, recalled doing the dance scene:

> There were all kinds of crazy dances going on back then, so Jules White hired a few professional dancers and asked them to demonstrate some of the silliest modern steps. He picked a few out and had them perform in the picture. Jules also wanted Andy and me to dance because we both had dancing in our background. So he hired an instructor for us. Andy was very light on his feet and learned quickly, so he helped teach me. Jules wanted me to jump up and wrap my legs around Andy while he spun me around. Well, I didn't want to do that. Jules and I argued, but Andy stood up for me, so I didn't have to. We had a great dance scene without my doing that.[34]

Lorna, who later acted as Adrian Booth, had nothing but happy memories of Andy Clyde. "It was my only movie with Andy, and I only worked on it a few days, but it was so much fun. Andy was wonderful to me, and a real professional. Of course, he was also very funny. I liked him a lot."

Everything comes to a head at the end. All five of the girls to whom Andy proposed are now interested in him and converge upon him at once. When he logically states that he can't marry all of them, they start tugging at him and eventually begin kicking and slapping each other. Andy escapes the melee by jumping out a window, but is intercepted by the tall girl with the deep voice. He runs and she chases after him as the picture fades.

Andy Clyde Gets Spring Chicken is a real *tour de force* for the comedian. He is not a part of a domestic situation with a wife and a conflicting situation. He is not an angry cuss putting up with kids. The film instead explores a tangential aspect of his character that is rarely explored. Andy is a man of some means with an eye for much younger women and an impulsive nature. It is atypical, but also quite effective and funny.

Andy Clyde Gets Spring Chicken continued Clyde's streak of successful shorts. It was very well received by moviegoers and Andy's popularity continued unabated.

Mr. Clyde Goes to Broadway

Directed by Del Lord; *Screenplay:* Elwood Ullman, Harry Edwards; *Produced by* Hugh McCollum, Del Lord; *Cinematography:* Allen G. Siegler; *Editor:* James Sweeney; *Cast:* Andy Clyde, Dorothy Vaughan, Vivien Oakland,

II. The Columbia Comedy Shorts

Andy introduces himself and mayor Vernon Dent while wife Dorothy Vaughan looks on in *Mr. Clyde Goes to Broadway* (1940).

John T. Murray, Vernon Dent, Richard Fiske, Eddie Fetherston, Don Beddoe, Cy Schindell, Ray Turner; *Shooting Dates:* November 15–18, 1939; *Released* February 2, 1940; *Columbia Production Number:* 466

Jules White didn't act as this film's producer, but he was still the man in charge of the short subject unit, and it is he who came up with the title, an obvious play on the then-popular feature *Mr. Smith Goes to Washington* (released a couple weeks before filming began on *Mr. Clyde Goes to Broadway*). Apparently MGM complained about White making sport of their titles with his short comedies, so this time the producer parodied the title of a feature released by his own studio, Columbia. *Mr. Clyde Goes to Broadway* is another of Clyde's best two-reelers, as it takes him back to his theater roots.

Andy and his wife run a boarding house, where a theater couple are staying but never paying their rent. Andy is prepared to throw them out, but they talk him into investing in their show. Andy, a former actor, likes the idea of reconnecting with the theater. However, on opening night, the sheriff shows up backstage and arrests the entire cast, indicating he has been chasing this show over several states due to their owing money everywhere. When Andy discovers what has happened, he and his wife get into costumes, go on stage and attempt to perform the show themselves in order to protect their investment.

There are many clever moments in *Mr. Clyde Goes to Broadway*, but the highlight is a long slapstick scene that allows Andy to exhibit how his background in silent comedy inspired his current work. After paying a $15 C.O.D. for a hat delivery, Andy smells something burning. He runs back to the kitchen where soup is bubbling over and a chicken is being overcooked in the oven. He burns his hand as he lifts the soup pot's lid, then turns off the burner and the stove. The doorbell rings. At the same time, the front desk bell is ringing. Andy stammers and walks back and forth, not knowing which to answer first. He chooses the doorbell, and he is met by the milkman and handed several bottles of milk.

While his arms are full of milk bottles, the front desk bell keeps ringing, adding to his pressure. An egg starts to roll off a table, Andy grabs a plate with his mouth, and catches the egg on that. He then opens the icebox door with his foot, jams the milk bottles into the opening, shuts the door hard, and hears all of the glass breaking. Milk starts to seep from the bottom edge of the icebox door. He then pulls the chicken out of the oven and tries to end its smoldering by pouring water on it. This causes a great deal of smoke, so Andy blindly reaches down and grabs what he thinks is the chicken, but it turns out to be the woman's hat he just paid for. When she comes in and sees what he has done, she charges him $20. So, he paid the $15 full price upon delivery, and another $20 after he ruined the hat.

Andy plays this remarkable scene perfectly, knowing how to use his full body for comedy, while also adding nuanced facial expressions when the camera closes in. Because there is no background music, Andy maintains a mumbling running commentary, which fits his befuddled character perfectly. It really is a particularly delightful scene, and one of the comedian's most impressive.

During the portion of the movie where Andy and his wife take to the stage and perform the play, we see them enlisting a janitor friend to act as prop man, struggling through the dialogue and generally lousing up the production. They are worried not only about their investment, but the fact that nearly the entire town has packed the theater, including the mayor. The stage antics are all quite funny, as Andy and his wife struggle through their roles with little frame of reference. At one point, Andy fires a gun that actually shoots real bullets at a prop moon dangling behind him, giving the moon (which is a face) a black eye. They are effectively destroying the original intention of the production, but their antics are so funny, the audience laughs and believes this is how the show is supposed to be performed.

The only drawback is its abrupt ending. The moon prop is on fire from the blast, so when it is set aside, it burns a rope holding a curtain weight, which falls on Andy's head and knocks him through a trap door. It is at that point that the film ends, without tying up any loose ends. It is almost as if they simply ran out of film.

Still, this is one of Clyde's most enjoyable comedies, and the kitchen highlight is exceptionally well performed and funny. Also, Clyde grew up as a stage performer and worked in theater for years before entering movies, so a film about performing in a play has a distinct connection to his past.

As the 1930s ended and the 1940s began, the budgets for short subjects were cut significantly. Things like location shooting and big gags that required extra production became a thing of the past. Eventually, films would have to be on standing sets available on the Columbia lot. However, the Columbia team was creative enough to still work their magic within these more limited parameters. *Mr. Clyde Goes to Broadway* is something of a portent of that. Its highlight is limited to a kitchen set, a few props and Andy Clyde's very real talent.

Money Squawks

Produced and Directed by Jules White; *Story and Screenplay:* Ewart Adamson; *Cinematography:* Benjamin H. Kline; *Editor:* Mel Thorsen; *Cast:* Andy Clyde, Shemp Howard, Vernon Dent, Bud Jamison, Eddie Laughton, Richard Fiske, Charles Dorety, Cy Schindell, Lynton Brent, Bert Young; *Shooting Dates:* January 27–30, 1940; *Released* April 5, 1940; *Columbia Production Number:* 459

Of the four films in which Shemp Howard appeared with Andy Clyde, *Money Squawks* is perhaps the best. Andy and Shemp are station agents at a railroad depot who must watch over a $10,000 payroll overnight because it can't be picked up until morning. This results in a series of complications involving everyone from innocent hunters mistaken for crooks to actual gangsters believed to be the rightful owners.

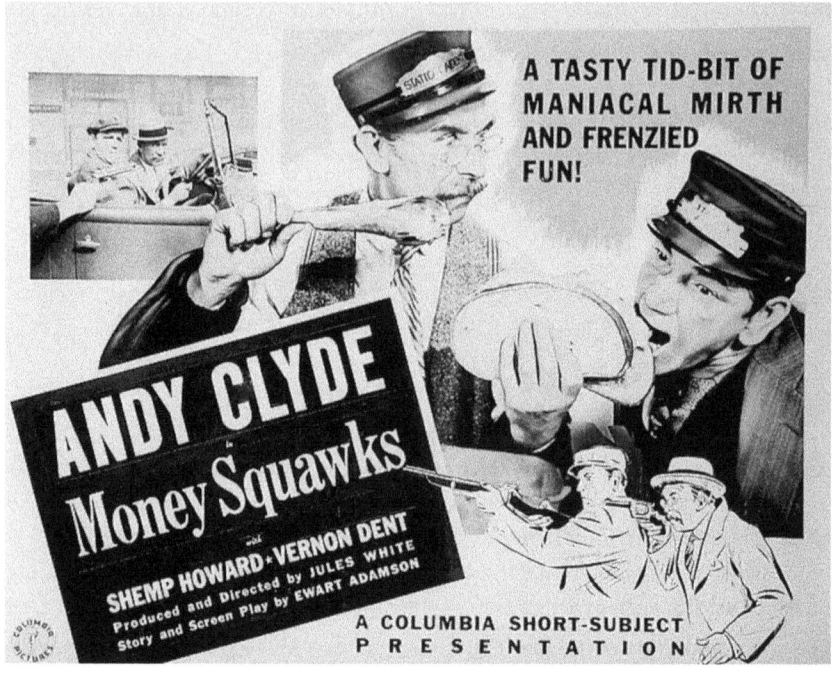

Lobby card for *Money Squawks* (1940).

The Andy-Shemp dynamic is not adversarial in *Money Squawks* as it had been in *Not Guilty Enough* and *Home on the Rage*. This time they function as a team, and any conflict between them stems from their connection as friends and co-workers.

While Jules White is noted for a very hands-on approach to directing, expecting the actors to perform according to his strict vision, there is at least one scene where both Andy and Shemp appear to have some creative freedom. As they eat their lunch, Andy sloppily gnaws away at a turkey drumstick while Shemp devours a sandwich. During the course of this, the two old pros inject little bits of comic business. Shemp grabs at a piece of skin hanging from the drumstick Andy is eating. Andy does a double take, looking at Shemp as if to say "Stay away from my food." Shemp starts talking with his mouth full, ad libbing nonsensical conversation by stating, "I'll never forget the time my father met my mother...." The only comic business that must have been worked out ahead of time is when a bullfrog comes hopping into the station and Shemp mistakes its croaks for Andy belching.[35]

Two hunters drive up and check the train schedule. Their car backfires as they stop, startling Andy and Shemp inside. The car radio is blasting a crime program, which Andy and Shemp overhear, so they follow the radio actor's instructions to get down on the ground. A hunter changes the station to an exercise program, so Shemp and Andy are now lifting their legs up and down as per the radio's instructions, believing themselves to still be in the clutches of gangsters. The hunters see that they have a half hour wait before the next train, so they decide to go into the depot. They are startled to see the two men exercising on the floor. They are even more startled when Andy and Shemp grab their guns and start blasting, believing the hunters to be crooks.

Responding to a radio voice as if it was actually nearby is an old gag that was used often in the pre-television era. Lou Costello famously used this premise for one of the highlight scenes in the Abbott and Costello comedy *Who Done It?* (1942). And W.C. Fields had a scene in *Tillie and Gus* (1933) where he is mixing paint according to a radio announcer's instructions when a baby changes the station to an exercise program, causing Fields to respond to the exercise directions and concluding "I never knew it was so difficult to mix paint!" In the hands of Andy Clyde and Shemp, it is also very funny.

At the time this is all happening, some actual gangsters are preparing to come in and steal the loot. But when they see how aggressive and impulsive the two are with their firearms, the crooks decide to go up to the mine and wait for the payroll to be delivered.

Andy and Shemp fall asleep. Shemp sleeps holding his rifle in his arms with the gun barrel pointed at his face, while Andy gets up and starts sleepwalking. While doing so, Andy takes the payroll envelope from the safe and slips it into his pocket. In a complicated, outrageous sight gag, something falls, the noise startles Shemp and his gun goes off. It knocks the phone off the wall, causing it to fly across the room and hit the sleepwalking Andy in the head. Only a few seconds long, this last bit is the sort of violent slapstick at which Jules White was a master, so it is staged and shot perfectly

Andy and Shemp go looking for the missing payroll money, not realizing it is in Andy's shirt pocket. A duck gets out of its cage, knocks over some glue, steps in this glue and gets small slats stuck to its feet. The noise it makes while walking makes Andy and Shemp think there's an intruder. They try to hunt him down, but only succeed in ramming against each other and falling to the floor. A derby falls onto Andy's foot. He raises his leg, sees the hat, mistakes it for one of the crooks and shoots his own toe![36]

Having had enough trouble, Andy and Shemp decide to take the payroll money to the mine themselves. As they leave the station, they see the hunters have come back with the sheriff. Believing the bandits have returned with reinforcements, Andy and Shemp open fire, then hop into their car and drive around the station building, with the sheriff and hunters in pursuit. Andy and Shemp drive off, leaving the others circling the station.

Andy and Shemp crash their car, which propels Shemp up into a tree. The resourceful Andy gets in a horse-drawn wagon and hurries to the mine. Footage from Andy's 1936 comedy *Old Sawbones* is used here, and blends nicely in this new framework.

By the time Andy arrives at the mining company, the gangsters have taken over. Believing them to be the mine operators, Andy gives them the payroll money. They write his receipt on the back of a wanted poster that displays the face of one of the gang members. Andy sees it, realizes what he's done, draws them to the window, hits them over the head and closes the window on them. While they are bent over and stuck in the window, Andy goes inside, retrieves the payroll money, grabs a large board and starts spanking them. The last shot of the film is the sheriff and hunters' car, still circling the train station.

Money Squawks garnered some of the best audience reaction of any Andy Clyde comedy. Theater owners reporting to *Motion Picture Herald*'s section "What the Picture Did for Me," which gauged audience reaction, said such things as "Had the house in an uproar," "Everybody loves Andy and this is his best" and "This short even beat the Stooges. Andy Clyde really made one when he made this one."[37]

Money Squawks is not only a particularly strong Andy Clyde comedy, it is also a good example of Jules White's work. Gag-for-gag sequences stemming from a basic narrative was always White's idea of comedy, and his vision is evident here. This style always works well for silent screen veteran Andy, while the boisterous Shemp plays his part well. Andy and Shemp are even funnier as a team than they are as adversaries, but apparently Jules White did not agree. The two co-starred once more, and for the final time, in Andy's next comedy *Boobs in the Woods*.

Boobs in the Woods

Directed by Del Lord; *Story and Screenplay:* Harry Edwards, Elwood Ullman; *Produced by* Jules White; *Cinematography:* Henry Freulich; *Editor:* Arthur Seid; *Cast:* Andy Clyde, Shemp Howard, Esther Howard, Bud Jamison, Bruce Bennett, Jack "Tiny" Lipson, Mariska Aldrich, Al Thompson; *Shooting Dates:* February 15–19, 1940; *Released* May 31, 1940; *Columbia Production Number:* 476

In another one of the most outrageously funny Andy Clyde comedies, Shemp Howard makes his fourth and last appearance in a Clyde short, once again as the shiftless brother-in-law. Shemp's character's full coterie of negative traits—laziness, obnoxiousness and stupidity—are all in full force as he gets Andy fired from his job, then ruins a camping trip.

The film opens with Andy at home, his wife prepared to serve brother Gus in bed. It is established that Gus has been sponging off of the Clydes for some time. Andy's wife is holding a tray with a towering stack of pancakes, a full bacon and eggs plate, a bowl of fruit and a pot of coffee, referring to it as a small snack because "Gus hasn't been feeling well." Andy diagnoses his malady as "laziness."

Andy's penchant for masterful double takes is given its best opportunity when he finds that his suit jacket has the elbow ripped out. Gus explains that he got into a scuffle with the cops while wearing it the night before. It is further explained that he rammed into a cop car while driving Andy's car. Andy's reaction is brilliant. His entire body staggers back as his eyes widen and his head shakes. The scene closes out with Andy throwing debris at Gus.

Director Del Lord offers a nice establishing shot for the next scene, showing Andy trying to carry on a phone conversation in the middle of a noisy music store. One woman is testing a radio, a man is trying out a trombone, another man is banging a drum, and another woman is taking a singing lesson. People are milling about during this commotion and Andy is at the left of the frame, leaning over a switchboard. It really is a nicely framed shot. We cut away to a close-up of Andy and the switchboard as the trombone slide extends to hitting him in the head. There is a bit of knockabout slapstick as Andy heads in to see the boss without removing his headset. It catches on something, and he falls into a bass drum. Seeing he has cymbals stuck to his feet, he kicks them off. One breaks the glass of the boss's door while the other hits the boss in the head.

For all the noise, movement and tumult that is already taking place, when Gus and Andy's wife come in, they become the central part of the action. Insisting that Andy leave work and take a camping trip, Gus demonstrates the effectiveness of his new fishing rod by casting in the crowded store. It hooks onto the skirt of a large, haughty woman taking singing lessons and rips it off. Gus hands the pole to Andy as he goes to talk to Andy's boss. Of course the woman confronts Andy, takes back her skirt, and hits him. Shortly thereafter, Gus announces that Andy's boss said he can go on the trip. He's been fired.

All of the aforementioned is merely a set-up for the body of the film, which takes place at a campground. The opening footage established the characters and their relationship. Once again Andy is a hard worker with a job that affords him little appreciation, and a home life that he has trouble controlling. He is not henpecked, his wife is actually quite kind and supportive. But her allegiance to her brother enables his laziness and ability to take advantage of both of them. She cannot see his faults. This allows Andy's masterful ability to exhibit rising frustration.

As the camping trip begins, Andy's car is practically buried under equipment. Gus goes to the other side to tie it off, and ends up roping Andy around the neck and fastening him to the equipment. This gag would later be used in the Three Stooges comedy *Pardon My Clutch* (1948) after Shemp had become a part of that trio. Gus, taking for granted that Andy is comfortably in the back seat, drives off with Andy still tied by his neck to the back of the car, knocking into the garage door and a trellis as he drives off.

The difference between Andy and Gus is especially evident in a scene where the car, now with Andy driving and Gus in the back, is stopped by police. About to get a ticket, Andy asks for compassion, indicating it is his first vacation in 20 years. Andy's kindly demeanor and advanced age is enough to soften the cop, who is about to let him go with a warning. Gus pops his head out from the back seat window and insults the cop, and Andy ends up getting a ticket.

Once the camping trip scenes begin, the film relies mostly on mechanical slapstick gags, but in the hands of Andy and Shemp they become hilarious. From hunting mishaps, chopping down trees, to pitching a tent, the gags are wild and violent, and all stem from the dynamic of Gus getting Andy into trouble. A run-in with a forest ranger almost gets Andy a citation, but once again Andy offers his plea of being on his first vacation in 20 years. And once again Gus' interference gets Andy a ticket when the softened-up ranger was prepared to instead allow him a permit to camp and conduct himself on the premises.

The only real drawback to this very funny two-reeler is its abrupt ending. Andy, sitting on the hood of the car as a lookout while Gus drives, ends up on a wild bull that goes running off into the darkness as THE END appears on the screen. Columbia comedies often ended this way, and it is always a problem, despite how good the comedy is until the end.

Critics were rather dismissive of *Boobs in the Woods*, but audiences loved it. It really is an audience movie with its relentless slapstick offering one big laugh after another. The strength of both Andy and Shemp is formidable, but support from Jack "Tiny" Lipson, Bud Jamison and Bruce Bennett is also impressive, even with little screen time for each. Esther Howard, who co-starred often with Andy in his Columbia comedies, is given little to do as Mrs. Clyde, other than act as the connection between Andy and Shemp.

Andy was beginning to use his old man character in situations where his advanced age was a focal point, and not always for comedy. For his next, *Fireman Save My Choo Choo*, Andy Clyde's old man character battles to retain his traditional means of transportation.

Fireman Save My Choo Choo

Directed by Del Lord; *Produced by* Jules White; *Cast:* Andy Clyde, Esther Howard, Richard Fiske, John Tyrrell, Roscoe Ates; *Shooting Dates:* April 2–5, 1940; *Released* August 9, 1940; *Columbia Production Number:* 478

A remake of Educational Pictures' Andy Clyde comedy *The Cannonball* (1931).

Fireman Save My Choo Choo is still another Andy Clyde comedy where the sound and picture negatives are housed at the Library of Congress, but no screening print exists in their archives. The film appears to be an interesting comedy about the aging process and support of traditional ideas that remain solid despite new ideas that seem fleeting.

Fireman Save My Choo Choo was inspired by a 1931 Andy Clyde comedy, *The Cannonball*, which Del Lord also directed. Andy inherits a very old railroad, one of the first tracks laid in America. There is only one train car. He soon learns that the train is about to be discontinued as a method of transportation, in favor of a new bus line. The railroad commissioner orders Andy to race his train against a bus line to determine which mode of transportation will be awarded a franchise. The two go on a wild race. Andy wins with his train, but the franchise ends up going to an airline.

It appears that much of the slapstick and excitement occurs during the race, which takes up the body of the film. At one point, Andy puts rocket fireworks in his boiler for fuel, while the bus line rival ends up

Andy inherits an old locomotive in *Fireman Save My Choo Choo* (1940).

running into a beehive, which fills his bus with angry bees. After this wild ride, Andy's train is wrecked at the junction, but the determined Andy believes he'll get a newer and better car with the franchise money.

This short seems to have a lot of interesting potential. First, it puts Andy in the position of an older man who appreciates the old ways and who truly believes in the enterprise he inherited despite it being woefully out of date. It also supports the idea that something newfangled is not necessary better than an old tried-and-true item. Finally, with Lord directing, the idea of a race between a train car and a bus seems quite promising, considering the director's skill at helming such scenes.

Fireman Save My Choo Choo completed filming on April 5, 1940, after which the Columbia shorts unit did its annual shutdown. Columbia's short subject production had vacation time during the summer months, allowing some acts, like the Three Stooges, to do personal appearances, while others, like Andy Clyde, sought work in movies at other studios. During his time off, Andy appeared in *Cherokee Strip*, a Paramount-Harry Sherman western featuring Richard Dix.

On April 6, 1940, *Motion Picture Herald* announced that Andy Clyde would take over for Gabby Hayes in the Hopalong Cassidy features:

> Producer Harry Sherman announced that he has signed Andy Clyde, old time comedian, for the comedy role in the Hopalong Cassidy series. As usual, William Boyd will have the top spot with Russell Hayden as his sidekick.[38]

Andy also lost three friends, two of whom he'd been acquainted since silent movie days. Charley Chase, who was active at Columbia and worked on several of Andy's comedies, died on June 20, 1940. Just over a week later, Clyde acted as pallbearer at his friend Ben Turpin's funeral. Ben died on July 1, 1940. Andy and Ben became good friends when both worked at Mack Sennett's studio during the silent era. Ben was best man as Andy's wedding to Elsie Tarron, while Andy returned the favor when Ben married Babbette Dietz after the death of his first wife Carrie. Finally, on August 15, actor Gene Morgan, who supported Andy in his recent films *Ankles Away* and *Home on the Rage*, died suddenly of a heart attack.

A Bundle of Bliss

Directed by Del Lord; *Screenplay:* Ewart Adamson, Ben Roberts; *Story:* Ben Roberts; *Produced by* Jules White; *Cast:* Andy Clyde, Esther Howard, Dorothy Appleby, Fred Kelsey, Vernon Dent, Bruce Bennett, John Tyrrell,

II. The Columbia Comedy Shorts

Blanche Payson, Eugene Anderson, Jr.; *Shooting Dates:* September 6–10, 1940; *Released* November 1, 1940; *Columbia Production Number:* 490; *Remade by* Andy Clyde as *A Blissful Blunder* (1952)

As mentioned earlier, Andy Clyde and his wife Elsie Tarron became parents fairly late in life. Both wanted a family, and while she could have no more children, they were very happy with young John Clyde, named for Andy's father. Andy doted on his child and would sometimes bring him to the set. So when Jules White came across a story idea by a young writer named Ben Roberts that dealt with an older couple wanting a child, he commissioned the writer to collaborate on a screenplay with Columbia shorts veteran Ewart Adamson. Roberts would later go on to create the TV series *Charlie's Angels*.

On her way home from a trip, Andy's wife sends him a telegram telling him she is going to give him something he has wanted "since we've been married." Jumping to the conclusion that she is going to have a baby, Andy has the guest room redecorated as a nursery. When his wife comes home and delivers authentic Scottish bagpipes, Andy is pleased with the gift, but disappointed it is not the child he so badly wants.

Andy is in trouble with officer Fred Kelsey as Dorothy Appleby looks on in *A Bundle of Bliss* (1940).

These opening scenes are played for comedy (Andy hearing the noise from the bagpipes, which are wrapped in a blanket, and reacting comically), but there is also an underlying poignancy. While his wife appears to take things in stride and accept them, the narrative tells us that this isn't the first time Andy has redecorated the room in anticipation of a child on the way. It's a nice contrast between the wild comedy and slapstick of the rest of the film that makes you realize how much having a baby means to him.

The transition of poignancy to comedy is nicely handled by director Del Lord. Andy is shown walking the streets, still glum about yet another disappointment. Spotting an unattended baby in a buggy, he starts to play with the child. Director Lord transitions to slapstick when a boy riding a bicycle bumps Andy, who falls down and knocks into the carriage, causing it to roll down the street. Andy chases after it and catches up to it at a construction site. The mother shows up, accusing him of kidnapping, and a nearby cop comes along. While the mother believes Andy's stammering explanation, and is understanding, the cop does not and threatens to take Andy to jail.

The dynamic offered here is significant in that the cop maintains his status as a comic heavy, while the child's mother is sympathetic. Andy is his delightfully amusing, flustered self. This sets up the premise that will continue when Andy discovers this very child on his doorstep with a note from the mother stating that she and her husband are splitting up and she will be financially unable to care for this child. She perceives that Andy is a good man who will care for the baby properly.

Andy believes the right thing to do is to report the abandoned child, but he must avoid the cop he'd run into the day before, who continues to believe he's a kidnapper. This results in a chase that ends up at an orphanage where Andy drops the baby off in a room filled with several other children. When he returns home, the couple is there to indicate they have patched things up and want the baby back. Andy goes to retrieve it and this sets up a fascinating scene that is also quite revealing in regard to Clyde's screen character.

Andy enters a nursery area (curiously without any adult supervisor present) where several babies and toddlers are stationed. Looking for the baby he needs to return, Andy crawls around and visits with all the other children. The infants respond very naturally to him, of course, as they are too young to respond much to Del Lord's direction. Clyde is able to respond humorously to whatever circumstance are presented. Some of it is clearly set, such as a child playing with a hammer pounding Andy's foot, or when another youngster gives Andy a hug, his wet lollipop gets stuck in Andy's hair. But when Andy painfully removes the sucker, pulling out some of his hair, he tries to hand it back to the child. The youngster cringes at the candy now filled with

Andy's hair and says, "No!" Andy crawls away from the child and mutters "Yeah," clearly ad-libbing a response to the child's natural reaction.

This quaint scene is interrupted by a rather big gag once Andy finds the baby he seeks. A door opens and knocks him out of the top floor window, Andy holding the baby while trying to also hold onto the ledge to keep from falling. When he is pulled back in to safety, the cop accuses him of jumping out the window and trying to escape with the child.

The film concludes on an amusing note, but an oddly courageous one. The cop suggests that Andy simply adopt some children. Andy responds by adopting virtually every child in the orphanage, and there is a neat visual showing him pulling a wagon that turns out to be a veritable train of several youngsters, with the cop helping out at the end. Andy hears another baby crying and sees a black infant in a nurse's arms. Andy smiles and says, "I'll take you home too!" The child responds with an overdubbed "Yeah, man!"

The idea of Andy agreeing to adopt an African-American child in a 1940 movie makes a point that the filmmakers probably weren't intending. It is far more likely they just wanted to have a funny ending. But Andy Clyde exhibiting complete comfort at the idea of adopting a child of another race as his own has a multicultural triumph borne of the poignancy of his inability to have children, as established earlier in the film. They could have easily taken that gag in a different direction that ended with Andy not accepting the child by reacting with a comic double take upon seeing it is black, but in the film he seems quite enthusiastic about including the child among his adoptees. It's a lovely moment, only seconds long, and offers an extra level of charm to an already charming short.

By 1940, budgets were tightened on short subjects, with Columbia among the few studios still operating a unit specifically for slapstick comedies. No longer able to engage in location work or expensive gags, the filmmakers used their creativity to work within stricter budgetary parameters. *A Bundle of Bliss* has a narrative that allows for amusing situations that are punctuated with slapstick gags. And the slapstick is never forced. It always acts to embellish the humor of the situation. For instance, when Andy is accosted at the construction site by the cop, he falls backwards on a board, which causes a bucket of cement to fly into the air and land over the cop's head. Gags like that help to enhance sequential points in the narrative situation, making the entire film that much more amusing.

The method of establishing a narrative conflict and punctuating it with slapstick gags became the structure of subsequent Andy Clyde comedies. This method is especially effective in his next Columbia comedy, *The Watchman Takes a Wife*.

The Watchman Takes A Wife

Directed by Del Lord; *Story and Screenplay:* Elwood Ullman; *Produced by* Jules White; *Cinematography:* Benjamin H. Kline; *Editor:* Arthur Seid; *Cast:* Andy Clyde, Betty Compson, Matt McHugh, Eddie Laughton, Bud Jamison, Robert McKenzie, Jimmie Dodd, Dorothy Vernon; *Shooting Dates:* September 17–20, 1940; *Released* January 10, 1941; *Columbia Production Number:* 489

The brilliance of *The Watchman Takes a Wife* is the structure that has settled into a norm for Andy Clyde comedies. The film has a general basis from which it derives situations and punctuates those with slapstick gags. This method works better here than in perhaps any other Clyde comedy up to this point. The *Watchman Takes a Wife* setting is the usual small town. The opening features Andy, late for his wedding, riding up on a bicycle and flipping it over head-first as he arrives. Andy is a night watchman, so punc-

Best man Jimmie Dodd suggests groom Andy wear a girdle in *The Watchman Takes a Wife* (1941).

tuality at daytime events is difficult. This wild slapstick pratfall is a good portent for what is to come.

Andy is getting dressed in a room adjacent to where the wedding party is impatiently waiting (the justice of the peace has a hog sale pending). With the help of his best man (a young Jimmie Dodd, who would later co-host television's *Mickey Mouse Club*), Andy dons a girdle to keep his shirt front down, struggling with the item that simply does not belong in the groom's ensemble.

During the ceremony, Andy complains about the tightness of his shoes, and is advised by his best man to simply slip them off. Because he is standing too close to the ant-infested peonies decorating the area, an army of black ants crawls down his back, causing him to react big and run back into the dressing room hollering, "I've got the jitters!" which seems to indicate he is getting cold feet about the marriage. When the door of the dressing room is opened, Andy, in his underwear, is trying to rid himself of the insects, with the help of his best man. When he sees the wedding party watching him, he offers one of his specialty double takes and quickly pulls up his pants. The film then cuts to the ceremony having ended and the wedding party leaving the house. Andy realizes he never put his shoes back on, so he hastily puts on a pair that are tied to the back of the car. Once he gets them on, the car takes off, dragging him down the street.

This series of outrageous slapstick gags does not come off as trite or mechanical in the hands of Andy and director Lord. Their being veterans of the silent Keystone comedies gives them both experience in filming such sequences. Lord offers a closer shot of Andy as he puts the shoes on, then cuts back to a long shot with both Andy and the car in the frame as it drives down the street. Clyde's brilliance at reacting to this series of frustrations further enhances the effectiveness of each gag.

On the train, Andy is resting his stocking feet in front of a fan. His foot gets a bit close, and a thread from his sock gets caught in the propeller, causing the sock to unravel from his foot. Andy then tries to climb up into his upper berth, and keeps falling down. When he does, the alarm clock in his suitcase goes off, further disturbing the other passengers trying to sleep. These gags continue with the slapstick motif of the short, as well as continuing to allow Andy to react in his inimitable fashion to each frustration.

The plot of the short is finally revealed when Andy runs into an old friend, now a divorce lawyer. The obnoxious friend sees that Andy is a newlywed, married to a younger woman, and works nights—all ingredients that, he states, keep his business thriving. This extends to a transition showing Andy at work on the phone talking about how much fun he and his wife had on his honeymoon. His friend drives up just as Andy's shift is ending, and continues to put ideas in his head, increasing his paranoia.

The film wraps with the lawyer seeing a handsome man enter Andy's home. He races to tell Andy, who hurries home on his bicycle with the lawyer in tow. They arrive, and discover that Andy's wife was merely talking with a man who sells motor scooters. She wanted to buy one for Andy to replace his bicycle. Incensed that the lawyer put negative ideas in his head, Andy chases him away with a rifle.

Even after *Watchman Takes a Wife* settles into its sitcom conflict of a husband suspicious of his wife and getting the wrong ideas from various clues, the slapstick continues. Andy is listening at the door, the wife shuts it, and a loud crash is heard. When Andy hurries back on his bicycle with the lawyer, he crashes as he arrives home.

There are also some subtler funny moments. Andy is listening to his wife talk to the salesman about the scooter. She keeps referring to his bike as ancient and an old antique and that they need to get rid of it, and Andy thinks she's talking about him.

Andy's wife is Betty Compson, who had been a leading lady in such

Lobby card for *The Watchman Takes a Wife*.

silent classics as Lon Chaney's *The Miracle Man* (1919) and director Josef von Sternberg's classic drama *The Docks of New York* (1928). She received an Oscar nomination for her performance in *The Barker* (1928) and was called "the prettiest girl in pictures." She had a villa, a fleet of automobiles and several priceless antiques, but lost them all when her estranged third husband, director James Cruze, was sued for back taxes; her financial connection to him cost her her fortune. By 1940, the middle-aged Compson was playing smaller roles. She left movies for good in 1948, going into business with her third husband, achieving success outside of movies and recouping some of her fortune.

Columbia comedies were noted for their violent slapstick, and *The Watchman Takes a Wife* is pretty much a textbook example of their method. It is done with perhaps their best director and one of their finest solo comedians. While Buster Keaton and Harry Langdon were also working in Columbia shorts at this time, and were perfectly capable of adapting to Jules White's slapstick vision, their background was of a more refined comedy than the knockabout slapstick of the Keystone era. (Langdon also worked for Sennett, but not until after the more raucous Keystone period, and he used a quieter character that he'd honed on stage.) Andy Clyde was the perfect comedian for this style, and in *The Watchman Takes a Wife* he is at his best.

Critics were less enthused with this short for the very reason it holds up so well today. They were dismissive of the more blatant slapstick. Audiences, however, responded very well, as they invariably did to all of the Columbia product. Andy Clyde continued to offer some of the top short comedies of the era.

The Ring and the Belle

Directed by Del Lord; *Screenplay:* Harry Edwards; *Story:* Andy Clyde, George Gray; *Produced by* Del Lord, Hugh McCollum; *Cinematography*: Benjamin H. Kline; *Editor:* Arthur Seid; *Cast:* Andy Clyde, Vivien Oakland, Jack Roper, Dudley Dickerson, Vernon Dent, Eddie Lughton, Sammy Stein, Jack "Tiny" Lipson, Hank Mann, John Tyrrell; *Shooting Dates:* January 6–9, 1941; *Released* May 2, 1941; *Columbia Production Number:* 494

With the budgets reduced on short subjects across the board, the Andy Clyde comedies had to rely more on the sort of violent slapstick that was Columbia's forte. It was usually production head Jules White who engaged in the more violently funny outings, while producers Hugh McCollum and Charley Chase would have a subtler approach. By the time McCollum and

Lobby card for *The Ring and the Belle*.

Del Lord produced *The Ring and the Belle*, Charley Chase had died. It appears he was the one who favored a more subtle approach, because this short is every bit as violent in its slapstick gags as anything White might have done.

The original story for *The Ring and the Belle* came from Clyde and his friend George Gray, with whom he'd acted in some of the Sennett comedies. Their idea was to put Andy in the boxing racket and, through a series of circumstances, have him enter the ring against a champion prizefighter.

The plot has Andy running a barber shop, but also managing a fighter whom he dubs the Masked Marvel. Andy arranges for a bout against the champion and brings his protégé home to be trained. His wife balks at having an intrusive houseguest and threatens to leave Andy. Andy pretends to toss out the fighter and quit the fight racket, but his wife finds out he is lying. She goes down to the arena on fight night and knocks out the fighter in the locker room. As a result, Andy has to take his place in the ring.

The Ring and the Belle is filled with slapstick gags and many opportunities for Andy to utilize his skills as a comedian. He always worked best with Del Lord and had the greatest creative input. That he had the original idea for this film makes even more of a difference.

One of the best scenes features Andy getting dressed for work and engaging in several minutes of pantomime, punctuated by his character's muttering of ad libbed lines. First he is unable to find the collar for his shirt (collars were separate features then). He looks in several drawers and finds it. Then he cannot find the button to fasten down the collar. He looks in several drawers even more hastily, throws contents of one onto the floor, and finally finds the button. He drops it, searches for it on the floor, finds it, then gets up and bumps his head on an open drawer. He pushes that drawer in, then rises and bumps his head on another open drawer higher up on the bureau. Andy continues muttering lines like "Everything happens when you're late," making this already amusing scene that much funnier.

Mrs. Clyde protests having to house the fighter and begins packing her things. Andy tries talking her out of it as he finishes getting dressed, but hastily puts on suspenders and catches them on one of the bureau drawer handles. When he walks toward his wife, the drawer comes flying out, hits him in the head, and he falls into her, crashing into the bed and catching her head in the bed frame. He tries to extricate her, and starts pulling on her head, making matters worse. It is brilliant how the physical comedy in this scene escalates and becomes more ridiculous, but the action builds on itself in a way appears perfectly natural. Once her head is freed, she insists Andy throw the fighter out of their house.

There's more good slapstick when Andy pretends to throw the fighter out. Initially the humor is dialogue-oriented: The fighter is still in bed as Andy explains that his wife has threatened to leave, so their association must be undercover. The boxer, lying in bed, replies, "I am under the covers." "No," says Andy, "undercover!" The boxer is confused and asks, "So I am only supposed to have one blanket?" Throughout this exchange, Andy embellishes the verbal humor with his artful double takes.

The slapstick occurs as Andy attempts to make noise as if he is beating up the fighter and throwing him out of the house. However it is Andy who falls out the second floor window. He climbs back up the trellis as the fighter is working out with a barbell. The banging of the barbell is shaking the house. Mrs. Clyde is shown on the lower floor, dealing with the entire room vibrating including all of the fixtures and furniture. Finally, a piece of ceiling falls right on her head.

While at the barber shop, Andy not only discovers that his fighter's training consists of overeating, but also that he has a glass jaw and is easily knocked out. Having bet everything on him to win, Andy panics. When his wife stops in the barber shop to have the back of her neck trimmed, a distracted Andy cuts off a hunk of her hair.

There is one tangential scene that uses camera trickery for its gags, but relies enough on Andy's reactive humor to make it work. Andy goes in for a massage, and his body is twisted and contorted in the most awful and painful manner. He reacts with ad-libbed asides between comic screams of agony, while the masseur, played by Jack "Tiny" Lipson, a large Columbia shorts stalwart, goes about his business matter of factly, with no response to Andy's suffering.

On fight night, Mrs. Clyde hears Andy interviewed over the radio. Realizing he never left the fight game as he'd claimed, she goes to the arena and enters the locker room wearing boxing gloves. She easily knocks out the fighter, forcing Andy to take his place in the ring. Dudley Dickerson plays Andy's assistant at the barber shop who also helps out in his prizefight management. He has little to do in the film until the boxing match begins, when he loads up Andy's gloves with actual dynamite. Andy's punch connects with his opponent and there is an explosion. When the smoke clears, the referee and champion are lying over a beam on the ceiling as the champ is counted out.

The Ring and the Belle is funny, clever slapstick throughout until the boxing sequence. It is then that it gets rather mechanical with Andy getting bopped repeatedly like a punching bag (the action sped up), the fighter holding Andy at arm's length while he swings wildly and can't connect, and other timeworn boxing gags. There is the authenticity of having Sammy Stein play the opposing fighter, as he was an actual football player and wrestler. But, overall, the climactic bout is only interesting in that Andy does win and, although the film cuts out at that point, ostensibly wins whatever money he'd bet on the match's outcome.

Vivien Oakland once again plays Andy's wife, as she had in many other films, including *In the Dog House*, *Alimony Aches*, *Knee Action* and *Mr. Clyde Goes to Broadway*. She was Andy's favorite actress to work with, and he always requested her, but Oakland was often too busy working in the Leon Errol and Edgar Kennedy comedies at RKO. It's fortunate that she was available for *The Ring and the Belle*, because her prowess for slapstick comedy is certainly challenged. Vivien had started out in silent comedies for Hal Roach, appearing with Charley Chase and Laurel and Hardy, so her frame of reference was strong. And to have this diminutive, middle-aged woman wear boxing gloves and knock out a prizefighter is a hilarious set-up to the otherwise disappointing climax.

There is nothing subtle about *The Ring and the Belle*, but it is very funny. Andy has ample opportunity to engage in some of his comic specialties (his double take reactions to the wife after she knocks out his fighter are priceless), and it effectively maintains its plot and its pace.

Yankee Doodle Andy

Produced and Directed by Jules White; *Story and Screenplay:* Clyde Bruckman, Felix Adler; *Cinematography:* L.W. O'Connell; *Editor:* Jerome Thoms; *Cast:* Andy Clyde, Tom Kennedy, Dorothy Appleby, Fred Vogeding, Bud Jamison, Vernon Dent, Victor Travis, Charles Dorety, Cy Schindell, Johnny Kascier, Al Thompson, Fred Kelsey; *Shooting Dates:* March 31–April 3, 1941; *Released* June 13, 1941; *Columbia Production Number:* 498; *Working title:* Hic, Hic, Hooray

When *Yankee Doodle Andy* was filmed in the spring of 1941, the war in Europe was raging. America would not become involved until after the Pearl Harbor attack in December 1941, but the idea of enemy spies in America was all over the news. This Clyde comedy is topical in that it confronts this issue and uses it as comedy.

Jules White had already produced and directed a Three Stooges short satirizing Hitler, *You Nazty Spy* (1940), released months before Charlie Chaplin's noted *The Great Dictator*, which was also the comedian's first full talkie. Chaplin's project had been two years in production, and its publicity inspired White to do a similar comedy with the Stooges and get it out first. The Stooges even did a sequel, *I'll Never Heil Again*, a year later. For Clyde, the idea was for him to innocently run into Nazi spies and become their prisoner, and to end up escaping and overpowering them.

Yankee Doodle Andy opens with Andy, a night watchman in an airplane factory, gleefully announcing to his friend and co-worker Murphy (Tom Kennedy) that he has just gotten his citizenship papers. However, the wind blows his papers out of his hand and they end up in the sewer. After some trouble, he finally extricates them, but they fly out of his hand again and into the window of a building. He climbs a ladder, goes in the window and retrieves them, but is startled by a woman living there who holds a gun on him. He stammers out his identity, and when he reveals he works in an airplane factory, she and some male accomplices force him to take them to his warehouse so they can destroy it, as they are Nazi spies. This leads to a series of complications with Andy and Murphy ultimately thwarting the Nazis and emerging victorious.

As with most Clyde comedies of this period, the narrative structure is punctuated by slapstick sequences. In *Yankee Doodle Andy*, they are all quite funny. The first occurs when the citizenship papers are blown into the sewer. Andy tries reaching through the grate, but only succeeds in getting his hand caught. He borrows an umbrella from a bystander and only succeeds in destroying it. The man goes to hit Andy with what's left of the handle, hits a cop and gets hauled off to jail. A drunken man lifts the grate so Andy can reach down into the sewer, and then drops it on his head.

When the paper blows into a window on the second floor of a building, Andy takes a painter's ladder to climb into the room. The painter goes to step down and falls into a vat of whitewash. When Andy leaves the room, the painter has taken his ladder back and it is Andy who falls into the whitewash. He is knocked out by the fall, and wakes up in the clutches of the Nazis. Now he is forced to take them to the airplane factory. They tie up Andy and Murphy and set explosives to blow up the factory with both of them in it.

There is a clever bit where the restrained Andy sees a lit cigar on the floor along with a scrap of paper. He crawls over to the cigar, moves it to the paper, starts a fire and lets the fire burn the ropes around his wrists, which frees him. He frees Murphy and they dismantle the timed explosive and head to the Nazis apartment. The slapstick fight that ensues features a lot of good physical gags. Andy, armed with a golf club, knocks out several of them, but also hits Murphy. When Murphy comes to, he also hits several people, including Andy. Among the more amusing bits, Andy holds up an unconscious Nazi, standing behind him and using his own hands to draw in other enemies. When another Nazi's pants are ripped off, we see the word HEIL printed across the backside of his underwear. Naturally Andy offers one of his artful double takes in reaction.

Like many Columbia comedies, *Yankee Doodle Andy* ends abruptly after Murphy hits Andy without realizing it and keeps looking around and calling for him. This ties back into Andy hitting Murphy earlier in the scene. What makes this gag amusing is that the entire time Andy is hitting Murphy with the club, he's calling out for Murphy to come help him, but is mistaking him for another Nazi henchman as he attempts to run in and offer assistance. The picture abruptly fades at that point, with the idea that the Nazis have been subdued, but no real conclusion.

The Scotland-born Clyde was not an American citizen when he filmed *Yankee Doodle Andy*. He would not become a naturalized citizen until 1943. But his performance here is quite good, showing a real determined enthusiasm for his having acquired his papers. The fact that he heroically works in an airplane plant that makes bombers for the war effort is also a pointed element of the narrative. The thwarting of the Nazis was a theme that Jules White revisited in various Columbia comedies until the war's end. As late as 1946, White made a Three Stooges comedy in which they played veterans confronted by a dwindling housing market, *G.I. Wanna Home*. However, the only other Clyde comedy that responded to wartime America was *Farmer for a Day* (1943), in which he plants a victory garden, with the usual complications.

Clyde was such a versatile comedian, he could work effectively as a single or as part of a team dynamic. Often he would be the solo comic beset by a wife and some troublesome situation. Other times, such as in *Yankee Doodle Dandy*, he'd be unmarried, and in his troubles would be accompanied by a partner of sorts, in this case Tom Kennedy. Kennedy's career, like Andy's, dated back to the silent comedies of Mack Sennett. So neither was a stranger to violent slapstick.

Yankee Doodle Andy was one of the most popular Clyde comedies. And the tireless Clyde continued to increase his popularity, not only with the Columbia comedies, but also his regular appearances as California in the Hopalong Cassidy western features for Paramount. In 1941 alone, Clyde appeared in ten Cassidy westerns, along with the four Columbia comedies.

Host to a Ghost

Directed by Del Lord; *Story and Screenplay:* Harry Edwards, Elwood Ullman; *Cinematography:* L.W. O'Connell; *Editor:* Burton Kramer; *Cast:* Andy Clyde, Dudley Dickerson, Frank Mills, Vernon Dent, Lew Kelly, Monty Collins, Bud Jamison, Johnny Kascier; *Shooting Dates:* April 8–11, 1941; *Released* August 8, 1941; *Columbia Production Number:* 509; *Remade as One Shivery Night* (1950) with Hugh Herbert

Screenwriter Elwood Ullman has stated that putting a comedian in a haunted house setting is surefire laughs. This is true. And a haunted house idea is perfect for someone like Andy Clyde, a master at the double take. But too often this concept results in mechanical gags and predictable situations. And that is the problem with *Host to a Ghost*.

Clyde, Frank Mills and Dudley Dickerson make up a three-man team dynamic so effectively, one wonders if *Host to a Ghost* was originally intended for the Three Stooges but ultimately reworked for Clyde. They play remodelers, and the slapstick begins right away with Dudley and Frank hammering Andy into a wall. They must then extricate him, and do so in a violent and slipshod manner, wrecking the wall they had been restoring. They attack the wall with a sledgehammer and a pick, smacking Andy every time they slam through it. Andy ends up with his head sticking out on one side and his feet on another. Frank pulls on one end, Dudley on the other.

Columbia's entire comic forte was based on slapstick and they regularly engaged in violent physical comedy, most notably with the Stooges. But the unit did not spare women from the same type of knockabout, nor old men. (Clyde was in roughly the same age group as the Stooges, but he wore makeup and played older.) As a comedian with silent movie roots, Clyde was accepting of the raucous slapstick, and director Del Lord was a master at it. The violence here is a lot of harmlessly sadistic slapstick comedy which does a good job establishing the team dynamic and the limitations of the workers.

After this opening scene, Frank Mills pretty much disappears from the team dynamic and Andy spends the remainder of the movie in a makeshift duo with Dudley Dickerson. Dudley and Andy head to a big house-wrecking job but end up working in a home that is said to be haunted. The film soon settles into a series of rather mechanical haunted house gags. While this is amusing at a superficial level, it lacks the creative substance that better Clyde comedies offer.

Andy and Dudley work at night in a house that includes a creepy inhabitant who tells them that the house is haunted by deceased confederates. When confronted by the Southern spirit, Andy and Dudley go into an improvised version of "Carry Me Back to Old Virginia." When confronted by the northern spirit, African-American Dudley states he is from Pittsburgh, "you can tell by the smoke all over my face!" Stereotyped humor was a frequent part of comedy from this era.

Most of the humor in *Host to a Ghost* is just typical goings-on that further frighten them (lights going off, things dropping from the ceiling, etc.). What the film relies on is how Andy and Dudley react to these situations. Dudley, who played everything from bit parts to co-starring roles in Columbia shorts, was known for his comical screams when in danger. Andy, as frequently noted, was the master of the double take. Their reactive humor bolsters the mechanical gags.

Andy and Dudley eventually discover that the noises they have been hearing came from a record, and that this condemned house is actually a hideout for a group of crooks. Soon the police converge upon the house and start shooting. Andy and Dudley run for cover, and the crooks are apprehended. More stereotyped humor is used to conclude the short when Andy, looking for Dudley, opens up a closet door and finds a black skeleton who greets him with Dudley's voice. Andy then jumps out a nearby window and flees.

It's not that *Host to a Ghost* isn't amusing, it's just that there is nothing terribly original or clever about it. Its reliance on the talent of the two actors can only go so far if their artfully comic responses are reacting to generally unimpressive situations. When the same concept was reworked a few years later in *One Shivery Night* (1950) with Hugh Herbert and Dudley Dickerson, it came off better. Perhaps this is because less was expected from Herbert, who was at the end of his career (and life) when he appeared in Columbia shorts and he was never the comedian Clyde was. We expect more from Andy Clyde.

Despite the limited budget, Del Lord manages to put together a good road chase scene, one of his specialties. It occurs earlier in the movie as Dudley and Andy are headed to their job. Without their knowledge, a cop gets caught on a board that extends from the back of their truck. The duo goes driving down the street with the cop protesting and blowing his whistle along the way. This scene is used for plot transition and it stands out as perhaps the funniest and most creative moments in the movie.

Host to a Ghost has potential. A scare comedy should work well for both Andy and Dudley Dickerson. And the two actors seem to play off of each other cohesively and they work hard to put over the material. But the gags are so mechanical, one can only derive superficial amusement from the proceedings. *Host to a Ghost* is not a bad film, but it is a very standard one.

Lovable Trouble

Directed by Del Lord; *Screenplay:* Harry Edwards, Ewart Adamson, Al Giebler; *Cinematography:* George Meehan; *Editor:* Paul Borofsky; *Produced by* Hugh McCollum; *Cast:* Andy Clyde, Esther Howard, Ann Doran, Luann Walters, Harry Seymour, Vernon Dent, Claire Carlton, Blanche Payson, Mary Jane Dolan, Stanley Brown, John Tyrrell, Eddie Laughton, Mary Louise Smith;

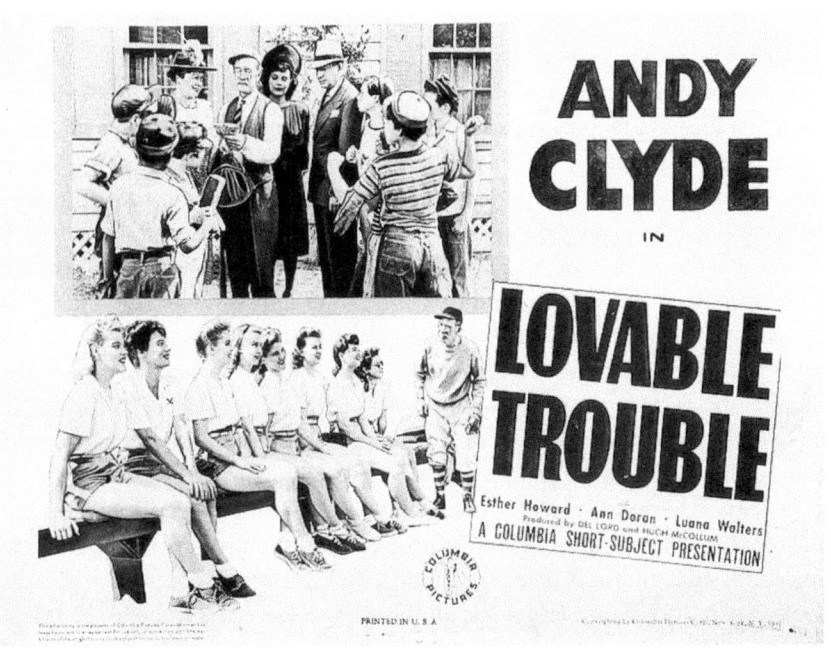

Lobby card for *Lovable Trouble*.

Shooting Dates: August 21–25, 1941; *Released* October 23, 1941; *Columbia Production Number:* 516

The idea used in the earlier Andy Clyde comedy *Gracie at the Bat* is reworked in this short. In the previous film, Andy was an old ballplayer hired to coach a young team only to find out it is all girls. In *Lovable Trouble*, a group of chorus girls don't draw a crowd because women's softball has become a more popular attraction. Things are so desperate, they have to come and go through the window because "the wolf is at the door." Their manager decides to form them into a team, and hires veteran coach Andy to take charge. Once again, Andy doesn't realize it is a girls' team until he has the job. When he realizes this group of women has no talent for the game, he dons a girl's uniform and wig and joins the team himself.

The way Andy is hired for the job offers a neat set-up. Andy is coaching the neighborhood kids in a softball game and playing along with them. He bats the ball and it hits the chorus girls' manager, who is walking down the street. He confronts Andy, who is protected by the kids. What inspires the manager to hire Andy as coach is not so much his skill with the kids' team, but the money he receives from his wife to pay the mortgage and home insurance, as she is leaving for a trip. It is quite a bit, all in cash, and the manager talks Andy into handing it over to "invest" in the team, while also hiring him as coach. When game time finally arrives, Andy is told his bankroll was bet on this ramshackle team to win.

Before Andy realizes he is coaching a girls' team, he sets up his house for a first meeting by putting out several spittoons. He plans to have the team live in his home, stating, "I'll be eating with 'em and sleeping with 'em." When the team shows up, Andy opens the door and is stampeded to the ground by the girls. He is then told that this is his team, causing him to faint.

In *Gracie at the Bat*, Andy was hired to coach an actual team of women ballplayers who knew and could play the game. This time he is in charge of chorus girls who simply want to find an act that attracts attention. So his attempt to train them as athletes does not meet with success. In one of the more amusing scenes, Andy is out jogging with the team behind him. One by one, they put out their thumb and get picked up as hitchhikers, or hail a cab. Andy turns around and sees that he is jogging alone.

Andy is beset by typical women who have put up a clothesline in his living room and are washing and ironing. Slapstick abounds as Andy runs into the clothesline and falls backwards into a full washtub. When his wife calls the house long distance and hears all the girls—answering the phone and on the extension—she rushes home along with her mother, whom she had been visiting. Andy quickly cleans the house and the girls all hide.

This results in another amusing sequence when Andy is confronted by his wife while one of the girls is hiding under a chair. His wife, while bawling him out, keeps pushing Andy down onto the chair, knocking the wind out of the girl underneath. She pulls out a pin and pokes Andy every time he is pushed onto the chair, causing him to jump up. Finally the girl overturns the chair and reveals herself. Mrs. Clyde responds by pulling a gun out of the desk and firing, causing a trunk to open and several young ladies running out. Before the big game, the wife is given an explanation and is in attendance. But she doesn't realize that their mortgage and insurance money has been bet on the game.

Once Andy dresses up as a girl and starts playing for the team, desperate not to lose his bankroll, the film switches to farce. Andy tries to speak in a falsetto. He climbs into the bleachers to fight with hecklers. He runs around and single-handedly performs a triple play. He whacks the ball over the fence and slides into home plate, beginning his slide as he is approaching third and keeps going around the corner into home—a fun visual that was also used in *Gracie at the Bat*, though not as elaborately. But when he lands, his disguise comes off, and he is chased off the diamond by the other team.

Despite the budget limitations imposed on short subjects after 1940, *Lovable Trouble* does have some outdoor shots, with settings like the ball diamond and a sandlot game with the kids. While it was probably filmed on Columbia's back lot, it is still impressive to see this film expand its scenes beyond the parameters of a sound stage.

The humor fluctuates from situational to slapstick. And the girls are all acting as girls in the traditional sense: powdering their noses while on the bench, insisting "I should go first" when told to "play third," even forming a kick line to the rhythm of the claps from impatient fans in the bleachers. At one point, a girl player quits the team because Andy won't fire the umpire who called her out.

Lovable Trouble is amusing enough, despite its concept being a rehash. *Gracie at the Bat* is perhaps the better film, however. Although the premise of forcing chorus girls to play softball is amusing, in the previous film Andy's reluctance to coach girls evolved into a respectful admiration once he saw they could really play. We aren't offered that sort of character development in *Lovable Trouble*.

Sappy Birthday

Directed by Harry Edwards; *Story and Screenplay:* John Grey, Lloyd French; *Cinematography:* George Meehan; *Editor:* Burton Kramer; *Produced by* Del

Lord, Hugh McCollum; *Cast:* Andy Clyde, Esther Howard, Matt McHugh, Vernon Dent, Olin Howland, Victor Travis, Bruce Bennett; *Shooting Dates:* December 18–22, 1941; *Released* February 5, 1942; *Columbia Production Number:* 517

Sappy Birthday has Andy all set to play golf, as he does every Sunday. But when his friends cheerfully arrive to pick him up, they are sent away by his obnoxious brother-in-law. Turns out it is Andy's birthday, and his wife and her brother have a picnic planned to celebrate. After several complications packing the car to leave, they never even get out of the driveway.

One of the weakest of the Clyde Columbia shorts, *Sappy Birthday* uses a narrative structure that had been done before, and better, but really flounders due to Harry Edwards' direction. Edwards' movie career dated back to 1914, and he spent much of the 1920s with Mack Sennett, often working with Clyde. Edwards' best work was with Harry Langdon, his collaborator on such Sennett productions as *All Night Long* (1924), *Soldier Man* (1926) and *Saturday Afternoon* (1926). He also directed Langdon's First National feature *Tramp Tramp Tramp* (1926). Edwards got his job as a Columbia writer-director due to Langdon's influence. Clyde always welcomed co-workers from the Sennett days, and was pleased with the scripts Edwards submitted for such previous Clyde Columbia shorts as *Boobs in the Woods* and *The Ring and the Belle*, two of the funnier Clyde efforts. But those movies had been directed by others. Edwards did not write the screenplay for *Sappy Birthday*, but it is his direction that causes it to fail.

The opening scene shows Andy happily getting ready for his Sunday golf fame, something he looks forward to each week. We are shown that he is a top level golfer who has won a trophy that he is quite proud of. Edwards liked sequences where the star comedian was tangled or caught in something and must extricate himself. However, Edwards often rests too long on the sequence, without cutting away, and the potential for humor is milked away. In the opening sequence, Andy gets tangled in the blinds over his bedroom window, and spends several minutes trying to get free. He then puts on his jacket, discovers it to be inside

Andy Clyde studio portrait.

out and tries to make it right. While struggling to do so, he gets a phone call (a wrong number) and while addressing the call, gets the phone tangled up in the jacket. Clyde does its best to work through these protracted situations, muttering asides and responding to his predicament in a humorous manner, but the director simply allows things to go on too long.

A full reel has gone by before Andy and his brother-in-law Matt McHugh begin packing the car for the picnic. McHugh is not quite as talented or charismatic as Shemp Howard had been playing the same role in previous Clyde films, but he does offer an obnoxious presence to counterpoint Andy's frustrated befuddlement. Edwards uses the idea he'd created for Andy and Shemp in *Boobs in the Woods*, where the two men pack far more than would reasonably be needed for a mere picnic. Of course Andy gets entangled in a large beach umbrella, and later a fishing boat, as he tries to somehow fasten them to his automobile for transport.

The script offers an extra dynamic to the proceedings with Andy's neighbor, Vernon Dent, playing a cop on the night shift who must sleep during the day. Naturally the noise the two men are making loading up the car continues to disturb his attempts to rest. Dent had appeared in many of the Harry Langdon comedies that Edwards directed for Sennett, so he also was happy to work with the director, and it is his scenes that come off best. A lot of it is mechanical. At one point Andy sits on a teetering board that propels a watermelon through Dent's window and onto his head. In another gag, Andy stands too close to a propeller, gets the seat of his pants caught, is spun around and propelled into Dent's window and under his bed. When Andy tries to sneak back out, he finds the seat of his pants are snagged by a bedspring.

Perhaps what is most unsettling about *Sappy Birthday* is its ending. Andy is thrown into Vernon's house once again. Fed up with his brother-in-law's antics, Andy grabs Vernon's pistol and shoots out the window. We hear the brother-in-law, off-screen, moan and fall. Satisfied that he has killed his annoying in-law, Andy climbs into bed with Vernon, wishes him good night, the bed breaks, and the two lie down and go to sleep as the scene ends.

Perhaps one can approach the ending as surrealism, similar to the type of bizarre humor Edwards utilized with Harry Langdon in the silent days. But in an otherwise typical slapstick with Andy Clyde, it comes off as rather desperate and confusing. Nothing in the film concludes or is resolved. Nothing is developed. Esther Howard, playing Andy's wife, is given nearly nothing to do.

McHugh tries hard to push his personality with loud guffawing, violent backslapping and noisy jokes. There is an early scene where Matt gets a commission for tricking Andy into buying a cemetery burial plot. But that sequence does not connect to any other part of this film, and just lies there with no point.

The screenwriters might have envisioned a much different concept before Harry Edwards got hold of their material. Lloyd French had written one of the Stooges' best shorts, *An Ache in Every Stake* (1941), coming to the Columbia unit with a résumé that included work on several Laurel and Hardy movies at Hal Roach. John Grey had a long history of penning solid short comedies at RKO and Columbia, including the Stooges' *False Alarms* (1936) and what is perhaps Charley Chase's strongest Columbia two-reeler *The Heckler* (1940). It would seem, with their track record, the *Sappy Birthday* story and screenplay they submitted to Edwards held together somewhat better than the resulting movie. In their book *The Columbia Comedy Shorts*, Ted Okuda and Edward Watz stated:

> Harry Edwards holds the unenviable title of the department's worst director. By the time he began working at Columbia, a bad drinking problem coupled with an insecurity about his advancing years, resulted in disappointing and frequently disastrous pictures.[39]

The Stooges refused to work with Edwards after two films with him; Barbara Jo Allen (who played the comic character Vera Vague) did likewise after only one. The Vera Vague short that Edwards helmed, *Strife of the Party*, features a protracted scene where she gets caught in a tile rack, another example of Edwards' comic vision failing to understand the concept of camera placement and editing.

Despite Edwards' botching this short's potential, *Sappy Birthday* was still accepted by moviegoers and Andy Clyde himself had no misgivings over working with Edwards again.

How Spry I Am

Produced and Directed by Jules White; *Story and Screenplay:* Jack White; *Cinematography:* Benjamin H. Kline; *Editor:* Jerome Thoms; *Cast:* Andy Clyde, Mary Dawn, Betsy Gay, Nat Bunker, Paul Clayton, Dorothy Anne Seese, Eileen O'Hearn, Ned Glass, John Tyrrell, Eddie Laughton, George Gray, Gwen Kenyon, Al Thompson, Daisy; *Shooting Dates:* January 7–10, 1942; *Released* May 7, 1942; *Columbia Production Number:* 524; *Reissued theatrically in* November 1963

Cranky hotel proprietor Andy dislikes children so much, they are not allowed to stay at his establishment ("I hate kids, who invented them anyhow?"). When a nearby orphanage burns down, he is forced by the sheriff to take in several kids at 50 cents a day. Andy can use the extra money, as he is currently having trouble keeping up with his expenses. When one of the children throws a ball into a bucket of paint, the paint splatters on his face, and Andy believes the red dots are scarlet fever. Andy's hotel is quarantined, causing him to lose revenue and putting him in even worse financial straits. When he finds that it is just paint, he is angered by yet another unnecessary setback. He is told that he has 48 hours to pay his back taxes or he loses the hotel. The kids feel sorry for him and put on a stage show which raises enough revenue to get Andy back in good financial shape.

Betsy Gay with Andy in *How Spry I Am* (1942).

Perhaps the weakest of the Clyde comedies thus far, *How Spry I Am* includes a few throwaway slapstick gags in the earlier portion, and then settles into being a musical that spotlights the kid performers. While such a thing might have a certain appeal in some quarters, it doesn't do much for Andy Clyde's comedies.

The children react to Andy's ire by praying for him while one of the girls (Mary Dawn) goes to the piano and sings the hymn "Lord, Lead Me." The black kid in the group continues his prayer by asking God for "fried chicken, and while you're at it, throw in a slice of watermelon." A live chicken comes wandering into the hotel and the child states, "It ain't fried, Lord, but it'll do."

Andy has a breakdown over his financial situation and goes to bed. While he's resting, the kids come in to give him a footbath. They argue whether it should be hot or cold, so they bring both and take turns dunking his bare feet in each. A frustrated Andy chases the children out with a rifle. The black kid says, "He sho' got da misery—ah's got it, let's put on a show and charge remission."

Perhaps the musical show that concludes the short is Jules White's response to the popular Our Gang series. In similar fashion to the Our Gang musicals where they put on a show, several novelty acts are performed. Betsy Gay does her comical "She'll Be Comin' 'Round the Mountain" number that she continued to do throughout her career, which lasted well into her adulthood. The black child, Paul Clayton, does a tap dance bit. Mary Dawn does an opera number.

In the early 1950s, after the Our Gang comedies became a hit on TV as the Little Rascals, Jules White made a short called *Kids Will Be Kids*. That film has the distinction of being perhaps the worst shot comedy the Columbia unit ever produced.

There are a few minor highlights in *How Spry I Am*. The gags in the earlier portion of the film, with Andy trying to care for the youngest child whom he believes is sick, offer the most laughs. He tries to give the kid medicine, but the spoon is knocked into Andy's mouth and he swallows it. Andy is also punched in the nose by the child and hit on the foot with a hammer. Andy calls the doctor, who appears behind him before he even hangs up to phone. The kids make a sign for their show that says "Bring your dog or your husband."

But overall, *How Spry I Am* is comparatively disappointing. *Variety* called it "mighty thin fare" in its May 6, 1942, issue.[40] In the October 21, 1942, *Motion Picture Herald*, a New York exhibitor opined, "[T]he acting is hammy and the picture laid an egg. This sinks to the lowest depths. People coming out of my theater had the looks of martyrs and I was the cause of it all."[41]

All Work and No Pay

Directed by Del Lord; *Story and Screenplay:* Monty Collins, Elwood Ullman; *Produced by* Del Lord, Hugh McCollum; *Cinematography:* George Meehan; *Editor:* Burton Kramer; *Cast:* Andy Clyde, Frank Lackteen, Duke York, Eddie Laughton, Vernon Dent, Bud Jamison, John Tyrrell, Johnny Kascier, George Ovey, Blanche Payson; *Shooting Dates:* January 19–22, 1942; *Released* July 16, 1942; *Columbia Production Number:* 516

While not among Clyde's very best Columbia shorts, *All Work and No Pay* is still a vast improvement over *Sappy Birthday* and *How Spry I Am*. It is essentially a pure slapstick outing, the body of which is one long chase. The lack of a budget forces it to often rely on studio-based settings and back projection. However, it still comes off as competent and enjoyable.

Andy, a night watchman, listens to a mystery radio drama. Distracted

II. The Columbia Comedy Shorts 127

by the radio, he is fooled into believing a couple of crooks wanting to steal a valuable ruby are men hired by his boss to fix the safe. However, a phone call from the boss reveals that no repairmen have been sent. The two men blow open the safe and steal the jewel, but Andy pursues them all the way to an ocean liner. When the ship's security is alerted to the possibility of crooks on board, they search the passengers, and Andy is forced by the burglars to swallow the ruby. When they later want to cut the jewel out, they tie Andy down, but are chased away by a gorilla that has escaped its cage. When Andy breaks free and escapes the ship on a lifeboat, he notices, while rowing away, that the gorilla is in the boat with him. He jumps overboard as the film concludes.

Bolstered by the creative direction of Del Lord, *All Work and No Pay* is fast-paced and filled with some wild slapstick ideas. Lord's creative penchant for road chase scenes is once again exhibited when Andy pursues the two crooks. He falls into a street sweeper's mobile garbage unit, which wheels into the road and is hit by a police car chasing the fleeing criminals. With the garbage unit in front of the speeding cop car, Andy is pushed along the road and caught in the crossfire between the police and the robbers. Even though the aforementioned budgetary limitations force Lord to rely on back projection and stock shots, he keeps his edits quick, while Andy's reactions further bolster the effectiveness of the scene. It is a highlight of the movie.

Aboard the ship, the film becomes one long chase with several clever gags along the way. Andy, a stowaway, must avoid the ship's security, while at the same time he must attempt to retrieve the ruby from the crooks. Andy goes to search their stateroom, and hides in a trunk when he hears them approaching. He is discovered and is forced by the robbers to swallow the diamond so they can evade being searched by ship security. The captain and purser come in to search the room, and, recognizing Andy as the stowaway, prepare to take him away. Andy goes willingly, seeing this as a way to escape with the swallowed jewel. One of the crooks ruins this idea by claiming that Andy is his valet and agrees to pay his fare. This is followed by some funny bits where a seasick Andy tries to vomit over the side of the ship, but is stopped by the criminals, who don't want him to regurgitate the ruby into the ocean.

The gorilla comes into play when a fleeing Andy seeks refuge in what he believes to be a hiding place, not realizing it is a gorilla's cage. When he runs out, he leaves the door open and the ape follows him. There are some cartoonish sight gags when Andy's neck is caught on deck as his legs dangle below, and the gorilla twists his legs as his head remains stationary.

The bit where Andy is tied down so the crooks can surgically remove the ruby, and is confronted by the gorilla after it chases the criminals away, would later be used by the Three Stooges in their short *Crime on their Hands* (1948) and its remake *Hot Ice* (1955). Andy is allowed to display his brilliant double takes and reactive humor through this scene, as the gorilla finds a knife and starts cutting off his shirt buttons as poor Andy lies tied to a table. His slapstick escape, due to adrenal desperation, is another good sight gag as he leaps from the table and breaks his bonds.

The fact that it is a standard comedy doesn't keep *All Work and No Pay* from standing out, mostly because director Lord maintains a consistent comic rhythm and the cast, especially Andy, perform at the necessary brisk pace. The chase never becomes protracted because it is broken up into a series of different sight gags, and stops to breathe during scenes such as Andy's capture by the crooks and confrontation with the gorilla. The fact that it opens with Andy getting into a mystery show on the radio establishes that he likes such stories. So naturally he is inclined to pursue the crooks and be part of one of these stories in reality. And so much about the rest of the film features the sort of exaggerated occurrences that would take place in a fictional radio drama, from the gorilla to something as simple as one of the bad guys menacingly sharpening his knives.

Often Columbia comedies are criticized for having abrupt endings that leave a lot of loose ends, and there is no shortage of Andy Clyde comedies that do so. However, this film ending when Andy jumps overboard from the lifeboat at least ends, however abruptly, with Andy having escaped the ship, escaped the gorilla on the lifeboat, and with the ruby in his possession, however tenuously.

While no better than an average Andy Clyde comedy, *All Work and No Pay* still succeeds due to the real talent involved in its concept and execution.

Sappy Pappy

Directed by Harry Edwards; *Story and Screenplay:* John Grey, Lloyd French; *Cinematography:* George Meehan; *Editor:* Charles Hochberg; *Produced by* Jules White; *Cast:* Andy Clyde, Barbara Pepper, Vivien Oakland, Vernon Dent, Marjorie Deane, Julie Duncan, Bertha Priestley, Lois James, Dorothy Kelly; *Shooting Dates:* May 19–22, 1942; *Released* October 30, 1942; *Columbia Production Number:* 540

Sappy Pappy is another of Andy Clyde's comedies that is inaccessible. The sound and picture negatives are housed in the Library of Congress, but no screening print exists in their archives. Harry Edwards, noted in the chapter on *Sappy Birthday* to be the Columbia shorts unit's worst director, was again at the helm. However, co-producer Del Lord stepped in and directed some scenes that proved to be too difficult for Edwards to effectively handle. It would be interesting to see just how effectively *Sappy Pappy* came off as a result.

In this one, Andy is the 1905 bicycle champ who now rests on his laurels by operating a sporting goods store. An attractive new bride comes in to purchase a pair of cowboy boots and claims to be a size smaller than she really is. Edwards liked doing scenes where people get stuck and must struggle to extricate themselves, and the first comic scene in *Sappy Pappy* is just that. The woman cannot get the cowboy boots off, Andy tries to help her and the two struggle to remove the boots in what is likely a typically protracted scene under Edwards' supervision.

During this struggle, the woman accidentally sits on some soot-filled gloves, resulting in a couple of dirty hand prints on the back of her blouse. When the disheveled woman returns to her husband, he sees the prints on her back and concludes that innocent Andy made a pass at his wife. The jealous husband goes after Andy with a gun, and he attempts to escape with trick bicycle maneuvers. It is here where Del Lord likely took over direction, as he excelled in chase scenes involving various vehicles, proving such prowess in other Andy Clyde comedies that he'd directed.

As per the structure of many Clyde comedies, it appears that once the conflict is established, the remainder of the film features the irate husband pursuing a fleeing Andy, with gag ideas along the way. *Film Daily* stated in its review that *Sappy Pappy* was "for those who like literally knock-em-down-drag-em-out entertainment completely devoid of subtlety."[42] *Showmen's Trade Review* said, "It should amuse the kids and adults who like to get their laughs the easy way."[43] It likely follows the same basic structure as *All Work and No Pay* where the body of the film is essentially a long chase punctuated by sight gags at various levels of creativity.

It appears, based on what we know about the film, that *Sappy Pappy* was supervised by Edwards during its first half and Lord during its second. How cohesive that turned out to be can only be determined by screening the movie. This is, unfortunately, not a possibility at the time of this writing.

Wolf in Thief's Clothing

Produced and Directed by Jules White; *Story and Screenplay:* Jack White, Ewart Adamson; *Cinematography:* Philip Tannura; *Editor:* Charles Hochberg; *Cast:* Andy Clyde, Emmett Lynn, Esther Howard, Stanley Brown, Vernon

Emmett Lynn and Andy Clyde fight for the attention of Esther Howard in *Wolf in Thief's Clothing* (1943).

Dent, Spec O'Donnell, Bud Jamison; *Shooting Dates:* November 4–9, 1942; *Released* February 12, 1943; *Columbia Production Number:* 538

While not a sequel to the connecting trilogy of early Andy Clyde comedies *Love Comes to Mooneyville, Stuck in the Sticks* and *He Done His Duty, Wolf in Thief's Clothing* does return to that setting and character dynamic. Once again we have a rural Andy Clyde comedy set in Mooneyville with Esther Howard playing a widow named Ivy and Andy vying for her hand in marriage with a rival, this time played by Emmett Lynn. And once again we have a series of gags punctuating that conflict. No story, no plot, just a series of knockabout gags derived from the central conflict, but with some truly creative ideas.

Wolf in Thief's Clothing responds to the wartime rubber shortage. Most of America's rubber came from rubber tree plantations in Southeast Asia, but after the Japanese occupied this area in early 1942, rubber became dangerously scarce. Military production needed all the rubber they could get, and American citizens were asked to donate old tires, raincoats, garden hoses, etc. As a result, being able to purchase a tire for one's car became almost impossible. People would stuff their tires with newspaper in hopes of making them last longer.

In *Wolf in Thief's Clothing*, Andy is, for once, with the times rather than behind them. He owns a car repair service. His rival Si is a blacksmith who deals in horse and buggy transportation. Because of the wartime rubber shortage, most of the small town of Mooneyville have reverted back to buggies, so Andy's business is failing while Si's is thriving. Si lords this over Andy, who is his rival for the hand of the widow Ivy (Esther Howard). Ivy has resorted to riding in a horse and buggy herself because her car has had a blowout. Andy knows where he can get a nice whitewall tire, but for the expensive price of $37.50. (Shockingly, what $37.50 could buy in 1942, when this movie was filmed, is equivalent to roughly $600 by 2018.)

Andy decides he is going to put Si out of business by learning the process of shoeing horses. Si makes a bet for the $37.50 that Andy cannot shoe a mule, and brings over what appears to be a gentle animal when in fact it is very aggressive. Andy attempts to shoe the mule, but Si keeps upsetting it with a peashooter and making it kick wildly. In one of the film's more amusing moments, Andy gets the clever idea of gluing the horse shoes on the ceiling, with nails protruding downward, so that when the mule reacts, it kicks the shoes onto its hooves. The idea works, Andy gets his money and buys a tire. There is another funny bit when Andy stores the tire in a closet that has an entire row of locks along the door—another comedic reference to the current rubber shortage.

It is amusing how Si and Andy's methods of transportation are as much at odds as their rivalry for widow Ivy. Si always has his horse and buggy, but Andy utilizes a variety of different methods, from a bicycle (that he doesn't realize is chained up, resulting in a pratfall) and a child's scooter that he pushes with his foot. It is a scooter that gets Andy to Ivy's house so he can court the widow. Si gets him out by ringing the town fire alarm (Andy is the volunteer fire chief). This works, and Si takes his place at Ivy's home.

Perhaps the cleverest scene in the film is Andy's method of getting Si out of Ivy's house once he realizes there is no fire. Si is an air raid warden, so Andy stages a mock air raid by standing outside Ivy's house making the sound of bombs dropping. He lets out a long, descending whistle sound, and follows it by hitting a hammer on a washtub. To punctuate his sound effects, he tosses small rocks onto Ivy's roof. Si is convinced of an air raid and hides under the couch. Ivy looks out the window, sees what Andy is doing, and is amused. This bit not only continues the narrative conflict, but shows Andy's resourcefulness with a clever comic idea.

Andy finds a ketchup bottle in the trash and creates a "head wound," further fooling Si, especially when the savvy Ivy goes along with it. But Andy is eventually found out, and the two are ready to fight, when Ivy simply states that the first one who brings her the needed whitewall tire will win her hand. Andy already has a tire, and Si realizes how difficult it will be to get one, but agrees to the deal. Somehow, Si does obtain a tire and is shown rolling it down the dirt road to Ivy's house, alongside Andy who is doing the same with his tire.

The visual of the two men rolling tires down the road is very funny, as each wants to move more quickly but are limited not only by their own energy but also by the difficulty in controlling the tire. A distracted Si bumps into a post. When Andy loses his tire, it bounces off a man and lands in a well. By the time Andy fishes it out, Si is already at Ivy's with his tire and a waiting justice of the peace. Andy is stopped by the sheriff, who accuses him of stealing the tire, but Andy can prove he purchased it. It is Si who stole a tire, so Andy brings the sheriff to Ivy's house. Si jumps out a window. While Si is being pursued by the sheriff's bullets, Andy gets married to Ivy.

Perhaps the first thing to address is Emmett Lynn playing Si instead of Robert McKenzie as in the earlier films that utilized this comic dynamic. McKenzie was still active in Columbia comedies, appearing in Harry Langdon's *A Blitz on the Fritz* (1943) and the Three Stooges' *The Yoke's on Me* (1944). He was a busy actor in small parts at many studios, playing cab drivers, bartenders and storekeepers. He even appeared with Andy in some of the Hopalong Cassidys. But somehow he wasn't cast in this short, playing the same type character he had originated in the earlier trilogy. Perhaps McKenzie was busy in other projects and unable to take the role. McKenzie would remain active until 1946 when he retired from the screen after over 30 years in movies. He died in 1949. Emmett Lynn made a career out of playing comical rustic types in many shorts and features throughout the 1940s and '50s, ending his career with his sudden death in 1958 after many television appearances. He had a flair for comedy and worked very well with Clyde in this two-reeler. Jules White must have liked the idea of Lynn being the rival of another comedian for a woman's hand, because he repeated this business in the Columbia short *Bachelor Daze* (1944) with Lynn and Slim Summerville.

White's penchant for violent slapstick is evident throughout *Wolf in Thief's Clothing*. Andy is doused with gasoline and is chased by Si with a blowtorch. Each man is hit with a buggy whip. Si gets a hot horseshoe down the back of his pants and is stabbed with a pitchfork. Each man is kicked by a mule. Andy mistakes a wrench for his cane, twirls it and hits himself in the face. Si rides his buggy into a clothesline and is knocked off. Si steps on a loose board, causing it to rise up and hit him. Andy's pants come down as he is running, causing him to trip and fall face-first into a mud puddle. But it is this kind of knockabout comedy that defined Columbia short subjects, and why they were so popular with moviegoers.

Shot conveniently and economically on the Columbia western set, *Wolf in Thief's Clothing* is fast-paced and funny, with a lot of well-performed slapstick and some clever comic ideas. It is decidedly an improvement on the trilogy of similar comedies Andy made with the same setting and character dynamic.

A Maid Made Mad

Directed by Del Lord; *Story and Screenplay:* Monty Collins, Elwood Ullman; *Produced by* Del Lord, Hugh McCollum; *Cinematography:* George Meehan; *Editor:* Paul Borofsky; *Cast:* Andy Clyde, Barbara Pepper, Mabel Forrest, Vernon Dent, Gwen Kenyon, Blanche Payson, Shirley Patterson; *Shooting Dates:* December 15–18, 1942; *Released* March 19, 1943; *Columbia Production Number:* 547; *Remade in* 1946 with Joe DeRita as *Slappily Married*

With budgets getting even tighter due to wartime shortages, the Clyde

Lobby card for *A Maid Made Mad* (1943).

comedies settled into the inexpensive structure of a conflict resulting in a long chase punctuated by slapstick gags. Usually Andy is mistakenly accused of flirting with a woman who has a jealous boyfriend, and circumstances keep coming up that make it appear he is guilty. That is the structure of *A Made Maid Mad* and it is the talent of the director, the star and the supporting cast that make it work as well as it does.

The film opens with Andy operating a women's clothing store. He's ready to close the store for the day and go back to bed because it's Friday the 13th. The wife scoffs at her husband's superstitious silliness and heads off to do some volunteer sewing for the war effort at a nearby women's hotel.

The gags begin when a woman customers asks for a pair of shoes, describing them as "two-toned brown suede with a French heel, open toe, and gold nail head trim, size 3A." Andy, who is used to the peccadilloes of lady shoppers, agrees to look for the shoes, but it ends up with him being bombarded by an avalanche of shoeboxes that knock him to the floor. The customer points out that she saw the exact shoe on a mannequin outside. Andy goes outside, mistakes an actual woman for a mannequin, and pulls her shoe off her foot, much to the chagrin of her nearby fiancé.

Introducing the film as taking place on Friday the 13th, along with Andy's superstitious reaction, is a nice basis for things to go wrong. Director Del Lord stages the shoeboxes falling very effectively. It is an entire wall of shoeboxes, along with a ladder that Andy almost walks under. When he climbs the ladder, he strains to reach the shoebox he wants, and ends up causing the avalanche that practically buries him. It is neat visual gag and one of the film's highlights.

The mistaken circumstance is established here too when Andy takes the woman's shoe and raises the ire of her boyfriend. The woman is Barbara Pepper, who would frequently be allowed to show her flair for comedy, right up to playing on TV's *Green Acres* before her death. She had already acted with Andy in the elusive short *Sappy Pappy*. Vernon Dent portrays her husband; Dent's career was defined by being at odds with the star comedian.

The customer changes her mind and decides to buy a hat instead. After choosing one, she gets into a fight with the woman with the jealous boyfriend. She wants the same hat, and their conflict erupts into violence. The women battle over the hat, ripping it apart as Andy tries breaking up the fight, but only getting himself shoved around. It ends with the woman with the jealous fiancé falling on top of Andy. Her boyfriend walks in to find the two of them sitting on the floor together, and hits Andy

The women's battle is merely a set-up for Andy to be once again in something of a compromising position with Barbara Pepper's character (she is

II. The Columbia Comedy Shorts 135

never addressed by name). The women are violent, pulling and tearing at each other, but there isn't any inherent comic element to their battle, except for Andy getting in the way. A tangential gag sequence has Andy attempting to prepare waffles and the waffle iron exploding. While Clyde is often at his best improvising little bits of business in such scenes, this one tends to distract from the flow of the action.

Andy goes to the hotel to pick his wife up from a women-only hotel but is not allowed entrance because she isn't finished with her Red Cross volunteer sewing and left word not to be disturbed. He tries to be aggressive, but is stopped by a large female house detective. Undaunted, Andy grabs a few linens from the lobby area and dresses up like a woman, and is shown to a room. When he stands too close to the elevator, part of his costume gets caught in the doors and comes off as the elevator ascends.

Another great visual is Andy's entire bit with the makeshift women's costume. He resourcefully improvises with whatever materials are available (including a live talking parrot balanced on his head), and has enough linens to cover the lower half of his face and hide his mustaches. This visually impressive sequence is highlighted when part of the costume gets caught in the elevator and the entirety rips away from his body as the elevator car ascends. He stands there in men's clothes, no hat, his pants legs rolled up, as his entire costume has disappeared.

Andy runs into a room to hide, and it turns out that it belongs to the woman with the jealous boyfriend. He covers himself with a blanket and bends over so that he looks like an ironing board. The woman, however, decides to do some ironing, burning Andy's back in the process. When he reveals himself, she reacts angrily and won't listen to his explanation. She starts throwing things at Andy, who ducks, causing the debris to go out the window and hit her boyfriend on the street below. Andy and the woman look out the window and he sees them together. Andy tries to escape, but is caught by the house detective. He turns and runs again, and ends up in a room where his wife is phoning him for a ride. He explains his predicament to her, and she tries to help.

Usually these chase-oriented shorts begin with one conflict and extend to others. Andy must avoid the house detective and the jealous fiancé. The bit where he is hiding as an ironing board is a neat twist on the usual, which would have the comedian posting as a chair. His reaction to the hot iron going over his back is shown in close-up, and allows for his always-welcome double takes.

The film concludes when Andy is on a cart that rolls across the room and deposits him out the window, where he is stuck on a flagpole sticking out of the building high above the street. He makes his way back in and grabs his wife's hand, and they flee as the movie ends.

While the ending is characteristically abrupt, it really is a case of Andy escaping from all of the conflicts he unwittingly caused despite his innocence. Del Lord has some fun with the visual dynamics in several scenes, and this extends to the casting of the characters. The hotel detective is tall, imposing Blanche Payson, another Sennett alumnus who had worked with Andy in silent movies. Payson had also appeared with Andy in his Columbia comedies *Lovable Trouble* and *All Work and No Pay*, but especially stands out here. Blanche had actually been both a prison guard and a policewoman before entering movies, likely drawing from her own experience to add greater effectiveness to her comic role here.

A Maid Made Mad is another long chase with limited sets, but the clever gags and fun performances make it a competent and enjoyable Clyde comedy. Confronted with wartime budget restrictions, the performers and filmmakers compensated ingeniously.

Farmer for a Day

Produced and Directed by Jules White; *Screenplay:* Clyde Bruckman; *Cast:* Andy Clyde, Betty Blythe, Jody Gilbert, Douglas Leavitt, Vernon Dent, Adele Mara; *Shooting Dates:* November 30–December 5, 1942; *Released* August 20, 1943; *Columbia Production Number:* 546

Just as wartime budget limitations forced many Andy Clyde comedies to rely on existing sets and perform essentially one long chase for the entire two reels after presenting a conflict, other Clyde comedies were essentially slapstick excursions based on a simple premise. *Farmer for a Day* is one example.

The war managed to open up a myriad of comic possibilities, including satire, military comedy and humor based on events at the home front. In *Farmer for a Day*, newly married Andy spends his honeymoon helping his brother-in-law Frank, and his sister Olga move into his honeymoon cottage with him and his new bride, so they can all plant a victory garden. With this premise, the film offers a series of outrageous gags and some of Jules White's most creative direction.

The first reel is the best, dealing specifically with moving the in-laws from their townhouse. Of course the moving of furniture in and out of doors and up and down stairs, has a lot of great slapstick potential, and *Farmer for a Day*'s visual gags are often quite clever. Perhaps the best bit features Andy

II. The Columbia Comedy Shorts 137

Jody Gilbert bangs Andy and Douglas Leavitt's heads together in *Farmer for a Day* (1943).

lifting an area rug while Olga is on a stepladder removing drapes from a window. Andy tugs at the rug, which is under the ladder, and causes Olga to fall out the second floor window and land on electrical wires. Andy attempts to rescue her by extending a ladder from the window to the wires and venturing across. He and Olga try to make their way back the same way.

The visual dynamic here is immediately interesting. Andy is small and slim and his sister-in-law is the heavyset Jody Gilbert, a character actress perhaps best known for her scene with W.C. Fields in *Never Give a Sucker an Even Break* (1941) in which she plays a wisecracking diner waitress. Andy struggles to lead Jody back in through the window, but she panics and falls on him. When instructed to "pick her up and bring her in," Andy responds, "Pick her up? With what?" White inserts a couple of outdoor long shots of the two teetering on the wires high above the ground, and cutting back to close-ups of their struggle to get to safety. It is a very funny scene that is nicely mounted.

Another visual has the gang, all packed, driving to the cottage. Their furniture is piled several feet high atop the car, and Andy must ride at the top to weight down the load and stabilize it. Frank drives, and the two women ride in front. White has to rely on rear projection effects for most of the shots, but there are a few cutaways to the car going down the road (a medium tracking shot from the front of the vehicle) that enhances the action. The comedy is further enhanced by Andy's reactive humor throughout this scene.

We are almost into the second reel by the time Andy and his brother-in-law are planting a garden. Some typical gags like a chicken following behind Andy and eating every seed he plants are amusing enough. When hot peppers are consumed, the chicken reacts by bouncing up and down. Andy and his brother-in-law throw things at the bird to get it out of the yard, unwittingly picking up a stick of dynamite and blowing up the fence separating them from an irate neighbor. After the neighbor (played by a well-cast Vernon Dent) beats them both up, Frank responds, "It's a good thing he left, I was getting mad!"

The film concludes with Andy and Frank trying to blow a stubborn tree stump out of the ground, using several sticks of dynamite. The stump blows into the air and crashes through the roof of Andy's new home. Irate, he knocks out both Frank and Olga with a pick handle and announces to his wife that they'll spend the rest of their honeymoon at Niagara Falls.

Of course this is not the first time Andy dealt with a troublesome brother-in-law in one of this short comedies, but what is interesting is that actor Douglas Leavitt, who plays Frank, approaches it much differently than Shemp Howard and Matt McHugh in earlier films. Not a loud, obnoxious back-slapper with a cackling laugh, Frank is just as lazy, but not nearly as boisterous. He is actually a bit low-key. When his own wife is in danger on the wires outside the house, he finds it to be a bother that he must assist her, sending out a ladder after he casually stops to light a cigarette. He then instructs Andy to rescue Olga. His approach to the role is quite effective and offers a much different perspective on a familiar character in the Andy Clyde comedies.

Director White often boasted that he made sure his comedies moved quickly, with the understanding that if they're going fast and have a lot of gags, one won't be able to tell if it isn't very good. However, with *Farmer for a Day*, White approaches the material more carefully with his choice of shots and his visual presentation. Even an establishing scene in the second reel, showing Andy and Frank in the garden, is a long shot that takes in their entire yard and working area within the frame.

Cast as Andy's wife is Betty Blythe, who had enjoyed a brief period of stardom during the silent era. Her big film was the lavishly produced *The Queen of Sheba* (1921), which was quite a hit for Fox studios, and made quite an impact on period audiences due to Ms. Blythe's very revealing costumes. (Only a few minutes of this lost film survive.)

Belying the many studies that claim Columbia shorts were no longer as creative or interesting when limited by budget restrictions, *Farmer for a Day* is a consistently enjoyable effort that kept Andy among the most popular comedians of his time. Andy came up with the idea for this short and took it to White, who responded favorably. Andy was a gardening hobbyist. As far back as 1938, a reporter interviewing him stated,

> Mrs. Clyde, the pretty Elsie Tarron, who was once a Sennett comedy girl, saw to it that we were served strawberries. They were the biggest this writer has ever seen. Andy said, "All my life I've yearned to have a little farm. I dreamed of growing the biggest and the best of everything good to eat."[44]

He Was Only Feudin'

Directed by Harry Edwards; *Screenplay:* Michael Ernse; *Produced by* Hugh McCollum; *Cinematography:* John Stumar; *Editor:* Paul Borofsky; *Cast:* Andy Clyde, Gwen Kenyon, Barbara Pepper, William McHenry, Snub Pollard,

Lobby card for *He Was Only Feudin'* (1943).

Bobby Barber, Bess Flowers; *Shooting Dates:* February 11–15, 1943; *Released* December 3, 1943; *Columbia Production Number:* 561

The title of this short would lead one to believe it is another rural outing with Andy involved in a feud between family dynasties. In fact, it is merely a domestic situation comedy with slapstick that offers a new character-driven dynamic for the comedian. In most of his films up to this point, the characters Andy mainly has to deal with are either his age or children. In this one, we see how he interacts with younger adults.

Andy is an apparently single father of a young lady who would like to marry. Andy likes Jack, her young man, but feels that they haven't known each other long enough. They have been dating for five years. Andy insists they wait at least 20.

This set-up shows old Andy to be the overbearingly protective father. He has gone so far as to steal off to a resort with his daughter, but she gets word to her boyfriend and he shows up. Jack talks a pretty young blonde into flirting with Andy, realizing the old man will respond to it. Jack comes in, clad in a cowboy outfit and a phony mustache as a disguise, and announces that he is the blonde's husband. Jack starts shooting blanks at a terrified, fleeing Andy. The film ends abruptly on a gag: When Andy, who is frantically packing to go home, is told by his daughter that Jack has fixed everything, he goes to thank him. However, Jack is still clad in the cowboy outfit and mustache. One look at Jack (whose mustache twirls around in another ineffective bit of post-production) and Andy escapes by running through a wall.

The first reel offers some typical slapstick sequences, but Harry Edwards' direction is slipshod. Andy tussles with a weight-pulling machine that hoists him to the ceiling, gets his face burned with a hot towel by a barber, gets hit by a ball that flies through the window, mistakes spilled mercurochrome on his razor for blood and thinks he cut his own throat, etc. None of these are particularly organic to the narrative and are tossed in haphazardly.

In an amusing scene, Andy is taking a bath when Jack confronts him. Andy is irate until Jack starts washing his back and feet with the brush; Andy now alternates between pleasure and ticklish laughter. Post-production adds a seal sound when Andy's comes up from being dunked in the tub water.

In the second reel, Andy responds favorably to the pretty blonde that Jack has recruited as a decoy. We see some throwaway mechanical gags, such as Andy jumping rope as the film is sped up, but the situation that is effectively part of the narrative has him losing his pants while in the girl's apartment. This is when Jack puts on a disguise and poses as her husband, in order to frighten Andy into a situation where he must be rescued.

The screenplay is credited to Michael Ermse, who is not on record for doing anything else in film, nor does research reveal anything about him otherwise. It is very likely a pseudonym, probably for Harry Edwards. It could also be Jack White, but his usual *nom de screen* was Preston Black, which he still occasionally used as late as the 1940s. In any case, the name Michael Ermse is something of a mystery.

Critics did not care for this Clyde effort, with *Film Daily* calling it "so-so" and stating that "the fun is mild in this Andy Clyde comedy.... Clyde isn't able to get many laughs out of the material given him."[45] As mentioned above, *He Was Only Feudin'* allows Andy to play an older adult whose ideas are considered amusingly archaic by the young couple. Andy makes such ridiculous statements as a couple courting 20 years before marrying. The main problem with the short is how disjointed it is in structure, due to director Edwards being so ineffective. Edwards would again direct Andy in his next comedy.

His Tale Is Told

Screenplay and Directed by Harry Edwards; *Produced by* Hugh McCollum; *Cinematography:* Arthur Martinelli; *Editor:* Paul Borofsky; *Cast:* Andy Clyde, Mabel Forrest, Christine McIntyre, Ann Doran, Vernon Dent, Snub Pollard, Heinie Conklin, John Tyrrell, Jack Norton, Bud Jamison, Sam Lufkin; *Shooting Dates:* August 31–September 3, 1943; *Released:* March 4, 1944; *Columbia Production Number:* 4007; *Partial remake of* Andy Clyde's short for Mack Sennett, *Taxi Troubles* (1931); *Remake of* the Andy Clyde Columbia short *It Always Happens* (1935); *Remade by* Bert Wheeler as *Innocently Guilty* (1950)

Perhaps it was partially due to budget restrictions, but *His Tale Is Told* reworks an earlier Clyde comedy, *It Always Happens*. Perhaps because Harry Edwards was so inept as a director, it was believed that an already constructed film that he could pretty much copy was an easy way to give him work. At this point, Andy, Hugh Herbert and Harry Langdon were virtually the only Columbia comedians who'd work with him (Herbert was so apathetic and lackadaisical about his comedies, he didn't care how they turned out). *It Always Happens*, directed by Del Lord, was one of the funnier Clyde comedies. This remake has some amusing moments, but pales by comparison.

In *His Tale Is Told*, inventor Andy's new coffee pot does a myriad of different things such as boiling eggs and warming up baby bottles. There is even a setting where it becomes a radio. He goes to the big city to secure a deal but is told that his scheduled appointment has been postponed to the following day.

As in the previous film, Andy is once again married to a supporting and trusting wife whose sister is suspicious. The women decide to go to the city and "surprise" Andy. Again a drunk meets up with Andy on the street and clings to him, despite Andy's efforts to avoid him. When Andy stumbles and falls, the drunk leans over to help him up, and a bottle of liquor falls out of his pocket and smashes on the street. A cop comes along, sees the shattered liquor bottle and Andy on the ground, believes him to be the intoxicated one and takes him to jail. Meanwhile, Andy's wife and her sister are in his room, wondering why he hasn't come home. Andy is returning the following morning when a woman across the hall asks if he can help her with a leaking bathtub. He falls in the tub, his clothes get soaked, and he waits in the woman's bathrobe while they dry. Of course the wife and sister-in-law run into him as he leaves the woman's apartment. He greets them happily and says he spent the previous night in jail. They pull him into the room and there are sounds of him getting beaten up as he protests.

Andy makes up with his wife in the car later that day, as he goes to the patent office and she and her sister go shopping. Andy leaves the office having secured the deal, and once again runs into the across-the-hall neighbor woman. She wants to apologize, but he wants to get avoid her in case his wife comes by. Andy closes the car door on the woman's dress and drives away, tearing off the woman's clothing. She hides in the back seat and the patent office man comes out just as his wife comes up the street. He pulls the man into his car and drives off, not realizing it is that man's wife in the back seat. As with the previous movie, this film concludes with Andy in the woman's apartment trying to get something for her to put on, getting caught there by his wife and by the woman's husband.

It Always Happens and *His Tale Is Told* are basically identical. There are a few elements that are a bit different. In *It Always Happens*, when the unknowing husband is in the car with his wife hiding in back, Andy pretends to be drunk and weaves all over the road, allowing Del Lord to engage in one of his specialties, a car chase sequence. When the same thing happens in *His Tale Is Told*, Andy pulls out in front of one car and makes a quick stop at his destination. There are no other visuals to indicate a wild ride in the streets had taken place. *It Always Happens*' car chase is a comic highlight; in *His Tale Is Told*, it is more of a transition between scenes than a funny sequence in and of itself.

His Tale Is Told's ending is also different. Andy is hiding in the woman's bathroom as her husband breaks down the door. It knocks into Andy and the impact causes him to fly out the window and land on a flagpole high above the street. His wife, down on the sidewalk, pulls out the hem of her skirt to create a makeshift net, and tells Andy to jump. Andy does so, and as he lands on his wife's skirt, it tears off of her body, leaving her in her underwear. Andy gets up staggering and discovers he is wearing his wife's dress.

While it is fairly amusing, has a few clever gags and offers some neat visuals, *His Tale Is Told* is nowhere near as good as its predecessor. It is interesting to see how this pared-down comedy relies on back projection, studio sets and the studio's back lot. Its predecessor had a larger budget and more freedom to expand. It also had Del Lord at the helm, rather than Harry Edwards.

The supporting cast is completely different. Bud Jamison played the jealous husband in the earlier film, but here that role goes to Vernon Dent. Jamison does appear as a cop in this one. Classic movie drunk Arthur Housman played his usual role in the first movie, but he died in 1942. Actor Jack Norton took over the type of roles Housman played, and became the perennial drunk in movies during the 1940s. In real life, Norton didn't drink at all.

When budgets for short films became even tighter, producer Jules White would often remake films and use footage from the previous one. But *His Tale Is Told* is a rare remake that contains no shots from its predecessor. It also offers less of the earlier film's consistent humor.

You Were Never Uglier

Produced and Directed by Jules White; *Screenplay:* Felix Adler; *Cinematography:* George Meehan; *Editor:* Charles Hochberg; *Cast:* Andy Clyde, Emmett Lynn, Esther Howard, Buz Buckley, Ida May Johnson; *Note:* Judy Malcolm appeared in a scene that was shot but not included in the movie; *Shooting Dates:* October 20–25, 1943; *Released* June 2, 1944; *Columbia Production Number:* 4008; *A remake of Gobs of Trouble* (1935) with Collins and Kennedy; *Remade by* Andy Clyde as *Hooked and Rooked* (1952)

Andy and Emmett leave their ship after having spent 30 years working at sea. Emmett tells of two "dolls" he has set up as their dates now that they're ashore. They both long for a home and a family. After a month, Andy is ready to propose to his intended but gets tongue-tied. He tries to do so with a record, but botches that. Finally, in desperation, he angrily yells his frustrated proposal and she accepts. Emmett also proposes. Once married, Andy and Emmett are henpecked husbands forced to do all domestic chores. When the clothing on the line outside gets too close to an active fire pit, the resulting blaze not only ruins the clothes but gets them thrown out of their apartment. They are relegated to a rundown rooming house. While the wives are out shopping, Andy and Emmett make a mess of moving in, destroying furniture and wall structures. The wives come home, go to hit the boys with a board, but end up hitting each other. Andy and Emmett run back to their docked ship so they can return to sea.

The film's first comic sequence is situational, when a bashful Andy uses a record machine to propose. Andy speaks into a microphone, and what he says is recorded on a record for immediate playback. To test the device, Andy reads a random car ad from the newspaper, stating, "Do you think it's time to have your body washed and polished?" Pleased with how he sounds, Andy then records his proposal. He becomes quite romantic until Emmett burns him with a cigar and he shouts, "I'd like to give you a good swift kick." Of course, when he plays the record for his intended, she hears the suggestion that she have her body washed and polished, and then on the other record his outburst at Emmett. It is then that Andy offers his now-angry lady friend a hollering proposal by stating, "I'm trying to propose to you, you old mud hen!" She accepts, just as loudly, capping a very amusing sequence that is very clever in presenting two older gentlemen trying to interact with a piece of then-modern technology they don't fully understand, with comic results.

Andy and Emmett's women seem kind and loving in their establishing sequences; that changes once they are married. The next scene show both men dealing with household drudgery, from washing clothes by hand on a washboard to taking out the trash to be burned. The scene where the clothing on the line gets burned is very well filmed. Jules White shows the clothing getting caught by the fire, and cuts to a wider shot to show how the flames have quickly spread and are out of control. Andy tries to put out the fire by spitting on it!

The slapstick continues in the new home when Andy and Emmett try to put the furniture in the correct rooms. Each comedian is allowed to react to a different inanimate object. Andy is struggling with a bedframe while Emmett tussles with a chest of drawers. The set-ups are pretty standard: Andy gets the bed to stay up, while every time Emmett closes one drawer, another pops out and hits him. But the talent of the performers and the director's shot composition makes them work so well. The wives enter with their best china and place it on a teetering table, only to have everything go crashing to the floor. That is when they attack the boys. White uses cinematic effects when the women go to hit the boys with boards and end up hitting each other. The action is sped-up and both women drop to the floor on impact.

The film closes with a gag. Andy and Emmett go running to the ship just as it is leaving the dock. They grab a rope that is fastened to the ship, but end up plummeting into the ocean. As they emerge, Andy has a lobster perched on his head.

A wildly funny slapstick romp, *You Were Never Uglier* is a good example of White's fast-paced directorial method and his staging of the gags, as it is a showcase for the talents of both Andy and Emmett Lynn. White seemed to enjoy experimenting with Andy in team situations, as he paired Andy with another actor. The results varied, but Clyde was very adaptable to any situation. He could work effectively as part of a team, and just as well as a solo comic.

Lynn was best known for playing a rustic old codger in western films, adding comic relief to the proceedings. While he didn't have Clyde's veteran background, entering films in 1940, his approach to his character was similar to Andy's with mussed hair and a grizzled look. They had effectively played comic adversaries in a previous film, *Wolf in Thief's Clothing*, so White tried them in a team dynamic. Having worked often with Clyde, Esther Howard responds effectively, in both the early scenes when she bubbly and coyly expresses affection, and the second reel which finds her overbearing and shrewish.

A child was added to this ensemble cast, Buz Buckley playing Howard's son. He introduces the boys to the record machine, then makes no other real contribution to the proceedings. Even when the women leave the boy behind with Emmett and Andy, he never gets in the way or creates further conflict. The only time he gets any footage is when he stands by while Emmett mixes paint, stifling his laughter when the paint splatters up into Emmett's face.

Writer Felix Adler dated back to the silent era, and had penned a few Sennett comedies in which Clyde appeared. His understanding of comic nuance was an asset as he wrote for Harold Lloyd, Laurel and Hardy, the Three Stooges and Buster Keaton. As with his previous script for Clyde, *Yankee Doodle Andy*, Adler stressed slapstick situations. *You Were Never Uglier* is filled with clever physical comedy that embraces the silent movie roots of its writer, director and star. *You Were Never Uglier* is one of the most enjoyable Andy Clyde comedies from this period.

Gold Is Where You Lose It

Produced and Directed by Jules White; *Story and Screenplay:* Elwood Ullman; *Cinematography:* Glen Gano; *Editor:* Charles Hochberg; *Cast:* Andy Clyde, Emmett Lynn, Gertrude Sutton, Mel Blanc, Hank Mann, Bud Jamison, Eva McKenzie, Cy Schindell, Frank Mills; *Note:* James C. Morton is seen in archive footage. He was already dead by the time they shot this movie; *Shooting Dates:* February 25–March 1, 1943; *Released* September 1, 1944; *Columbia*

Emmett Lynn thinks Andy's being careless with that axe in *Gold Is Where You Lose It* (1944).

Production Number: 4009; *Working title: Gold Is Where You Find It; A remake of* Sidney and Murray's *Back to the Soil* (1934) *and the Three Stooges'* Yes We Have No Bonanza; *Remade as* Pleasure Treasure (1951). This short was later released by Excel Movie Products as a 16mm silent home movie entitled *Fools for Gold.*

Jules White explored the teaming of Andy Clyde and Emmett Lynn further with *Gold Is Where You Lose It*, a remake of two previous Columbia short comedies. While I could not obtain a reference print of the George Sidney-Charley Murray short *Back to the Soil* (1934), the Three Stooges version *Yes We Have No Bonanza* (1939) is readily available. The Stooges version had a bigger budget and more layered production, as well as Curly Howard's manic energy. The Andy Clyde version, made on a tighter budget, is mildly amusing.

II. The Columbia Comedy Shorts 147

Andy and Emmett own a pawnshop. Emmett considers it a success when they lose over $400 in a month, rather than $600 as in the previous month. To Emmett's thinking, that is a comparative $200 profit. Andy scolds him, stating they are losing money hand over fist. A townsman tells them about a bank holdup and then pays for his cigars, and outstanding bill, with a crate of guinea pigs, indicating that laboratories offer as much as $1.50 per animal.

While this sequence is a set-up for the ensuing narrative (and the closing gag), it is noteworthy that the townsman is played by Mel Blanc, who stutters through his dialogue in a Porky Pig voice and does the Woody Woodpecker laugh as he exits.

The two bank robbers come into the shop, asking to buy a pick and shovel. Their plan is to bury the loot, but Andy and Emmett believe they are prospectors so they plan to dig for gold themselves. They happen to go to a camping area and it is right where the robbers buried the money. They dig it up and believe they have become wealthy. The crooks return, but Andy and Emmett believe them to be claim jumpers. They capture them by creating a makeshift slingshot between two trees and slinging rocks at them. Back in town, Andy and Emmett are congratulated for capturing the men and recovering the bank money. Their only reward is "a nice write-up in the newspaper." They return to their shop and find it overrun with guinea pigs, the ones they took in having multiplied while they were gone. At $1.50 per pig, they will be wealthy men after all.

The body of this short contains a series of slapstick set pieces structured around camping out and digging for gold. Dangerous tools and physical activity results in a lot of comically violent banging around, director Jules White's specialty. When the boys dig in the dirt with their hands, they throw dirt at each other. Andy swings back with a pick axe and smacks Emmett. When Andy falls in a puddle, Emmett scolds him: "How can you take a bath at a time like this?" Andy then pulls Emmett into the puddle. There is a fun bit where a dog places lit dynamite into a box containing supplies, and when it explodes, some meat flies up and falls to the ground. Andy and Emmett believe they have blown up their mule. When they try to sleep in their tent, they hear the mule, look outside and believe it to be a ghost coming to haunt them.

The outrageousness of their discovery is never realized by either man. Why they would dig up gold that was already minted as coins, contained in sacks, and included actual bills in the form of paper money if it were natural and coming from the ground is not logically approached. Andy and Emmett are just too happy about their discovery.

Since the Three Stooges version *Yes We Have No Bonanza* is so accessible, fans will notice that the violent slapstick presented here is far more the Stooges' style than Andy's. Of course Andy excelled in slapstick too, and with a veteran status that dated back further than any of the Stooges. But *Bonanza*'s larger budget and direction by Del Lord (including a wild chase sequence with Curly on a fake horse being dragged by a car) resulted in a more expansive, elaborate and amusing production.

But *Gold Is Where You Lose It* is not a misfire. Andy and Emmett work well together, and this story depends on their ability to play off each other in these wild situations. As they both have similar comic styles, they can play allies without one actor overwhelming the other. Audiences still enjoyed the Clyde comedies, especially rural and small town moviegoers. In the December 30, 1944, *Showmen's Trade Review*, their critic stated: "There is plenty of hokum in this film, which may prove acceptable to small town and suburban audiences." So the demographic was certainly known in the trades.

One week after filming completed on *Gold Is Where You Lose it*, Andy Clyde's nine-year-old son contracted meningitis and died after only two days. Andy, who became a father late in life, was devastated. Filming on his next movie was postponed indefinitely.

Heather and Yon

Screenplay and Directed by Harry Edwards; *Produced by* Hugh McCollum; *Cinematography:* George Meehan; *Editor:* Henry Batista; *Cast:* Andy Clyde, Isabel Withers, Jack Norton, Vernon Dent, Heinie Conklin, Brian O'Hara, John Tyrrell, Snub Pollard, Cy Schindell, Wally Rose, Al Thompson, Johnny Kascier; *Shooting Dates:* April 18–21, 1944; *Released* December 8, 1944; *A remake of* the Buster Keaton comedy *Jail Bait* (1937); *Columbia Production Number:* 4021

Production was postponed on *Heather and Yon* due to the untimely death of Andy Clyde's only child. When John Clyde died at age nine after a two-day illness, production on this short was suspended. John died on March 10, 1944, and his funeral was held on the 14th. Andy was very well-liked, even beloved, by the film community, and his child's funeral was crowded with his comedy peers like Three Stooges, Shemp Howard, Harry Langdon, Jules White, Vernon Dent, Bud Jamison, many of his old friends from the Sennett days and several new friends from the Hopalong Cassidy westerns.

Andy was told to take all the time he needed, but after a month he felt he was ready to get back to work. He was warmly welcomed on the set, but Andy was still so distraught he had trouble getting through the movie. A fairly lackluster film hampered by Harry Edwards' limited directorial skills, *Heather and Yon* features Andy in a performance that is still good, as he was a trooper, but the inherent enthusiasm that is so evident in other films is not noticeable here.

In this remake of the 1937 Buster Keaton two-reeler *Jail Bait*, Andy agrees to help his reporter friend Scoop get enough information to obtain enough info to convict a murderer. Andy is in a good mood, having just proposed to the woman who gives him diction lessons, and has plans to open a school with her. Scoop indicates that the cops are baffled over a recent murder. Scoop, however, knows who did it and where he is hiding. So, before the police get on the killer's trail, Scoop wants enough time to gather the necessary information himself. He talks Andy into confessing to the crime and going to jail so the cops stop investigating and Scoop is allowed to gather enough into to bring the actual killer to justice. However, while Andy is in jail, Scoop is injured in an airliner crash, leaving Andy stuck behind bars awaiting the electric chair. Scoop arrives just as a prison break occurs and clears Andy's name, allowing him to marry his intended.

A revamped script, a distracted lead performance and a limited director combine to make *Heather and Yon* one of the lesser Clyde comedies. Edwards' penchant for putting the lead comedian in situations where he is caught and must struggle to extricate himself, is evident with Andy's first scene. Resting in a hammock awaiting diction lessons, Andy gets his foot caught and must struggle to escape. While in jail, he gets his neck caught between two prison bars. Both of these scenes disrupt the flow of the narrative and are less-than-amusing distractions. The film also offers a very clumsily staged prison escape, with a lot of random running around and falling down that doesn't adhere to any real comic structure.

There are some funny scenes involving Andy's interactions with other prisoners, who unlike Andy are actually hardened criminals (there is an awkwardly amusing moment where Andy and another prisoner get their faces close together as Andy gets a light from the other man's cigarette). However, the idea of a story—a man confessing to a crime he didn't commit so his friend can investigate said crime—is funnier than the execution.

In perhaps the most amusing sequence, Andy shows up at the jail to confess. Policemen are running out of the building, knocking into Andy, who tries hard to stammer out a confession, but is being ignored. The Three Stooges would sometimes employ the idea of attempting to break into prison in order to expose corruption in the judicial or penal system, but Andy is merely acting as a decoy while Scoop "gets the goods" on the killer. He finally stumbles into a courtroom and is confronted by a judge, to whom he confesses. His sentencing to the electric chair takes place shortly thereafter. Andy exhibits a defiant and confident demeanor as he is sure Scoop will rescue him in time. While comfortably reading the newspaper in his cell, Andy discovers Scoop was in a plane crash.

Scoop is played by Jack Norton, known for playing comic drunks. He played such a part in a previous Clyde comedy. However, in this film he plays a straight character, coming off as both appealing and funny. Despite his limitations, Harry Edwards was a director Andy knew well, and he was also surrounded by old actor-friends like Vernon Dent, Snub Pollard and Heinie Conklin. But, according to Jules White,[46] "Hugh McCollum told me that Andy would have to stop scenes and take a few minutes. The poor man would be openly weeping on the set. After he finished this picture, I had him take about a year off." (It was actually six months.)

When Andy returned, he first took a small part in a Warner Brothers feature, his agent believing that it would be best if the comedian came back slowly before embarking on a starring short. He returned to Columbia to begin filming his next comedy, *Two Local Yokels*, in October 1944. Jules White claimed he was "his old self again," but added, "He never completely recovered from the loss of his son."

Two Local Yokels

Produced and Directed by Jules White; *Story and Screenplay:* Felix Adler; *Cinematography:* George Meehan; *Editor:* Charles Hochberg; *Cast:* Andy Clyde, Esther Howard, Charles Judels; *Shooting Dates:* October 21–November 3, 1944; *Released* March 23, 1945; *The working title* was *Bread and Butter*; *Columbia Production Number:* 4024. This short was later released by Excel Movie Products as 16mm silent home movies entitled *Hiss and Make Up* and *Servant Trouble*.

Director Jules White once again offers the idea of Andy Clyde in a rivalry for the attention of Esther Howard, with actor Charles Judels as his adversary, an actor who had been playing small parts in films for decades. Judels stopped by Columbia's shorts department in 1945 and appeared in two shorts. After a small role in Shemp Howard's comedy *Off Again On Again*, Judels essayed a larger role in this Andy Clyde film.

Andy's wife is annoyed that her husband spends more time with his friend Charlie than he does with her. She concocts a scheme to make the two friends angry with each other. She finds an excuse to divorce Andy. Andy, in his attempts to win back his wife, agrees to be her servant. However, when

II. The Columbia Comedy Shorts 151

she brings home Charles for dinner, Andy takes offense and a slapstick battle ensues, concluding with Charlie jumping out the window and Andy reuniting with his wife.

White's penchant for utilizing a basic conflict on which to hang a series of slapstick sequences is effectively presented here. It starts right off in the opening scene when Andy and Charlie are playing ping pong. The ball gets past Andy and rolls into a golf bag on the floor. Andy reaches in, pulls out a golf ball, and hits that to Charlie, bouncing it off his head. Andy returns the shot, Charlie ducks, the ball bounces off the wall and goes in Andy's mouth, getting stuck in his throat. Charlie is trying to help Andy cough up the ball, when Andy's wife walks in. Seeing what appears to be Charlie attacking Andy, she jumps in, wrestling Charlie away. Andy is still choking. Finally, some tongs are stuck in his mouth and they pull the ball out. White's extreme slapstick, involving all three characters, is at its violent best.

It is this bit of roughhouse slapstick that Esther uses to dupe Andy into thinking she is planning to divorce him and cite "cruelty" as her reason. When she scolds him, she punctuates her statements by poking him with the tongs. There is a clever gag where every time he is poked, Andy pulls out something that has been damaged. First, he pulls crushed cigars out of his pocket. Next, he pulls out his watch, which has been shattered. This scene extends from the ping pong game and the choking battle to effectively continue the visual humor on which this short concentrates.

There's more slapstick when servant Andy and guest Charlie become rivals for the attention of Andy's wife. Charlie is seated at the dinner table with Esther. Andy fills Charlie's water glass. When he asks for a refill, Andy pours water down Charlie's sleeve, director White cutting away to under the table where water is pouring from Charlie's pants leg. He then pours water on Charlie's head. Esther, seeing that her plan is effective, shows amusement at their antics.

Another impressive visual shows Charlie dropping his fork, and ordering Andy to pick it up. Andy bends under the table, Charlie stabs him in the butt with a knife, and Andy abruptly stands, the contents of the table balancing perfectly on his head. This scene concludes with Andy effectively beating Charlie up with a series of comically performed punches and Charlie's escape out the window. Andy and Esther kiss and make up as the picture fades.

Two Local Yokels is sustained by some clever gags, good performances and White's capable direction. This type of briskly paced slapstick is how White defined his Columbia comedy unit. The cast is small, just the three players, and there are no dull stretches. Even in transitional scenes, slapstick comedy prevails. Batter from a mixer splashes in Andy's face when he tries to bake a cake. He turns with the mop on his shoulder and hits Esther Howard, et al. It is consistently funny. Howard continued to be a good sport whenever she worked in the Columbia comedies, and her engagement in this film's raucous slapstick is a good example.

The only trifling quibble is the fact that Esther is successful in busting up a comfortable friendship. She plays the two men, they fall for it, and there is no comeuppance. Andy's relationship with his best friend is effectively ruined. It is done so in a comic manner, but perhaps threatening Andy and duping Charlie in order to destroy their friendship should have met with some comical payback of its own.

By the end of 1944, a smaller number of short comedy units were operating. Even the Our Gang comedies ceased production by 1944. RKO was still putting out Edgar Kennedy, Leon Errol and Gil Lamb comedies, but Columbia's short subject unit was the one that was thriving with several units active. Exhibitors continued to seek the Columbia comedies, with the Three Stooges remaining their top choice and Andy Clyde continuing as the close second.

A Miner Affair

Produced and Directed by Jules White; *Story and Screenplay:* Elwood Ullman; *Cinematography:* Glen Gano; *Editor:* Charles Hochberg; *Cast:* Andy Clyde, Charley Rogers, Robert Williams, Charles Bates, Gloria Marlen, Jack "Tiny" Lipson, Al Thompson; *Shooting Dates:* January 24–29, 1945; *Released* November 1, 1945; *A remake of* the Three Stooges *Cash and Carry* (1937); *Remade by* Andy Clyde as *Two April Fools* (1954); *Columbia Production Number:* 4040. This short was later released by Excel Movie Products as 16mm silent home movies entitled *Phony Treasure* and *A Blasted Hoax*.

About a month before embarking on his next comedy, Andy Clyde attended the funeral of his friend Harry Langdon, who died on December 22, 1944. Clyde had worked with Langdon in the Mack Sennett days and stayed connected to him while both were active in Columbia comedies. Harry was in attendance at the funeral of Andy's son.

A Miner Affair is a remake of an accessible and noted The Stooges short, *Cash and Carry*, and in a comparison, it holds its own reasonably well. Thee Stooges short was a bit too sentimental for the trio, even though it included their trademark slapstick. However, when this aspect was reworked for Andy (by one of the original film's screenwriters), the idea works more effectively. Andy is paired here with English comedian Charley Rogers.

II. The Columbia Comedy Shorts 153

Lobby card for *A Miner Affair* (1944).

Remarkably, Rogers receives above-the-title billing alongside Andy, as if they were a bona fide comedy team.

Andy and Charley return home to their shack in the middle of the city dump after spending time unsuccessfully prospecting. They find a young boy doing his homework in their shack and tell him to leave. However, they change their minds when they see he walks with a limp. When the men stumble across a can full of money in the dump, they conclude their luck is changing, until they realize it is money the boy and his sister are saving so he can have an operation on his leg. Andy and Charley are tricked into using the money to buy a "treasure map" to an old abandoned house where they believe a fortune is buried. After digging they find themselves in a bank vault and, once again, believe their luck has changed. Bank security stops them, and when they run away, they bump into the man who sold them the map. Since he had just committed a robbery, Andy and Charley are rewarded for "capturing" him, and it is enough for the boy's operation.

Most of the comedy in *A Miner Affair* is contained in the slapstick scenes while Andy and Charley are digging for the treasure. Buckets are dropped on heads, picks and shovels bang into the other man who is standing too close, and other knockabout fare. While this type of comedy worked will in the Stooges version, Andy and Charley are just as adept at physical humor of this fashion and just as funny.

The duo improves on the Stooges in the situational elements. While it can be argued that sentiment added another layer to the Stooges that gave them more depth than usual, Andy already fits neatly into such a situation. His reaction upon seeing the boy get up from his makeshift desk and limp is a good example. Understanding nuance, Andy's initial angry look upon finding the boy squatting in his shack softens discernibly as the boy gets up. He hastily stammers that it is okay if the boy and his sister stay.

The Stooges original was made in 1937 when America was still recovering from the Depression. This gives the poverty of the boy, and the Stooges, a bit more substance. The country was much more prosperous in 1945, so these are merely isolated poor people who are struggling. In *A Miner Affair*, the sister has a job, but one that pays poorly. In 1945 America, she could likely find more lucrative employment. In 1937, the lack of money afflicting the boy and his sister is due to there simply being no jobs available.

The Stooges film is a bit more grandiose in that they do not merely dig into a bank vault, they tunnel their way directly into Fort Knox. The film concludes with them, the boy and the sister pleading their case to the president, who indicates he will arrange for the child's operation, and extends executive clemency to the Stooges. The president at the time was Franklin Roosevelt, himself disabled, which adds further impact to the proceedings. (The actor playing the president, Al Richardson, appears with his back to the camera, but is affecting his vocal delivery to sound like President Roosevelt.)

The Clyde film has its own optimism. It ends with Andy and Charley playing a pickup baseball game in the junkyard with the boy and his sister. The boy hits the ball and runs the bases, indicating that his leg operation was a success. Andy announces that they now have a son and a daughter, Charley points out, comically, that Andy is the father and he is the mother.

The British Charley Rogers has an amusingly droll character that plays nicely off of Andy, so it is unfortunate that the two never worked together again. He had played small parts in films at the Hal Roach studios, but was most successful as a writer; he worked on several Laurel and Hardy films, including *Way Out West* (1937), *Blockheads* (1938), *A Chump at Oxford* (1940) and *Saps at Sea* (1940). He also directed the duo in several of their shorts, including *Them Thar Hills* (1934), *Tit for Tat* (1935) and *Thicker Than Water* (1935). This level of prestige was likely what allowed him such lofty billing.

A Miner Affair is a rather pedestrian effort, but the situations make the characters a bit more layered, and the slapstick is well-performed. It is an amusing movie with a gratifying conclusion.

Spook To Me

Screenplay and Directed by Harry Edwards; *Story:* Edward Bernds, Russell Malmgren; *Produced by* Hugh McCollum; *Cinematography:* Benjamin H. Kline; *Editor:* Henry Batista; *Cast:* Andy Clyde, Vie Barlowe, Dudley Dickerson, Frank Hagney, Wally Rose, Dick Botiller; *Shooting Dates:* February 6–9, 1945; *Released* December 27, 1945; *Columbia Production Number:* 4037; *The original working title was Be Prepared*; Reissued theatrically in June 1959

Spook to Me is another haunted house comedy that relies on pretty typical gags. At least it allows Andy to work with youngsters again. This one has Andy as the troop leader for the Bloodhounds, a Scout group. While on camping, the boys notice flashing lights on an old abandoned house that is rumored to be haunted. Andy is dismissive, but agrees to investigate. He is met by his friend Sam, a chauffeur, whose car broke down and who claims to have seen some strange occurrences. The Bloodhound troop goes to notify police, while Andy and Sam apprehensively approach the house. After a series of scares, they stumble upon some money and discover that the old house is a hideout for counterfeiters who have been pulling stunts in an attempt to scare them away. The crooks tie up Andy and Sam, but the Bloodhounds arrive and subdue the criminals even before the cops get there.

Andy worked well with youngsters, but hadn't done so at this level since *How Spry I Am* three years earlier. This time he is fully in charge of the troop, who respectfully address him as Mr. Clyde. The boys are often more resourceful and competent. Early in the film, when one boy is given a merit badge for subduing a criminal, Andy asks for a demonstration. The boy grabs Andy's wrist and tosses him across the room, in a neat slapstick visual. However, once they are outdoors in their tents, it is the boys who are unsettled about the lights flashing at the old house, and Andy who courageously agrees to go investigate. "Gosh," one of the boys exclaims, "you sure are brave!" Andy responds with the question, "You're just realizing that now?"

The film gets a bit convenient when the boys go to seek help while Andy and Sam venture on toward the house. This gets the youngsters out of the picture and allows Andy and Sam to engage in typical haunted house gags. (Sam was played by Dudley Dickerson whose specialty was reactive humor in scary situations.) Not a great deal of time is spent on Andy and Sam in the dark hallways, running into ghost-like images, but there is enough to provide some amusement. The Bloodhounds descend upon the house and gang up on the three criminals in the neat conclusion, and when the cops finally arrive, they are pleased that the counterfeiters have been apprehended.

Perhaps it would have been more interesting had the kids played a larger part in the film than Sam. The kids at least had a reason for being there, while Sam's introduction in the story is very random. And with the kids, there could also have been some different variations on the gags, instead of the usual haunted house fare, which is mainly amusing thanks to Clyde and Dickerson's expressive reactions. Some of the jokes are not as effective, but a scene where a dog-like head mounted on a wall actually grabs Andy's face is so weird, it works.

The original story was written by Edward Bernds and Russell Malmgren. Both were part of the sound department at Columbia and worked extensively for the short subjects department. While Malmgren collaborated on only one other story before returning to running sound, Bernds continued to write and also moved into directing at about this time. Perhaps Bernds had a hand in the direction of *Spook to Me*; it's helmed in a much more competent manner than the usual films credited to Harry Edwards. The shots are not held too long, there are no distracting instances where a character gets tangled up in anything, the pace is steady and breezy, and the flow of the film is consistent.

While *Spook to Me* was another popular Andy Clyde release, the postwar budget for short subjects was tightening even more. Fewer films were being released each year. While in the late 1930s Andy was averaging six Columbia shorts per year, he was now appearing in three. The Hopalong Cassidy series was dropped in 1944; not until 1946 did actor William Boyd bought the rights to the films and the character, resuming production and asking Andy to return to the series.

Clyde still found work in some films to supplement his income, so that wasn't a problem. But his specialty was the short comedy, and that seemed to be headed toward its last days.

The Blonde Stayed On

Screenplay and Directed by Harry Edwards; *Produced by* Hugh McCollum; *Cinematography:* Benjamin H. Kline; *Editor:* Henry Batista; *Cast:* Andy Clyde, Gladys Blake, Christine McIntyre, Vernon Dent, Dorothy Vernon, Robert Williams, John Tyrrell; *Shooting Dates:* February 26–March 1, 1945; *Released* January 24, 1946; *Columbia Production Number:* 4041

The Blonde Stayed On is one of Clyde's better comedies from this period, despite Harry Edwards directing from his own script. The comedy is consistent, the action flows nicely, and the succession of shots is clear and effective. Of all the Clyde comedies that Edwards directed, this is his best work. Some have opined that perhaps Edward Bernds directed most of the film, without credit, under Edwards' supervision. This film is more layered as per the style Bernds would later establish. But I could find no tangible evidence of that.

Andy, a clothing store owner, is in the middle of a move from his home to another. His absent-mindedness is identified when the movers show up and he has to be reminded he'd made arrangements to move. The new house is not ready, so during the interim, Andy and his wife must stay in a hotel. The wife doesn't want the movers to be in charge of her expensive mink, so she asks him to take it to the store that day. He does so, but inadvertently sells it to a woman, and must then go to her apartment and retrieve it. Turns out she has a jealous boyfriend, who is also an old friend of Andy's.

As with several of Andy's 1940s comedies, *The Blonde Stayed On* features a conflict that must be resolved, and is punctuated by a succession of slapstick gags that starts in the opening scenes. First, Andy drops a bottle on his foot while shaving, falls backwards into the bathtub, and turns the hot water on as he falls. Next, the movers come and, with no regard for the Clydes, start hauling things away, including rugs that are being stood upon and beds that are being sat upon. When Andy opens his store, a crowd of women bursts through the door and starts fighting over sale items. Andy gets knocked to the floor, stepped on, etc. It's all a lot of violent, crazy comedy in the classic slapstick tradition, and despite being past 50, Andy Clyde continued to do many of his own stunts.

Layers of mistaken conclusions ensue once a pretty blonde comes into the store looking for a fur. After she chooses the wife's coat, an unwitting Andy has his delivery boy bring it to her hotel—conveniently the same hotel where Andy and his wife are staying. There is a neat bit of comic nuance when Andy tries to check out the material on the pretty lady's stocking, and then slaps his own hand as he gingerly feels the fabric near her upper leg. He is also caught by a chance visit to the store by his wife, who angrily chases the blonde from the premises.

Andy realizes he sold his wife's coat and heads over to the hotel to retrieve it. In the lobby, he runs into an old friend, newly married, who complains about how jealous he is. Andy gives him a pep talk and cheers him up, unaware that the wife is the blonde who has the fur coat Andy. Andy sneaks into the room on a dinner dolly, covered by a sheet, but is quickly caught. He tries to explain his situation, but the woman wants to keep the coat she's paid for, stating that the transaction makes it rightfully hers.

One of the more clever bits of business occurs when the husband discovers Andy hiding behind the couch. He pulls out a gun and starts shooting, at fairly close range, but Andy deflects the bullets by using an operating electric fan as a shield. One of the bullets hits a clock that falls off the wall and knocks out the husband. Andy is able to retrieve the mink and hurry to his own room.

The movie ends on a gag. Andy and his wife decide to take their little dog for a walk, but don't notice that a black and white fur cap has fallen on him, making the pet look like a skunk. As they go down in the crowded elevator and entre the equally crowded lobby, they are bemused by the shrieks of the other people.

Apparently whatever talents Harry Edwards offered to such silent screen classics as *Saturday Afternoon* and *Tramp Tramp Tramp*, both with Harry Langdon, are evident in this well-directed Clyde comedy. So many comedians refused to work with Edwards, he was only kept on the Columbia payroll because Clyde and Harry Langdon were pleased with him, and he was among the few directors who could work with Hugh Herbert (a comedian who was difficult to deal with while at Columbia). With Langdon dead, it was only Clyde and Herbert keeping Edwards employed at the unit. But with *The Blonde Stayed On*, we have evidence that Edwards could still put together a nicely paced, steadily progressing comedy two-reeler.

Along with the slapstick, another fun aspect of *The Blonde Stayed On* is the occasional comic dialogue. Early in the film, Andy complains that he woke up late because he set the alarm for nine instead of for six. His wife opines that perhaps he set it while upside down. While in the woman's apartment as her husband is arriving home, Andy is told to jump out the window and escape. Andy replies, "It's 13 floors up! I'm superstitious."

Christine McIntyre, who plays the blonde, was an attractive Columbia stalwart whose popularity continued via her many appearances in the durable Three Stooges comedies. Vernon Dent, the all-purpose heavy of the Columbia shorts, is perfectly cast as the jealous husband. With Bud Jamison dead (as of September 1944), Dent was cast more frequently in these parts, which he'd once shared with the other actor. Gladys Blake, who plays Andy's wife, had a 20-year career playing small parts in movies. This is was her only Columbia short subject.

Despite lower budgets, personal tragedies and filmmakers with limited skills, Andy persevered.

You Can't Fool a Fool

Produced and Directed by Jules White; *Story and Screenplay:* Ewart Adamson; *Cinematography:* George Meehan; *Editor:* Edwin Bryant; *Cast:* Andy Clyde, Esther Howard, Vernon Dent, Fred Kelsey, Heinie Conklin, Ted Lorch, Joe Palma; *Shooting Dates:* February 6–9, 1946; *Released* July 11, 1946; *Columbia Production Number:* 4049

One of the wildest and most outrageous of all the Andy Clyde two-reelers, *You Can't Fool a Fool* rests almost completely on crazy behavior by nearly all of the ensemble cast.

Andy is once again a henpecked husband. His wife Ivy (Esther Howard again) has nominated him for mayor, much to his chagrin, because she wants her women's league to have more of a voice in the city's planning. Another problem for Andy, aside from simply not wanting the responsibility, is the fact that the current mayor is corrupt and not above arranging for his opponents to get injured or worse.

While Andy is in his backyard practicing casting with a new fishing rod, he casts a sinker through his neighbor's window and gives the neighbor a lump on his head. The irate neighbor gets a cop, convincing him that Andy is so crazy, he thinks he can fish in his backyard. When the cop tries to take Andy away, Andy's dog bites the cop's rear end, ripping away his pants.

Later that night, a man from the insane asylum, Dr. Strong, visits Andy. Andy believes Strong is there to discuss the mayoral race and says, "I am not going to be mayor." Strong believes this is just the ravings of insanity and humors him by asking, "Wouldn't you rather be Napoleon?" Andy laughs, thinking the man is making a joke. The conversation continues as Andy refers to an ivy branch tapping against his window: "I was just about to go cut up my ivy." The doctor mistakes it for a reference to Andy's wife.

Andy looks out the window, sees a car marked "Insane Asylum" and believes the man in his house is an escaped lunatic. Now the two men both think the other is insane and they try to humor each other. The dog once again comes to Andy's rescue. Just as this situation gets settled, a hit man sent by the acting mayor comes to Andy's house to rub him out. Andy prepares to defend himself, aiming a rifle at the door. When his wife comes home, he shoots off her hat. Finally having had enough, Andy turns his wife over his knee and spanks her until she agrees that he does not have to run for mayor and the two are going fishing. The man from the asylum returns just as Andy is spanking his wife and believes that act proves he is perfectly normal. The film ends with Ivy breaking a vase over Andy's head.

This delightfully outrageous comedy is filled with some of the most extreme ideas in all of the Clyde Columbia shorts. In the backyard scene, Andy's dog gets tangled up in his fishing line, starts running and causes the reel to turn rapidly, burning Andy's thumb every time he tries to stop it. When Andy and Dr. Strong each believe the other is crazy, their attempts to humor one another are especially amusing. The doctor, playing with the dog, starts pretending to be a cat. Andy concludes that the man actually believes himself to be a cat. Dr. Strong then tries to humor Andy by saying, "Let's play follow the leader," and begins dancing about the living room. Andy does not join in, and the doctor is disappointed. While the doctor believes he is controlling the situation due to his experience with such people, Andy is frightened, not knowing what will happen next. Andy finally orders the dog to attack, and the doctor is chased from the house. Vernon Dent plays off of Andy marvelously as Dr. Strong, and the two old pros bring many laughs to the wildest scenes in the movie.

Nothing much really comes from the set-up of a hit man headed to knock off Andy. The film concludes with the wife getting shot at and spanked, and knocking out Andy at the conclusion, triumphantly proclaiming, "You are still running for mayor," to reassert her authority.   Esther Howard always holds her own when cast as Andy's wife. Fred Kelsey as the neighbor and Heinie Conklin as the cop also offer formidable support.

Clyde followed up this crazy slapstick-filled comedy with a more story-oriented movie with a premise that once saw life as a full-length feature film.

Andy Plays Hookey

Directed by Edward Bernds; *Screenplay:* Clyde Bruckman; *Produced by* Jules White; *Cinematography:* George F. Kelley; *Editor:* Paul Borofsky; *Cast:* Andy Clyde, Geneva Mitchell, Minerva Urecal, Dick Wessel, Lorin Raker, Fred Kelsey, Emil Sitka, Heinie Conklin, Symona Boniface, Judy Malcolm, Frank Mills, Snub Pollard, Victor Travers; *Shooting Dates:* February 13–16, 1946; *Released* December 19, 1946 *The working title* was *Wilbur Goes Wild*; *A reworking of* Lloyd Hamilton's *Too Many Highballs* and W.C. Fields' *The Man on the Flying Trapeze*; *Reissued theatrically* in November 1958; *Columbia Production Number:* 4041

Andy Plays Hookey has an interesting backstory. In 1933, W.C. Fields was scheduled to appear in the Mack Sennett two-reeler *Too Many Highballs*. Creative differences resulted in Fields leaving the project and Sennett instead casting Lloyd Hamilton. In 1935, Fields took the idea for *Too Many Highballs*, hired its writer-director Clyde Bruckman, and expanded it to the feature-length *The Man on the Flying Trapeze*, which remains one of Fields' best films. Also scripted by Bruckman, *Andy Plays Hookey* is a remake containing the basic premise of *Too Many Highballs* and also retaining some of the gags in the Fields feature. The result is quite fascinating for those familiar with the earlier movies.

Andy is a hard working man whose home life is beset with a nagging wife, a shrewish mother-in-law and Claude, a spoiled, lazy brother-in-law. Andy has saved $50 so he can attend a championship prizefight, a lifelong dream of his. His wife finds the money hidden in an old suit and gives it to Claude. Claude reveals at the dinner table that he ran through several traffic lights and evaded police in a chase. Because he was driving Andy's car, the license plate is traced back to him, so an officer comes to the door and hands Andy five traffic tickets. Andy has to borrow Claude's car to get to work the following morning.

Andy receives a hot tip on the fight, so he makes a bet with ten dollars of the rent money and spends the rest on a ticket. He believes his winnings will cover the rent money he's spent. In order to get off work to attend the fight, Andy tells his boss that his mother-in-law has died. When sympathy wreaths start showing up at the Clyde home, Andy's wife calls the office and tells the boss that her mother is not dead. The boss then informs Mrs. Clyde that Andy is fired. When Andy arrives home, he is confronted by his angry family, but it is interrupted by another visit from the police. While driving Claude's car, Andy innocently got into a series of traffic mishaps and now it is Claude who is being blamed. He is hauled off to jail, while the mother-in-law follows in protest.

Andy's boss is helpless without Andy at the office (Andy's roll-top desk is cluttered with papers and only Andy knows where anything is). The boss calls and offers Andy a $10 raise if he returns. Andy agrees, but triumphantly states he is taking the next few days off with pay. He tells his wife that the worm has turned, that he is now head of the household and will be making all decisions.

While this is indeed enough material for a feature film, it somehow compacts quite successfully into a two-reeler. *Too Many Highballs* was a bit more streamlined and didn't include as many layers. *Andy Plays Hookey* has more in common with the W.C. Fields feature.

Perhaps the casting of Claude could have been better. Dick Wessel made a career out of playing slow-witted tough guys, and his bulky appearance and growling delivery don't come off too effectively as a pampered child-man. Grady Sutton, in the Fields feature, was also a big man, but more pudgy than husky, and much more effete. However, Andy is also a different screen character than the one played by Fields. Fields played his role as very quiet, put-upon, and averse to any sort of confrontation. Andy is feistier, so when a little guy like him goes to fight a big guy like Wessel, the visual is more amusing.

A lot of the humor comes from the scenes that establish how little say Andy has in his household. He cooks dinner and pays for it with his salary, but gets almost nothing to eat because Claude hogs it all. He is the one that needs to get to work, but can't shave because Claude's larger frame is taking up the bathroom mirror, even though he has nowhere he needs to be.

One element of the Fields feature that is missing from the Clyde short is the sympathetic daughter. But this was part of what effectively expanded the Fields film to feature-length. Andy does have a friend who serves as a sort of confidant for his family troubles and who goes on some of this adventure with him. It leads to fun interactions—like when the friend shows Andy the newspaper while he's driving, causing Andy to hit the police car in front of him. Andy tells the officer that he couldn't see him because he was looking at the paper, then quickly glances at his friend and mumbles, "I shouldn't have said that." There are other small differences between *Flying Trapeze* and *Andy Plays Hookey* (in the Fields film, it was a wrestling event, not a prizefight, etc.), but overall, *Andy Plays Hookey* is an impressive example of a two-reel version of a feature-length story.

Andy Plays Hookey was the first Clyde film to be directed by Edward Bernds, who had graduated from sound man to writer to director in the Columbia short subjects department. Bernds recalled Andy as "a good comedian and a good actor. He knew how to convey the right emotion for each scene, when to do a double take, and how to look. Most of that was instinctive on his part, and it made my job easier." The film also features the first appearance by Emil Sitka in a Clyde comedy. Emil joined the Columbia unit in 1946 and quickly became one of the most active members of the short comedy stock company; he's best-remembered for working in the Three Stooges shorts. Sitka truly enjoyed his first experience with Andy Clyde, and wrote in his diary:

> Watching this great artist, who puts makeup on to resemble an old man, made me want to be like him. The intense hours of waiting until I got to my "bit" almost had my tongue white again, but by gosh, when the lights were all set, cameras measured off and Ed Bernds directing I was there with my business well-planted in my mind. What gave me confidence was the director's liking my outline of what I showed him I'd do. Andy Clyde's car hits the one I'm writing out a traffic ticket to, knocking me on my fanny. My scene follows on his running board, which caused even Andy to congratulate me on![47]

Sitka would have more opportunities to work with Andy, and would consider him a good friend.

Andy Plays Hookey is not the wild slapstick romp that other Clyde short comedies of the period were. Largely situational, it depended a lot on the vision of the director and the talent of the performers. All of these are stellar. But what is perhaps most impressive is screenwriter Clyde Bruckman offering a third version of this story for another comedian, in another context, and making it work so effectively.

Two Jills and a Jack

Produced and Directed by Jules White; *Story and Screenplay:* Harry Edwards; *Cinematography:* George F. Kelley; *Editor:* Edwin Bryant; *Cast:* Andy Clyde, Christine McIntyre, Vernon Dent, Dorothy Granger, Johnny Kascier; *Shooting Dates:* January 6–9, 1947; *Released* April 14, 1947; *Columbia Production Number:* 4079; *Remade as Oh Say Can You Sue* (1953).

Another Andy Clyde comedy where a conflict is introduced and slapstick gags stemming from its complications are strewn throughout, *Two Jills and a Jack* shows this formula getting a bit thin.

This time Andy is a wealthy man who goes to the big city in search of the girlfriend who left him after a quarrel. Andy also visits Jack, an old friend from back home who is now happily married. Jack must hurry to an important meeting, and asks Andy to stay and visit with his wife, who has been in the bedroom changing. In the bedroom, she is visited by a girl friend who agrees to entertain Andy while Jack's wife goes to buy Jack a birthday present (luggage). The woman turns out to be Andy's girl who left him. They see each other, both apologize, and they embrace. However, Andy suddenly concludes this must also be Jack's wife, and flees from the house. Jack's wife comes over to explain, and is caught with Andy by Jack (he has seen the luggage in his apartment and concludes his wife is packing to leave with another man). When it is all explained in the end, Andy goes to kiss his girl, grabs and kisses Jack's wife instead, and is chased away by Jack.

Complicated, noisy and not particularly amusing, *Two Jills and a Jack* seems like a quickie two-reeler thrown together as cheaply and quickly as possible. This may be rather accurate in that Jules White was working under tighter budgets since 1940. But *Two Jills and a Jack* is not without merit. Andy playing a wealthy Southern oil man, with all of the lofty stereotyping, is a neat change of pace from his usual character. Andy always works well with

Vernon Dent, who plays Jack. Then there's the attractive presence of Christine McIntyre as Jack's wife (Christine was a game Columbia shorts actress who had a distinct comic flair) and Dorothy Granger as Andy's girl (a brunette actress whom Andy inexplicably refers to as a blonde, Dorothy was a veteran of Hal Roach comedies). Dent's heavyset, overbearing presence is a good visual contrast to the smaller, slimmer Andy. In the Jules White style, the film moves very quickly with fast movements and sharp edits.

The scene with Andy and Jack getting reacquainted is amusing, containing a running gag of Andy unsuccessfully trying to light his cigar while conversing about the folks back home (their old schoolteacher is 90 years old and entering jitterbug contests). White likes to get the women involved with slapstick so Dorothy Granger sneezes into makeup powder, Christine has her dress ripped off, and both start physically battling each other as the movie concludes.

Some of the comedy seems to be ad-libbed. When Jack's wife is in Andy's room attempting to explain and Jack comes pounding on the door, she begs Andy to hide her. Andy quickly opens the drawer of an end table, Christine lifts her foot, then quickly states, "I'll never fit." It is done very rapidly as per the pace of the short, and appears to be a quick idea by Clyde that McIntyre responds to effectively. This is a good example of capable performers bolstering standard material. One gag is lifted from the Laurel and Hardy film *Blockheads* (1938): Christine sits like a chair and is covered with a blanket to simulate an actual chair. Of course the comic complication is that someone unwittingly sits on her.

Film Daily called *Two Jills and a Jack* a "typical Andy Clyde comedy that should go over with his fans."[48] Despite the thinness of the material, the film did go over well with period audiences. Postwar moviegoers were weary after the Depression and a world war. By 1947, lighter fare was more welcome than heavier drama. *Two Jills and a Jack*, for all of its hectic silliness, continued Andy Clyde's steady popularity with audiences.

Wife to Spare

Directed by Edward Bernds; *Story and Screenplay:* Elwood Ullman; *Produced by* Hugh McCollum; *Cinematography:* Henry Freulich; *Editor:* Henry DeMond; *Cast:* Andy Clyde, Christine McIntyre, Lucile Browne, Dick Wessel, Vera Lewis, Emil Sitka, Murray Alper, Heinie Conklin; *Shooting Dates:* January 21–24, 1947; *Released* November 20, 1947; *Columbia Production Number:* 4096

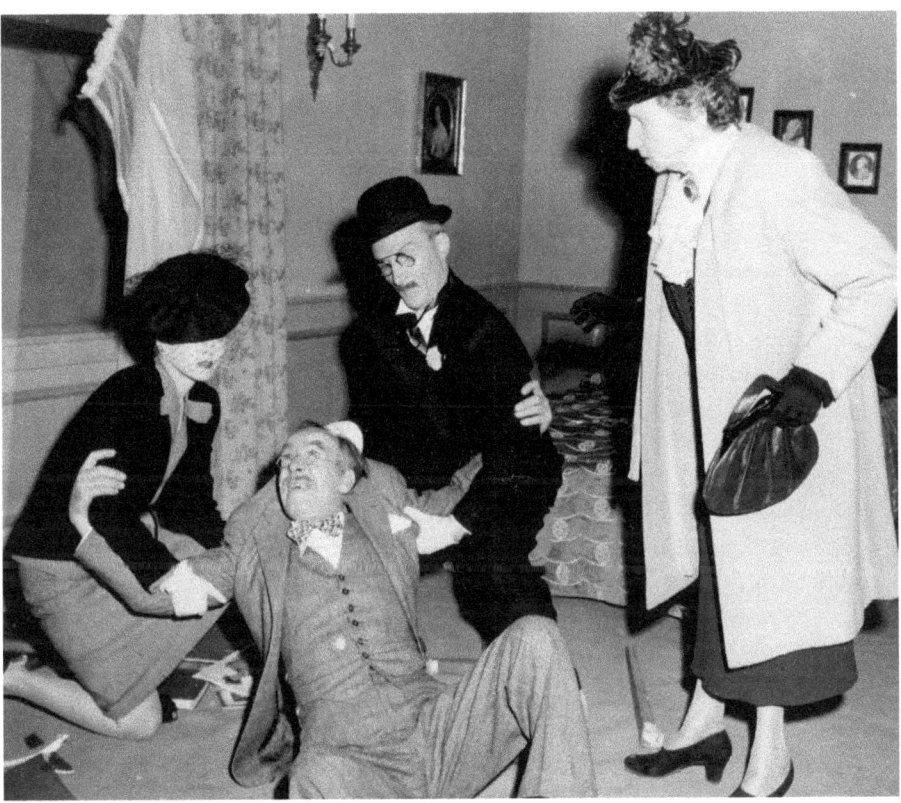

Lucille Brown and Emil Sitka help Andy up while Vera Lewis looks on in *Wife to Spare* (1947).

Another formula film, *Wife to Spare* at least offers some clever ideas to help enhance the run-of-the-mill material. Andy once again has a sponging brother-in-law and a cranky old mother-in-law. He again has to extricate his brother-in-law from trouble, and ends up getting himself into it. Typical of Columbia comedies from this period, it moves briskly and is filled with slapstick gags.

This time Andy's brother-in-law Claude gets involved with a woman who blackmails him. Andy goes to the woman's apartment to settle things, but gets involved with her himself, with the help of her boyfriend who was hiding in the next room. Apparently the entire situation is a set-up where men are easily duped by the beautiful woman. Now it is Andy being blackmailed, and when his mother-in-law picks up the phone and hears him plotting with the woman, she makes a call to her lawyer.

Dick Wessel, the actor who played the pampered brother-in-law role in

Andy Plays Hookey, repeats his role in this movie, including the same character name. *Andy Plays Hookey* was a two-reel adaptation of the W.C. Fields feature *The Man on the Flying Trapeze*, written by the same screenwriter, Clyde Bruckman. However, in *Andy Plays Hookey*, the part called for more of a namby-pamby like Grady Sutton in the Fields film. Wessel's husky frame and gravelly voice is better suited to tough guy parts, which is what he usually played. However, in *Wife to Spare*, it works. Claude in this movie is written in the same manner as the brother-in-law characters that had been portrayed by Shemp Howard or Matt McHugh in earlier Clyde comedies. Claude is still lazy, refuses to work, and sponges off Andy, but is revealed to be a ladies man who gets involved with them a bit too often (like the Doodles Weaver character in *Lodge Night*).

Christine McIntyre gives one of her best performances as the gold-digging Honey. When Andy arrives at her apartment, she talks like an innocent Southern gal, with affected accent and fluttery mannerisms. She believes Claude is wealthy, stating, "He told me he had a li'l ol' fortune." Andy truthfully reveals that Claude never had a job, "but I try to set a good example by working hard, investing, putting money in a bank account…" The term "bank account" attracts Honey and she starts turning on the charm. As Andy struggles to break free from her embrace, her boyfriend secretly takes photographs they can use to blackmail him. It is amusing how he's supposed to be secretly taking pictures, but with the size of the cameras they had back then, and the powerful flash, that's kind of hard to do. So he just keeps popping up quickly over the back of the couch, and Andy is confused about where the flashes are coming from. Honey tries to convince him that he's seeing things.

What is especially amusing about McIntyre's performance is that she lapses in and out of her Southern belle accent when she gets angry, such as when Andy tells the truth about Claude. With no accent, she yells, "Why, he told me…" and then quickly returns to her Southern belle persona to finish the sentence.

Edward Bernds had directed *Andy Plays Hookey* and allowed actors to experiment creatively with their roles. Emil Sitka, who played the lawyer, recalled:

> When I worked with Jules White, he acted out the part for me and I was to copy it just as he did it. When I worked with Ed Bernds, he let me play the character my own way. So I knew what to expect depending upon who was directing me.[49]

Sitka recalled *Wife to Spare* as one of his favorite experiences at Columbia. He always enjoyed working with Andy, and was inspired by him to play an old man character while still a young man, just as Clyde had done. He also liked working with Bernds and Christine McIntyre.

Two actors in *Wife to Spare* have especially interesting backstories. Lucile Brown, who plays Andy's wife, had a long career until she married actor James Flavin in 1938. After that, she returned only sparingly to movies, including this short. Flavin died in 1976 and a heartbroken Lucile passed away only days later. Vera Lewis, who plays the mother-in-law, played that role in the aforementioned W.C. Fields feature. She had been in movies since 1915 and was at the end of her career when she did *Wife to Spare*. Noted for playing shrewish landladies, gossips and judgmental old coots, Lewis was fondly recalled as being a very sweet, kind lady off-screen.

In his diary, which has been posted on the Internet, Sitka recalled the experience of making *Wife to Spare*:

> I was summoned immediately, in full and articulate dress, with perfectly groomed makeup, to appear as the dignified Lawyer "Mr. Pratt" in a scene with Andy and the rest. It is the scene where I get doused again with a fire extinguisher, but completely, and again for a close-up! Then I'm given another identical outfit of clothes to get into for my next scenes, which now will be those preceding the one just made! It's all fun and fascinating for me, though. And even though from the beginning Ed Bernds told me to play "straight" I still wound up making an "eccentric" out of the role. How could I help it? I end up with a bucket over my head in a heap of other people in the end. Certainly I love working in comedies, especially these kind. Every foot of film must be a laugh, or a build-up for a gag that leads to a laugh. And most laughs in these two-reelers are aimed for the belly regions! Andy Clyde always makes me think of his wise decision early in his career to keep his creation of the "old man" he does so well.[50]

Another typical slapstick excursion, *Wife to Spare* still seems to work within familiar parameters. This two-reeler can be considered one of the better Andy Clyde shorts from the postwar era.

Eight-Ball Andy

Directed by Edward Bernds; *Story and Screenplay:* Elwood Ullman; *Produced by* Hugh McCollum; *Cinematography:* Henry Freulich; *Editor:* Henry DeMond; *Cast:* Andy Clyde, Dick Wessel, Maudie Prickett, Florence Auer, Vernon Dent, Ralph Volkie; *Shooting Dates:* September 16–19, 1947; *Released* March 11, 1948; *Columbia Production Number:* 4113

The tradition of Andy Clyde having a nagging wife, a meddlesome live-in mother-in-law and a lazy, pampered brother-in-law continues with *Eight-Ball Andy* and again Dick Wessel is cast as the good-for-nothing Claude. This time, the Clydes have been thrown out of their rented home because Claude keeps playing his trombone. This is moving day, and Claude is in the city trying to join a band. As the family is moving into their new rented home, Claude shows up announcing he has chosen chemistry as his next venture. After some experimenting, he believes he has created the ultimate termite destroyer. Inviting Andy's boss to dinner so Claude can convince him to invest in the product results in the usual slapstick.

Claude's inventing of the bug spray is central to the film's plot, but Andy's slapstick fumbling during the moving process offers most of the highlights. Along with the usual bits about carrying too many items, turning with a broom over his shoulder and hitting others, etc., Andy also repeats a bit he did in *Mr. Clyde Goes to Broadway* where he tries to get several bottles of milk into his crowded refrigerator, while also keeping an eye on a chicken that is roasting in the oven. As with the previous performance, Andy recalls his silent movie training and performs this set piece beautifully, offering a shifting balance that results in one bottle dropping and shattering on the floor, and then another, until he quickly crams all of the bottles into the fridge, and the noisy crash as he slams the door results in several quarts of milk spilling out of the refrigerator door.

Another fun sequence has Claude spreading his termites over a piece of wood Andy has straddling between two ladders so he can paint the ceiling. He sprays them with his invention and it starts to eat the wood. Claude leaves the area to experiment further and Andy comes in. He climbs the ladder, steps on the board and causes it to split as he crashes to the floor. Andy replaces the board and leaves to get painting supplies. Claude returns, sees the new board and concludes that his bug spray made the termites disappear.

The plot picks up when the boss (played by the ubiquitous Vernon Dent) visits and expresses some interest in Claude's termite invention. To demonstrate that it is otherwise harmless, Claude sprays all the chairs at the dinner table. When the boss sits down, the chair shatters under him. He tries another chair and it happens again. He uses an end table to lift himself up, and knocks over the jar of termites that Claude planned to use for his demonstration. The bugs crawl up his sleeve and he runs off screaming. Defending Claude, the mother-in-law insists the boss was too heavy for their chairs, sits in one herself, and it shatters the same way.

The succession of shots used by director Edward Bernds is worth noting here. Bernds was always keenly aware of how to structure a gag based on what was seen on the screen. When Dent lifts himself up and knocks the bug jar over, the effect would be successful if Bernds held a medium shot. But he cuts to a close-up of the insects entering Dent's sleeve, further enhancing the gag, and breaking up the shots with the same rhythm as the gags. It's all quite effective and funny.

The boss threatens to fire Andy unless he disassociates with Claude. Andy gladly does so, especially after his mother-in-law gives him an "If he goes I go" ultimatum. Once they've left, an explosion is heard. A dazed Claude, his face blackened, comes staggering in holding a steering wheel. Apparently he put one of his concoctions in her gas tank. Mother then comes in, yanks Claude into a room and starts hitting him as he protests.

Dick Wessel's approach to the Claude role continues to be similar to how Shemp Howard and Matt McHugh played similar characters in earlier Clyde comedies. The feisty Andy often becomes so frustrated that he is ready to hit the much larger Claude. A frightened Claude then retreats behind his mother despite being much larger and more powerful looking than Andy. The visual contrast between the two men is part of the underlying humor.

Maudie Prickett, who plays Mrs. Clyde, was in the midst of a career where she made short comical appearances in various feature films, usually as an uptight spinster. She was currently active at Columbia in westerns featuring Charles Starrett. Prickett later had an extensive TV career. Florence Auer, who plays the mother-in-law, was also active in both shorts and features at Columbia at this time. She appeared in Andy's next film, *Go Chase Yourself*.

Go Chase Yourself

Produced, Directed and Screenplay: Jules White; *Cinematography:* Rex Wimpy; *Editor:* Aaron Stell; *Cast:* Andy Clyde, Florence Auer, Patricia Barry, Ferris Taylor, Gay Nelson, Symona Boniface, Dudley Dickerson, Al Thompson; *Shooting Dates:* February 17–20, 1948; *Released* October 14, 1948; *Columbia Production Number:* 4118; *Working title: Oh Professor! ;A remake of* the Charley Chase short *The Nightshirt Bandit* (1938); *Remade by* Andy Clyde as *Pardon My Nightshirt* (1956).

Jules White decided to remake the only Charley Chase short that he directed, and make it as an Andy Clyde vehicle. Chase was a funny man, but the material seems to work even better with Clyde, who responds better to White's more aggressive approach.

Andy is Professor Clyde, a criminology professor at an all-girls college who lives on campus. He has been sleepwalking in his nightshirt and stealing things. Nobody suspects that he is the culprit whom they refer to as Nightshirt Bandit. He's asked to assist in capturing the culprit, due to his knowledge of criminal behavior. Andy realizes it is he who has been sleepwalking and stealing because of some of the clues left behind.

Andy offers some amusing comic nuance to the scenes that show him sleepwalking. He moves slowly and stares straight ahead, and although he has his mouth shut, he is audibly snoring through his nose, as he walks through rooms and removes items. He never steals anything for which he'd have any real use, and when he awakens, he tries to quietly sneak the items back where they belong.

There are some fun moments when Andy tries to prevent himself from sleepwalking. He chains himself to a chair but, in his sleep, he removes the chain and continues on. When Andy awakens, he sees all manner of stolen items around him and exclaims, "I sure must have been busy last night."

Things become serious when sleepwalking Andy steals treasury money. When he awakens and realizes this, he sticks the money in his shoe so he can return it the next day. A dog and cat are making noise outside, so Andy's wife picks up one of his shoes and flings it out the open window at them. Of course she threw the shoe with the money, so Andy jumps out the window after it. The dog takes the shoe and jumps through another window inside the girls dormitory. Andy follows him, but as one of the girls wakes up and screams, he dives under the bed. Andy manages to escape from the screaming girls by sitting in a chair that is booby trapped to cause the person to fall through the floor and plummet into a fountain.

When the dean sits in the same chair, he finds Andy and inquires why he isn't dressed. Andy cleverly states that he wore his nightshirt to catch the Nightshirt Bandit, as part of the criminological process. He also reveals that he has the stolen money and turns it over to the dean.

The fast pace and the slapstick that permeate *Go Chase Yourself* make this a fun short, and the appearance of Dudley Dickerson as a night janitor trying to be cautious about running into the criminal adds more fun to the proceedings. The problem with this film is that it resolves almost nothing. Andy does return the money that he himself stole, but he never figures out a way to stop himself from sleepwalking. Nobody knows it was Andy all along. The original Charley Chase version had the same loose ends.

Jules White would direct the remaining Andy Clyde comedies, taking over the unit from Hugh McCollum who was busy with the Hugh Herbert and the Three Stooges comedies that he and White shared. In 1952, McCollum would be fired and White would be the sole director for the few remaining short comedy series that continued to produce new films. The idea of recycling older material would become pretty standard at this point, which is made very evident with the next Andy Clyde comedy.

Sunk in the Sink

Produced and Directed by Jules White; *Screenplay:* Jack White; *Cinematography:* Rex Wimpy; *Editor:* Edwin Bryant; *Cast:* Andy Clyde, Margie Liszt, Mark Roberts, Frank Mills; *Shooting Date:* September 29–30, 1948; *Released* March 10, 1949; *Columbia Production Number:* 4069; *A remake of the Andy Clyde comedy* Mister Smarty *(1936); Working title: What's Cookin'?*

A *Sunk in the Sink* negative exists in the Sony archives, there is no screening print available. It is the first in a series of remakes using older Andy Clyde comedies as their source. In the 1936 short *Mister Smarty*, Andy insists to his wife that he can take care of household chores more efficiently than she. He sends her off shopping and proceeds to attend to matters himself, with disastrous results. In this remake, some of the dynamic has changed. New footage is shot where Andy makes the same lofty claim to his daughter (Margie Liszt) and tells her to go off with her boyfriend while he takes care of things. From this point, Jules White uses ample footage from the earlier film including a scene where Andy gets himself locked in his own bedroom closet while trying to put up shelves.

Mister Smarty was a movie where everything seems to go wrong and Andy responds with mounting frustration rather than his usual resourcefulness. *Sunk in the Sink* is the same, except a few factors are changed. It is now a daughter, not a wife. He does not have young sons selling his items to the junk man as in the earlier movie. There is new footage of a dishwasher destroying dishes and a cake exploding in the oven.

This practice of remaking movies and using footage from the former became the norm for Columbia as a cost-cutting measure. Production costs were going up, and it became more difficult to create a two-reeler with all-new footage. By 1949, Columbia was producing only a few series. The Three Stooges remained popular, and series featuring Joe Besser, Hugh

Andy tries to handle the household chores himself in *Sunk in the Sink* (1949).

Herbert, the team of Gus Schilling and Richard Lane, and the team of Wally Vernon and Eddie Quillan were still active at Columbia. At RKO, Leon Errol and Gil Lamb kept busy in shorts (Edgar Kennedy died in 1948). In comparison to what the comedy field once boasted, this is a small number of active units.

Jules White had once been an editor, so he knew how to shoot new footage that could be blended with an older movie and released as a new short. He recalled for Okuda and Watz:

> We were always fighting the budget and the time. I had a month's pay on the line with every picture, so I had to pinch every penny. That's a hell of a burden to have on your shoulders. I wince when I see some of the comedies now—if only I didn't have to skimp on them.[51]

Some of the remakes were shot in only one day. In Andy's next film, there's hardly any new footage at all.

Marinated Mariner

Produced, Directed and Written by Jules White; *Original Story:* Albert Ray; *Cinematography:* Rex Wimpy; *Editor:* Edwin Bryant; *Cast:* Andy Clyde, Jean Willes, John Merton, Blackie Whiteford, Kit Guard, Johnny Kascier, Ethan Laidlaw, Sam Lufkin, Al Rosen. Appearing in older footage: Al Thompson, Harry Keaton, Bert Young, Heinie Conklin, Tom Dempsey, Idalyn Dupre, Ethelreda Leopold, Charles Phillips; *Shooting Date:* December 5, 1949; *Released* March 30, 1950; *Columbia Production Number:* 4153; *A remake of* the Andy Clyde comedy The Peppery Salt (1936); *Re-released in* 1962

The Peppery Salt (1936) was a fun comedy in which Andy longed to be at sea and would regale the children visiting the shipyard where he worked with stories about his seafaring exploits. Andy is delighted to receive word that he has

Andy in *Marinated Mariner* (1950), a remake of *The Peppery Salt*.

inherited from a late uncle "the *Admiral Dewey*" as he concludes it is a ship he can have for his very own. He buys an elaborate admiral outfit, only to discover that the Admiral Dewey is a diner. When his dock boss' daughter is kidnapped, Andy goes to her rescue.

While roughly 90 percent of *Marinated Mariner* is just stock footage from *The Peppery Salt*, a major character from the previous movie was recast. In *The Peppery Salt*, the kidnapped daughter was played by Mary Lou Dix. Here she is portrayed by Jean Willes. All scenes featuring the daughter had to be replaced. In an establishing scene in *The Peppery Salt*, Mary Lou Dix is talking to Warner Richmond, playing her father, who is chagrined that Andy is telling stories to kids and not getting any work done. In this remake, that scene is played by Jean Willes, and an unknown actor with his back to the screen represents her father. Now we go to *Peppery Salt* footage where boss Richmond confronts Andy. It is not Richmond in the new footage, as he had died over a year before this scene was shot.

Andy's scenes in the diner, his falling into the ocean and finding rescue on the ship that is holding the daughter are all footage from the earlier movie. When he discovers the daughter, it is new footage as it features Willes. It is fascinating when one considers that Jules White had to find the same set and Andy's old admiral costume from the previous movie in order for the new footage to match the older film.

In other new footage, the crooks are overpowered and Andy and the woman escape. These scenes feature Willes and are shot with a different group of actors playing thugs, although some scenes from the older film contain different actors. It is all fairly elaborate and quite impressive that an entirely new short can be produced this way, but White did this with all the existing series at Columbia, including the Three Stooges. Oddly, there are times when the remake works better than the original. However, in the case of *Marinated Mariner*, the previous film *The Peppery Salt* is the better effort.

A Blunderful Time

Produced, Directed and Written by Jules White; *Original Story:* Searle Kramer; *Cinematography:* Rex Wimpy; *Editor:* Edwin Bryant; *Cast:* Andy Clyde, Margie Liszt, Christine McIntyre, Al Thompson, Dick Curtis; *Shooting Dates:* December 6–7 1949; *Released* September 7, 1950; *A remake of* the Andy Clyde comedy *Trouble Finds Andy Clyde* (1939); *Columbia Production Number:* 4160

It is especially frustrating that there is no screening print available for

Officer Dick Curtis collars Andy (right) and his twin brother Al Thompson in *A Blunderful Time* (1950).

A Blunderful Time. It is a remake of *Trouble Finds Andy Clyde*, and that film is also inaccessible. So we have no way to screen either film to assess them as part of Andy Clyde's filmography, or to compare how each version holds up.

As with the original film, *A Blunderful Time* involves Andy getting mixed up with his twin brother by friends, co-workers, cops, even his wife. Andy does not play two parts, his twin being played by Al Thompson, who wears the same type makeup. Thompson, eight years Andy's senior, was Andy's stunt double. The two look remarkably alike. Looking at the cast list that our research has found, neither Christine McIntyre nor Margie Liszt, both of whom are credited in this film, appear in the earlier one.

Between this and *Marinated Mariner*, Clyde got only three or four days work at Columbia for all of his 1950 output from the studio. Fortunately, he had already established himself in westerns. After the Hopalong Cassidy movie series ended in 1948, Clyde signed to play Winks in the Whip Wilson western series. In 1950 alone, six Whip Wilson cowboy features were released, and Andy was in every one.

Even though short subjects had been replaced in theaters by cartoons, and were becoming even more archaic as a result of television becoming predominant, research tells us that *A Blunderful Time* received decent bookings. It showed up on marquees advertising such features as *At War with the Army*, *The Story of G.I. Joe* and *Halls of Montezuma*, usually also accompanied by a cartoon.

According to Okuda and Watz:

> While filming these crazy-quilt efforts, Jules White had a Movieola on the set, making sure the new scenes matched the older footage, right down to the smallest details. Says Emil Sitka, "I remember Jules once wanted to add some new shots of me to a sequence I had appeared in some years before. He wanted me to look exactly like I did in the earlier picture, so he told me to lose ten pounds in one week!"[52]

Blonde Atom Bomb

Produced, Directed and Written by Jules White; *Original Story:* Ewart Adamson; *Cinematography:* Rex Wimpy; *Editor:* Edwin Bryant; *Cast:* Andy Clyde, Jean Willes, Emil Sitka, George Chesebro, Minerva Urecal, Billy Frandes, Clay Anderson; *Shooting Dates:* November 27–30, 1950; *Released* March 8, 1951; *A remake of* the Andy Clyde comedy *Lodge Night* (1937); *Columbia Production Number:* 4160

Blonde Atom Bomb is another film for which we have no available screening print, and, perhaps as a result, it has been misidentified in other studies. In *Blonde Atom Bomb*, Andy tries to help his nephew deal with a gold-digging blonde, which is similar to the plot of *Wife to Spare*. As a result, other studies, including books and online sources, have identified *Blonde Atom Bomb* as a remake of *Wife to Spare*. In fact, it is a remake of *Lodge Night*. It is not a nephew in *Wife to Spare*, it was a brother-in-law. Plus, this film refers to the gold digger as a nightclub singer, which relates to *Lodge Night*.

In the original film, Joan Woodbury played the gold digger, but this time it is Jean Willes, clad in blonde wig. Doodles Weaver had been the nephew in *Lodge Night*, but he is replaced by Clay Anderson here. Emil Sitka is added to the cast as a lodge brother of Andy's, and Minerva Urecal is on hand as his meddling sister-in-law who tries to convince Andy's wife that his lodge meetings are just an excuse to step out and see other women.

Just as with the earlier film, Andy's attempt to help gets him mixed up with the woman himself, and when his wife finds the address and goes to confront Andy, she jumps to the wrong conclusion. Andy must also avoid the gold digger's jealous boyfriend, a fellow club entertainer. So, once again, it is basically one long chase, with a lot of confusion and mistaken identity.

While we don't have a film to screen in order to make an assessment, the fact that *Blonde Atom Bomb* was allowed three days of production, whereas *Marinated Mariner* only needed one, would indicate that less stock footage was used. This makes sense, as so many key cast members of the previous film have been recast. It appears that the only stock footage used is from the chase, especially when Andy and the jealous boyfriend are clad in masks and costumes that hide their features. That way, the viewer cannot tell it is a different actor playing the boyfriend in the older footage.

While eventually all of the Columbia shorts would be relegated to remakes with stock footage, many were still producing new films at this time. For instance, Three Stooges films also released in 1951 included *Three Arabian Nuts*, *Baby Sitters Jitters* and *Scrambled Brains*, none of which were remakes nor used any stock footage. The Joe Besser series, launched in 1949, would not begin doing remakes with stock footage until 1955. The Hugh Herbert series never did remakes with stock footage (Herbert died in 1952).

Perhaps because Andy was active in other films for other studios, and always could rely on steady work, his Columbia comedies were made as quickly and cheaply as possible. Clyde was a trooper and did as he was instructed. Nobody who saw *Blonde Atom Bomb* realized that some of the footage came from a Clyde comedy made over a dozen years earlier, so the comedian's Columbia shorts continued to get good bookings.

Pleasure Treasure

Produced and Directed by Jules White; *Screenplay:* Ewart Adamson, Jack White; *Story:* Elwood Ullman; *Cinematography:* Rex Wimpy; *Editor:* Edwin Bryant; *Cast:* Andy Clyde, Emmett Lynn, Margie Liszt, Tom Kennedy, Emil Sitka, Babe London, Johnny Kascier; *Shooting Date:* November 30, 1950; *Released* September 6, 1951; *A remake of* the Andy Clyde comedy *Gold Is Where You Lose It* (1944); *Columbia Production Number:* 4160

This remake of *Gold Is Where You Lose It* uses footage from the previous movie for its body, but offers newly shot footage for its opening and closing. In the first film, Andy and Emmett run a pawn shop that isn't making money. When crooks who robbed a bank walk in and indicate they got their money from prospecting, Andy and Emmett go out into the woods and dig for gold. They find the bandits' hidden loot and think they've struck it rich, but end up discovering their error, capturing the bandits and returning the money.

In this remake, Andy and Emmett are featured in new footage working for the bank run by Tom Kennedy. They are distracted from their duties by Tom's daughter, played by Margie Liszt. While they flirt with her, crooks rob the bank. As a result, they're fired. The film then switches to older footage, as they go into the hills and discover the bank's money which had been buried by the crooks. The same situations ensue as in the previous film as the only new footage that occurs is when a shot of Andy or Emmett is shown referring to the bank robbery or getting fired. Otherwise, this is all repeated footage from *Gold Is Where You Lose It*. The ending is newly shot footage of Emmett and Andy returning the loot to the bank and turning in the criminals.

Pleasure Treasure works as well as the previous film, because the opening footage with Andy and Emmett fighting over Margie helps to define their characters and their relationship effectively. The actors play off each other nicely. And even though this new footage is just a means to transition to the older material from an earlier film, it has its own charm, and it could be argued that it even improves upon the original.

A Blissful Blunder

Produced and Directed by Jules White; *Screenplay:* Jack White; *Story:* Clyde Bruckman, Ben Roberts, Ewart Adamson; *Cinematography:* Henry Freulich; *Editor:* Edwin Bryant; *Cast:* Andy Clyde, Esther Howard, Fred Kelsey, Ruth Godfrey, Bonnie Bennett, Barbara Lande; *Shooting Date:* February 12, 1952; *Released* May 8, 1952; *A remake of* the Andy Clyde comedy *A Bundle of Bliss* (1940); *Columbia Production Number:* 4190

What is most interesting about this remake of the 1940 Andy Clyde comedy *A Bundle of Bliss* is that two actors from the previous film, Esther Howard as Andy's wife and Fred Kelsey as his cop nemesis, were hired to repeat their roles. Thus, bridging the new footage with the old is more seamless, and it can be argued that *A Blissful Blunder* is every bit as good as its predecessor.

As with the earlier movie, Andy gets a telegram that he interprets to mean he is about to become a father, but it turns out to be the wrong conclusion. He despondently walks the streets, happening upon a baby carriage. He starts to play with the baby, but the carriage gets bumped and rolls away. Andy catches up to it at a construction site, and is confronted by the mother as a kidnapper, thus attracting the ire of a policeman. Only the footage of Andy running down the street after the carriage is used from the earlier

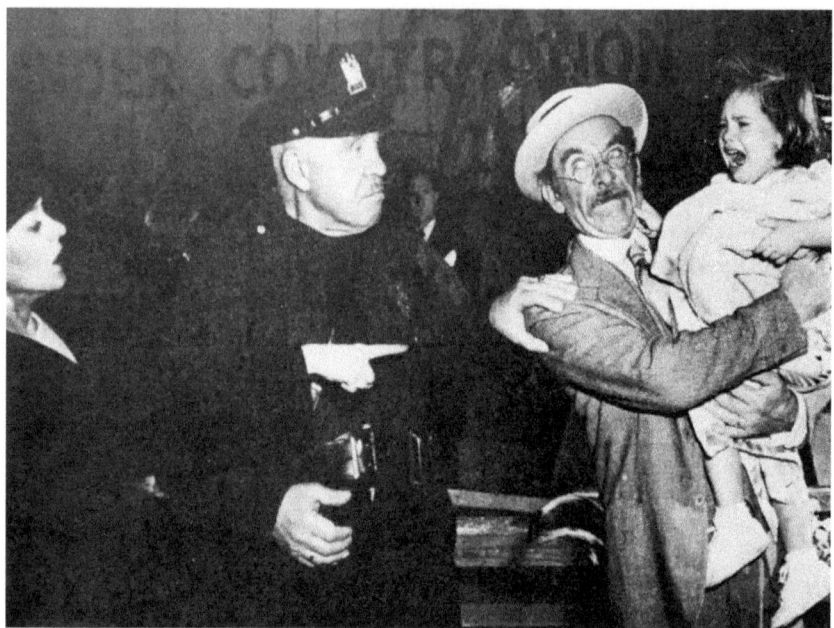

Ruth Godfrey tells officer Fred Kelsey that Andy is a kidnapper in *A Blissfull Blunder* (1950). Child actor unindentified.

movie. The mother confronting Andy is Ruth Godfrey, replacing Dorothy Appleby from the previous movie, while the aforementioned Fred Kelsey repeats his role as the cop.

Ruth splits with her husband, leaves a baby on Andy's doorstep, Andy takes it to the adoption center, Ruth makes up with her husband, returns to Andy for her baby, and he must go to the center and retrieve it. As he attempts to do so, he is noticed by cop Kelsey, who believes the worst.

All the adoption nursery footage with Andy and the children is lifted from the earlier film. That it also includes Kelsey doesn't matter because his presence in the new footage allows for such a transition. The film ends the same, with Andy adopting a parade of youngsters himself.

Despite the replacement of one of the supporting actresses, and having to rely solely on new footage when the story dealt with her character, *A Blissful Blunder* managed to get its new footage shot in one day. Carefully editing it into the older film, Jules White managed to produce yet another "new" film out of older material.

By 1952, White had the short subject market pretty much to himself. Hugh McCollum had been fired, Leon Errol at RKO had died, and that studio limped along for one more year with Gil Lamb shorts until closing its shorts department. Although the Clyde series was relying more and more on stock footage, the shorts continued to secure decent bookings.

Hooked and Rooked

Produced and Directed by Jules White; *Screenplay:* Jack White; *Story:* Felix Adler, Clyde Bruckman, Ben Roberts, Ewart Adamson; *Cinematography:* Henry Freulich; *Editor:* Edwin Bryant; *Cast:* Andy Clyde, Emmett Lynn, Margie Liszt, Maxine Gates; Shooting Date: September 11, 1951; *Released* May 8, 1952; *The working title* was *Bridal Wails*; *A remake of You Were Never Uglier* (1944) and Collins and Kennedy's *Gobs of Trouble* (1935); *Reissued theatrically in* December 1959; *Columbia Production Number:* 4191

This remake recasts two major characters and uses them only in new footage. In the original, *You Were Never Uglier*, Andy and Emmett leave a ship after having lived and worked on the sea for 30 years. They meet up with two women, propose, and end up being henpecked and having to do the chores. This new version has the same premise, but re-casts the roles of the wives. So, the opening scene of Andy and Emmett getting off the ship is from the earlier movie. Their arrival at the apartment, although they do essentially the same thing as in the older film, is newly shot footage. Throughout this short, any time the wives are on camera, it is new footage. When Andy and Emmett are alone, it is stock footage from the older movie.

Once again Andy is too bashful to propose to his girl so he records a proposal on a record. However, unlike the first movie, Andy does not need a youngster to walk him through how to use the recording device. By the early 1950s, they were common enough and Andy would have some idea how to work one.

The footage of Andy and Emmett washing clothes, hanging them on the line and causing a fire is used from the earlier movie, but naturally the cutaways in the house to the wives' reaction are new footage. When they are forced to move into another home due to the fire, the wives are present, so it is newly shot footage, but when they leave, the film returns to older footage of Andy and Emmett attempting to get the place in shape. When the wives come home, the new footage copies the old, with Andy and Emmett leaving out the window and returning to their ship in the harbor.

Perhaps the most interesting transition is in regard to the youngster character played by Buz Buckley in the original. A stand-in is used for the new footage, with his back to the camera. He has some dialogue early in the film when he answers the door as Andy and Emmett arrive, and also when they move into the new place, but the only times his face is seen is when old footage of him with Andy or Emmett is used. Since he had little to do with the previous movie, Buckley's role was not re-cast in the remake, just filled out with a stand-in for the new footage.

While on the surface it might seem lazy to re-release old shorts with new footage as a cost-cutting measure, there is a creative process involved in seamlessly blending old footage with new and releasing it as new product. Audiences were satisfied, and the movies continued to secure good bookings. Margie Liszt and rotund Maxine Gates have great comic flair and, therefore, make *Pleasure Treasure* an even better effort than its predecessor.

Love's A-Poppin'

Produced and Directed by Jules White; *Story and Screenplay:* Jack White; *Cinematography:* Henry Freulich; *Editor:* Harold White; *Cast:* Andy Clyde, Margia Dean, Phil Van Zandt. Appearing in stock footage: Dorothy Appleby, Eva McKenzie, Lorna Gray, Suzanne Ridgeway, Ethelreda Leopold; Shooting Date: March 18, 1953; *Released* June 11, 1953; *The original working title was Lover Boy; A remake, with stock footage, of Andy Clyde Gets Spring Chicken* (1939); *Columbia Production Number:* 4206

There is no available screening print for *Love's a-Poppin.'* There is nothing for this title in the Library of Congress. This remake of *Andy Clyde Gets Spring Chicken* once again shows Andy being so affected by the season, he proposes to women at every turn. A young actress who believes him to be wealthy accepts his proposal. Complications ensue because he has proposed to many women—and they all have accepted for the same reason.

Unlike the first film, in which Andy played a man who actually was wealthy, in this remake he is only perceived as such, adding another complication. Based on existing stills, much of the footage in *Love's a-Poppin'* comes from *Andy Clyde Gets Spring Chicken*. Dorothy Appleby, Lorna Gray, Ethelreda Leopold, Kay Vallon and Eva McKenzie all appear in stock footage from the earlier movie, but do not appear in any of the new scenes. New footage features Margia Dean (as the actress) and character actor Phil Van Zandt, who was in many Columbia comedies.

Having adapted to many changes in movies since his start back in the silent film era, Clyde was, by now, supplementing his income with TV appearances. When William Boyd bought up the Hopalong Cassidy franchise and began producing shows for TV, Andy was hired to once again play sidekick California Carlson. His experience in westerns also got him a role on TV's

Death Valley Days. And, along with his Columbia appearances, he went over to RKO, then in its final year of producing live action short comedies, and appeared in two Gil Lamb two-reelers, *Fresh Painter* and *Pardon My Wrench*. Although his Columbia series had dwindled to only a couple days work per year, Andy remained in demand elsewhere.

Oh, Say Can You Sue

Produced and Directed by Jules White; *Screenplay:* Jack White; *Story:* Clyde Bruckman, Ben Roberts, Ewart Adamson; *Cinematography:* Gert Andersen; *Editor:* Edwin Bryant; *Cast:* Andy Clyde, Gus Schilling, Christine McIntyre, Vernon Dent, Dorothy Granger; *Shooting Date:* March 18, 1953; *Released* September 10, 1953; *The original working title* was *Bridal Wails*; A remake, with stock footage, of *Two Jills and a Jack* (1947); *Columbia Production Number:* 4207

In this remake of *Two Jills and a Jack*, Andy, his old buddy Jack, Jack's wife and Andy's girlfriend are all sitting in an attorney's office. Everyone is suing each other. As Andy explains what happened, the film flashes back and footage from *Two Jills and a Jack* is seen. In that film, Andy goes to the city in pursuit of his girl, who left him after a quarrel. While there, he stops in to see old hometown buddy Jack. Jack has to leave for a meeting, but says that his wife, who is getting dressed in the other room, will entertain Andy. Andy's girl is also at the apartment visiting Jack's wife. Jack's wife wants to pick up a birthday present for her husband, so her friend agrees to entertain. When she comes out of the other room, she discovers it is Andy, her boyfriend, but Andy concludes that she is now Jack's wife and leaves. Jack's actual wife comes to Andy's place to explain, complications ensue, her dress gets ripped off, Jack catches them together, and a slapstick chase follows.

Jules White intersperses occasional new footage into the old by cutting back to the attorney's office with Andy explaining. When a certain point in the older footage is reached, Andy concludes his story, everyone makes up, and the attorney cheerfully leaves them. The four actors then recreate the ending from the previous film where Andy accidentally grabs Jack's wife and starts kissing her, causing another slapstick battle as the picture fades out.

At about this same time, the TV series *I Love Lucy* was doing essentially the same thing with their episodes as White did with this short. Lucy was on maternity leave, so in her absence, the latest shows would present Ricky, Fred and Ethel sitting around reminiscing and the ensuing flashback would be an episode from a few seasons earlier. Reruns were not standard in these early days of TV, so viewers weren't used to seeing something for the second time, and the practice was accepted and even welcomed.

In the case of the Columbia two-reelers, White was resurrecting footage from years earlier that moviegoers would not likely recall. Thus, a film like *Oh Say Can You Sue* could appear as if it were a fully new two-reeler, especially when the four main actors from the previous movie also appear in the new footage. (Gus Schilling, as the attorney, is the only actor new to this remake.)

The new footage for this film was shot on March 18, 1953, the same shooting day as the new footage in *Love's a-Poppin'*. In one day, new footage for two Clyde remakes was filmed. This helped keep costs way down on the two-reel unit for Columbia, although television and animated cartoons caused bookings for the comedies to slow start to become more limited.

Tooting Tooters

Produced and Directed by Jules White; *Screenplay:* Jack White; *Story:* Ewart Adamson; *Cinematography:* Ray Cory; *Editor:* Robert B. Hoover; *Cast:* Andy Clyde, Gail Bonney, Barbara Bartay. Appearing in stock footage: Bennie Bartlett, Lynton Brent, John Tyrrell; *Released* May 13, 1954; *A remake, with stock footage,* of *Swing You Swingers* (1939); *Columbia Production Number:* 4219

In this remake of *Swing You Swingers*, Andy once again is a crotchety old man who hates both kids and swing music, and is stuck taking care of two boys. The older boy, Bennie, is a trumpet player who loves to play swing.

There is very little new footage in *Tooting Tooters*. There is an opening scene with Andy and his wife, played by Gail Bonney. Mrs. Clyde reads a letter indicating that her sister is too ill to take care of her children. Andy must care for them while his wife visits her ill sister. (In the first film, they were orphaned nephews who are placed with him by the State Department.) Andy reacts angrily saying he doesn't want them around. His wife overrules him, since the boys are waiting in the music store adjacent to their house. There is some perfunctory slapstick when Andy slams his hand down on a dish of butter, then picks up paper to wipe it away, grabbing fly paper instead.

In the store, Andy meets the boys. We cut from new footage of Andy and his wife, to footage of the boys from the original. The wife then conveniently goes to see her sister while Andy is left with the children. From this point, we see almost nothing but *Swing You Swingers* footage. To ease his uncle's financial woes, Bennie gets the idea to form a band so that the instrument rental and lessons will add some money to Andy's business. Then fol-

II. The Columbia Comedy Shorts   183

Andy conducts an all-kids band in *Tooting Tooters* (1954).

lows a scene from the original film where Andy conducts the boys playing Chopin's "Death March" to the bored musicians, and they following it up with a swing number once he angrily leaves, as discussed in the chapter for *Swing You Swingers*.

In another new scene, found midway through the short, a pretty young lady comes in looking to buy a piano and Andy shows her around. Meanwhile, the film cuts to old footage of the younger boy getting into mischief by covering himself with molasses and then the feathers from a pillow. He walks into the store and Andy hides him by sticking him in an upright piano. Back to new footage where the lady customer presses on the upright's keys and feathers come flying out of its top. She leaves in a huff. An angry Andy reaches into the piano saying, "Come out of there, you troublemaker." It cuts back to old footage of Andy cleaning the boy up.

There is no attempted purchase in the earlier movie. That is added here with new footage. The old footage of the child walking in and being placed in the piano is for another reason entirely in the first movie. The effect with the keys and feathers is fun, but when Andy angrily reaches into the piano, the scene cuts away. This is another good example of Jules White's keen attention to details from the 15-year-old movie he was remaking. The transitions and changing of footage is done seamlessly, and likely would be undetectable by the untrained eye.

The smallest child wanders off, worrying Andy, and then comes back as the boys are playing swing music in the store. This causes a relieved Andy to realize he likes swing. The next scene shows him conducting the band playing the music they love. A radio man happens by and offers them a spot on the air. However, in this remake, the dialogue is no longer, "How would you boys like to be on radio?" it's "How would you boys like to be on television?" The actor, John Tyrrell, had died about five years earlier, so Jules White himself overdubs the word "radio" (from the original soundtrack) with "television."

The final sequence of *Swing You Swingers* shows the band playing swing, with Andy conducting, in a radio studio. In the remake, that same scene is seen on a television screen with Andy's wife and her sister proudly watching. For a low-budget two-reeler, the effect of the 1939 footage appearing as if it were on a TV screen is nicely done.

By the time *Tooting Tooters* was in theaters, Bennie Barlett was no longer a 15-year-old trumpet player as seen in the *Swing You Swingers* footage. Bartlett was now a 30-year-old active member of the Bowery Boys, and in some theaters, *Tooting Tooters* was the short comedy playing along with Bartlett's latest feature *The Bowery Boys Meet the Monsters*. One wonders if any period moviegoers noticed that Bennie from the Andy Clyde comedy was the same man showing up twice that age in the Bowery Boys feature.

Another factor that might have dated the old 1939 footage 15 years later is the fact that swing music was rather passé by 1954. Pop hits by the Crew Cuts, Rosemary Clooney and the Chordettes were topping the charts that year, while rock 'n' roll's earliest influences were hitting the jukeboxes with songs like Big Joe Turner's "Shake Rattle and Roll," LaVern Baker's "Tweedlee Dee" and the Spaniels' "Goodnight Sweetheart Goodnight." Elvis Presley recorded his Sun label songs "That's Alright Mama," "Good Rockin' Tonight" and "Mystery Train." Music was on the cusp of a cultural revolution, and swing was no longer part of the mainstream.

Production costs continued to rise, while bookings for short comedies continued to become more limited. White made an unsuccessful attempt to create his own *Our Gang*-type series with *Kids Will Be Kids* (1954), and was resorting to remakes, with stock footage, on all of his remaining short comedy units, including Joe Besser, Vernon and Quillan and the Three Stooges.

Two April Fools

Produced and Directed by Jules White; *Screenplay:* Jack White; *Story:* Clyde Bruckman; *Cinematography:* Ray Cory; *Editor:* Robert B. Hoover; *Cast:* Andy Clyde, Charley Rogers, Robert Williams. Appearing in stock footage: Al Thompson, Jack "Tiny" Lipson; *Released* June 17, 1954; *A remake, with stock footage,* of *A Miner Affair* (1945) and the Three Stooges comedy *Cash and Carry* (1937); *Columbia Production Number:* 4220

For this remake of *A Miner Affair,* Jules White changed the set-up so that prospectors Andy Clyde and Charley Rogers do not find a disabled boy and his older sister living in their shack at the city dump, they find an abandoned baby. There is nobody around to care for the baby, it is just lying in a crib alone. No discussion is made as to the dangers of such a thing, it is just used casually as a set-up so that Andy and Charley can work the situation for gags.

Except for the first two minutes, showing Andy and Charlie driving into the junkyard, the entire opening features new footage. While Charley tries to find something for the crying infant to eat, Andy holds the baby on his lap and unbuttons his own shirt as if he's preparing to feed the child naturally. What he does is pull out his watch so the baby will play with it and stop crying. The usual gags, with the baby throwing its food back into the face of Andy and Charley, are good for laughs.

The stock footage comes up when Andy and Charley go to town to invest their $62 savings, hoping to let it gain interest so they can properly care for "their" new baby. All of the scenes of the duo digging up the house they foolishly bought, digging into a bank vault, escaping arrest and foiling an actual robbery, etc., are all here. New footage returns when Charley and Andy are shown caring for the baby in somewhat better surroundings than a shack at the junkyard.

It continues to be impressive that Jules White could shoot a few new scenes, add it to some old footage, and come up with a new two-reeler that offers a different dynamic. The footage that had been amusing in the first film, remains so here, but the idea of an baby being abandoned in a city dump shack for an undetermined time before being discovered is awkward. Andy and Charley's reactions to the baby are rather sweet and amusing. They are immediately excited at the prospect of suddenly being "fathers," and it doesn't seem to be a question in their minds that they will care for the child. But the fact that they also don't question where the baby came from, or try to find out, is unsettling. It is this element that makes *Two April Fools* inferior to its predecessor.

Scratch Scratch Scratch

Produced and Directed by Jules White; *Screenplay:* Jack White; *Story:* Clyde Bruckman; *Cinematography:* Ray Cory; *Editor:* Robert B. Hoover; *Cast:* Andy Clyde, Norman Ollestad, Carol Coombs, Doyle Baker. Appearing in stock footage: Esther Howard, Robert McKenzie; *Released* April 28, 1955; A remake, with stock footage, of *Love Comes to Mooneyville* (1936); *Columbia Production Number:* 4235

Scratch Scratch Scratch does a good job of using old footage for a flashback sequence combined with a beginning and ending comprised of newly shot scenes. Andy works at a soda fountain, and supports the romance of his nephew and a pretty girl, who are regular customers. A meddlesome bully with an annoying high-pitched cackle comes in and tries to attract the girl. She turns him away, so he grabs some itching powder and puts it down the back of Andy's nephew. While the nephew is frantically scratching, his rival takes the girl away. Andy reveals that the rival is Cy Ruggles, Jr., whose father once "tried to take your aunt away from me." As Andy tells the story, the film moves to stock footage from *Love Comes to Mooneyville* where Ruggles (Robert McKenzie) fights with Andy for the hand of Ivy (Esther Howard). Neither McKenzie nor Howard appear in the new footage (McKenzie had died five years earlier). We then see the footage as described in the chapter on *Love Comes to Mooneyville*, with occasional cutaways to Andy continuing to tell the story in new footage.

The film ends with a new scene. Andy invites his nephew, the girl and the bully over for dinner. While the bully has his back turned, Andy cuts his belt, causing his pants to fall down. The nephew then puts live bees in the bully's pants. When the bully sees his pants are down, he quickly pulls them up, and starts rolling on the floor reacting to the stings. The nephew exits with the girl. The then ends on a gag: An errant bee lands on Andy's forehead and he hits it with a hammer, knocking himself silly.

This short's use of footage from 18 years earlier likely didn't matter to moviegoers, especially young audiences who weren't around when the first film was produced. At this point, the main area where the Columbia comedies found bookings were for children's matinees, where they remained in demand. Perhaps the casting of teenagers in the new footage helped engage those younger audiences.

By 1955, the only active units in the Columbia short subject department were the Three Stooges and Andy Clyde. A couple of films from other series that had already been shot were released in 1956, but neither remained in production. It was due to the continued popularity of the Stooges and Clyde series that White continued to produce them as economically as possible.

One Spooky Night

Produced and Directed by Jules White; *Screenplay:* Jack White; *Story:* Elwood Ullman, Harry Edwards; *Cinematography:* Ray Cory; *Editor:* Tony DiMarco; *Cast:* Andy Clyde, Dorothy Granger, Dudley Dickerson. Appearing in stock footage: Monty Collins, Lew Kelly; *Released* September 15, 1955; A remake, with stock footage, of *Host to a Ghost* (1941); *Columbia Production Number:* 4234

Another rather clever use of old footage combined with new, this one opens with Andy coming to see his girl (Dorothy Granger). He proposes and she accepts, but as they sit together, he becomes frightened by every little thing, from her small dog to a young boy playing outside with a balloon. The child's balloon has a comical monster drawing on it, and it frightens Andy so much that he jumps out the window. The next scene shows Andy at work with his friend (Dudley Dickerson). His girl has returned the engagement ring, stating she can't be married to such a coward. To prove her wrong, Andy accepts a job to wreck an old house that is said to be haunted. Dudley unwillingly goes along.

From this point the film switches to archive footage from *Host to a Ghost* going through all the haunted house gags, the discovery of a record album, a shootout with police and the apprehending of the criminals hiding out in the abandoned home. The film ends with new footage of Andy and his fiancée drinking a toast to his bravery, but when they hug, clumsy Andy spills his drink down her back.

Host to a Ghost is one of the less interesting Clyde comedies due to its over-reliance on typical haunted house gags; somehow *One Spooky Night* is an improvement. While it incorporates the same haunted house gags from the previous film, its context being changed to Andy having to overcome crippling fear makes it work better. Of course, the older footage does not refer at all to this problem, but the fact that he and Dudley are continually scared by various goings-on in the house, confirming the haunted rumors, makes the new context effective. Andy isn't merely performing an assigned job, he is also proving something. That makes the eventual capture of the crooks more gratifying as well.

The older footage does contain the highlight gag from the previous film, when a board sticking out of the back of Andy's truck hooks onto a motorcycle cop, going up his shirt, so that when Andy drives off, the helpless cop goes with him. This footage had originally been shot by Del Lord.

Because of its theme, *One Spooky Night* secured somewhat better bookings, being used for midnight horror shows at theaters. The film being released in mid–September meant that it was hitting the smaller towns and neighborhood theaters by Halloween, and was a popular item, being perceived as a new two-reeler and not a re-release. That it had been made so economically further enhanced its profits.

Despite other studios shutting down their comedy shorts units, Columbia president Harry Cohn still felt the Andy Clyde and Three Stooges movies were bringing in enough profit to keep the series in production. The success of a film like *One Spooky Night* made Cohn feel like his choice to do so was justified.

However, Jules White's penchant for remaking older films and using ample footage from earlier ones did not go undetected by the filmmakers who worked on the earlier movie. Writer-director Edward Bernds told Okuda and Watz:

> When I saw *Fling in the Ring* [the Three Stooges, 1955], I couldn't believe what I was watching. Jules had taken *Fright Night* [1947], a Stooge short I directed, and just added a few new scenes. Columbia had the right to use the old footage, but I felt that I had the right to some credit. It upset me terribly that this much old footage was being passed off as new product. I handed the case over to the Directors Guild, claiming it was a cheat on exhibitors. I eventually got some money out of it, but not as much as I deserved.[53]

Andy Goes Wild

Produced and Directed by Jules White; *Screenplay:* Jack White; *Story:* Clyde Bruckman; *Cinematography:* Ray Cory; *Editor:* Robert B. Hoover; *Cast:* Andy Clyde, Maudie Prickett, Dick Wessel. Appearing in stock footage: Vernon Dent, Florence Auer; *Released* April 26, 1956; *A remake, with stock footage,* of *Eight Ball Andy* (1948); *Columbia Production Number:* 4220

This remake of *Eight Ball Andy* features a few new scenes that combine with the archive footage from the earlier movie. The opening is new, with Maudie Prickett repeating her role as Andy's wife, and Dick Wessel back as her sponging brother with big ideas. Wessel, sporting a large mustache, comes to the breakfast table in a loud and obnoxious manner, boasting about his experiments and inventions, and exhibiting hideous table etiquette. He eats hard-boiled eggs with the shells on, smothers his pancakes with ketchup, and drives a disgusted Andy from the table. He also scolds his brother to shave off the mustache, allowing for a more seamless transition to the older footage.

In another newly shot scene, Andy is at the office complaining to his secretary. The brother-in-law comes in, bumps into the secretary's desk as

Andy must put up with brother-in-law Dick Wessel in *Andy Goes Wild* (1956).

he tries to flirt, spills ink on his hands, then sneaks up behind Andy and playfully blinds his eyes with his inky hands. When Andy goes to smack him with a desk drawer, he rears back and hits the approaching secretary. As Andy attends to her, the brother-in-law sneaks into the boss' office.

We return to old footage after this scene: the brother's invention, Andy doing the slapstick bits while trying to paint the kitchen, the switching of the boards causing the brother to assume his termite spray works, etc., as outlined in the chapter on *Eight Ball Andy*. The dinner party where the boss sits in chairs that break, lifts himself and gets termites up his sleeve, etc., are all part of the recycled footage as well.

The ending is different. While the brother once again puts his newly invented gasoline in his mother's car, the subsequent explosion causes them both to be arrested. Andy gleefully watches from the window of his upstairs apartment.

Vernon Dent, who plays the boss, had retired by this time and only appears in the *Eight Ball Andy* stock footage. By the end of 1955, Dent was blind from poorly treated diabetes. Florence Auer also only appears in stock footage as the mother-in-law, having retired the year before.

In November 1955, Shemp Howard of the Three Stooges died suddenly of a heart attack. Moe and Larry fulfilled the remainder of their contract for 1956 by doing remakes of their older films. In new footage, Joe Palma replaced Shemp, carefully keeping his face hidden from the camera. When these shorts were produced, Jules White suggested Joe Besser as a replacement. Moe and Larry accepted and another 16 shorts were produced through 1957, but their release was staggered into 1959.

Because Columbia wasn't offering Andy Clyde much work any more, he was concentrating more on television opportunities. He had a role on the series *The Adventures of Rin Tin Tin* and was asked to return. He also was in talks with the producers of a new show called *Circus Boy*. This sort of steady work looked more beneficial. Clyde told Jules White he would fulfill the remainder of his contract, which was one more short for Columbia, and then he would be concluding this series.

The one day of new footage shot for *Andy Goes Wild* was filmed on February 15, 1956, coming well under budget. The one day of new footage for *Pardon My Nightshirt*, Andy's final short film for Columbia, was filmed the very next day, on February 16,1956. Interestingly enough, while Jules White was under budget on *Andy Goes Wild*, he went over budget for *Pardon My Nightshirt*. Fortunately, between the two films, Columbia still came out over budget, so White saved the studio money as he closed out this series.

Pardon My Nightshirt

Produced and Directed by Jules White; *Screenplay:* Felix Adler; *Story:* Allen Leslie; *Cinematography:* Irving Lippman; *Editor:* Harold White; *Cast:* Andy Clyde, Dudley Dickerson, Joe Palma. Appearing in stock footage: Symona Boniface, Ferris Taylor, Florence Auer, Dudley Dickerson, Patricia Barry, Diana Darrin, Al Thompson, Gay Nelson; *Released* November 22, 1956; *A remake, with stock footage, of Go Chase Yourself* (1948) and Charley Chase's *The Nightshirt Bandit* (1938); *Columbia Production Number:* 4248

Pardon My Nightshirt is comprised of nearly all of the footage from *Go Chase Yourself*, and includes only a few new scenes. The dynamic is also changed. In the first film, criminology professor Andy was the Nightshirt Bandit, committing robberies on campus while sleepwalking. In this remake, there is an actual bandit (Joe Palma). Other than the brief scenes with Palma and a couple of new scenes with Andy and Dudley Dickerson, this short is comprised of nearly all stock footage. It still works as an amusing effort, and concludes Clyde's long running series of short comedies for Columbia.

Pardon My Nightshirt is actually the better of the two films since, as indicated in the earlier film's chapter, there wasn't any closure in *Go Chase Yourself* with Andy being the Nightshirt Bandit. Here it's a bit funnier since we know Andy isn't the Bandit, but keeps getting mistaken for him while investigating. This was the final Andy Clyde Columbia short. The December 17, 1956, issue of *Box Office* called it "a good comedy ... [with] all the necessary ingredients for a lot of laughs."

While studio head Harry Cohn was sorry to see Andy go, Jules White understood his old friend's decision. Andy had been one of the very first comedians Jules had hired when starting the Columbia short subjects unit in 1934, and the larger budgets and producing several films per year were now a thing of the distant past. It wasn't worth continuing to be employed with Columbia for only a few days work per year, especially when other opportunities were on the horizon.

White was ready to call it quits as well. He worked another year on the Three Stooges comedies, with Joe Besser appearing with Moe and Larry, and because this was now the only active short subject unit at the studio, relying on stock footage wasn't as necessary. Of the final 16 films, nine were original scripts that were not remakes of previous Stooges comedies. However, the bookings became even more scarce. Jules went to see Cohn after finishing work on the Three Stooges comedy *Flying Saucer Daffy* in December 1957 and announced he was retiring. Jules recalled for Okuda and Watz:

> I went to Cohn's office and said, "The short subjects business has gone to hell. It's time to get out. I'm going to retire." "Retire?" he says. "You're crazy! You'll go nuts!" "No," I said, "you'll go nuts! I have hobbies, I know how to relax. But you'll wind up killing yourself if you don't get out of this office. Why don't you get out and do other things?" He just looked at me and said, "I don't know how to do other things."[54]

About two months later, Cohn died of a sudden heart attack at the age of 66. Jules White retired and lived to be 84.

III

Clyde in Feature Films

Andy Clyde would occasionally supplement his short subject income with appearances in features. When he signed his contract to do Columbia two-reelers, one provision he insisted upon was the freedom to appear in films outside of the studio.

At first, Columbia produced so many two-reelers, Andy only had time for very small parts. He did have a good supporting role in RKO's *Annie Oakley* (1935) with Barbara Stanwyck in the title role. Clyde's rustic look made him a good fit for westerns and he appeared in several during the next decade, including *Yellow Dust* (1936), *Bad Lands* (1939) and *Cherokee Strip* (1940), all while continuing to do shorts at Columbia.

In 1940, Clyde was hired to appear in the Hopalong Cassidy series, which featured William Boyd in the title role. George "Gabby" Hayes left the series in 1939 due to a salary dispute with producer Harry Sherman, and was replaced for a few films by Britt Wood before Clyde was hired. Clyde played California Carlson in the Cassidy western *Three Men from Texas* (1940) and stayed for the remainder of the series.

Andy's ability to play an old codger who was adept at being both comical and dramatic, and who could offset the serious plot and add comic relief, was considered very beneficial to the Hopalong Cassidy series. Audiences were familiar with Andy from his short comedies, and the western features expanded his audience and his fan base even further. Andy had a talent for getting along with everyone he worked with, and quickly became friends with William Boyd, Russell Hayden and Rand Brooks. Hayden told the author in a 1978 phone interview: "Andy Clyde was every bit as good a sidekick as Gabby Hayes was."[1] In 1944, when Andy's young son died, his Hopalong Cassidy cast mates attended the funeral along with his co-workers from Columbia and Sennett.

In 1944, the Hopalong Cassidy ceased production. Producer Harry Sherman wanted to produce other things, but William Boyd wanted the series to continue. Boyd took a real chance and mortgaged everything he owned to

Andy was as popular in westerns as he was in comedies.

buy the rights to the character from its creator, Clarence Mulford, and also buy all of the previous films from Harry Sherman. In 1946, Boyd resurrected the series and asked Andy to return. Clyde did, and remained until B westerns started to fall out of favor with audiences. The movie series ended in 1948.

In 1949, while still continuing his short comedy series at Columbia, Andy accepted a job playing Winks, the sidekick to cowboy actor Whip Wilson, in a series of films at Monogram. He left that series in 1952 when William Boyd brought Hopalong Cassidy to television and again asked Andy to return to his role as California. Along with shooting new half-hour shows, Boyd began a marketing campaign, selling lunchboxes, drinking cups, cereal bowls and other merchandise. It made him a millionaire.

By the 1950s, Andy no longer was appearing in feature films, and focused on his short comedy series and the new medium of television.

Andy's comic persona made him a good comic sidekick in features. He didn't actively look for roles that would give him star billing or a big paycheck, but was content with doing his best work in whatever roles came his way, and therefore was able to remain employed for so many years.

IV

Clyde on Television

By the 1950s, production costs for short comedies had increased and budgets became tighter. Producer Jules White cut costs by remaking older films and shooting a few new scenes, then marketing them as new product. Thus, Andy Clyde's workload at Columbia plummeted to only a few days per year.

To supplement his income, Clyde investigated opportunities in television. He agreed to repeat his role as California in the new *Hopalong Cassidy* TV series in 1952. He later appeared in other westerns (*Death Valley Days*), dramatic teleplays (*Santa's Old Suit*) and sitcoms (*My Little Margie*) until production on his short comedy series ceased completely in 1956. That year he sought steadier work in television, finally landing the role of Colonel Jack on *Circus Boy* featuring Micky Dolenz, who later became one of the pop group The Monkees. At the same time Andy was doing *Circus Boy*, he also appeared on the sitcoms *The People's Choice* and *The Bob Cummings Show* and played a featured role on *The Adventures of Rin Tin Tin*.

For the remainder of the 1950s and into the early 1960s, Clyde continued to freelance on various shows, including a recurring role on *The Tall Man*, a couple of *Gunsmoke* episodes and a memorable one-shot on *The Andy Griffith Show*. In 1963 he signed on to play the character of George MacMichael in the series *The Real McCoys*. Series star Walter Brennan told *TV Guide* in its November 19, 1960, issue: "Andy Clyde is a genuine professional, a joy to work with as an actor and to know as a friend. He can get laughs with just one look. He is a valuable part of the show"[1] Andy stayed with *The Real McCoys* from 1957 until 1963.

From 1959 to 1964, while appearing on *The Real McCoys*, Clyde was also featured as Cully Wilson on the *Lassie* TV series. Series star Jon Provost, who played Timmy, fondly recalled working with Andy:

> I adored Andy Clyde. The show had several adults, two dogs and me. Many of the adult actors responded to the series as just another job. They were professionals and did good work, but it was just work to them. Andy really seemed to love being there. He loved to work. He was a little guy, so as a kid I responded to that. And he always

made me laugh. Our director, William Beaudine, went back to silent movies and was pretty demanding at times. But Andy could always handle him. They understood each other. Andy was always adding little things to make the scene funnier. He was really wonderful to work with and to know.

After Andy appeared on *Lassie*, he played Grandpa on the *No Time for Sergeants* TV series (1964–1965). In 1966, he made one last *Lassie* appearance, but not in the Cully Wilson role. The series no longer featured Jon Provost as Timmy, and now starred Robert Bray as Corey Stuart. Andy did an episode where he played a farmer in a dispute with another over the possession of a cow.

Andy and Jon Provost share a laugh on the *Lassie* set.

Clyde remained active until his death on May 18, 1967. He was not ill, he just passed away peacefully in his sleep of a sudden heart attack. His wife (since 1932), Elsie Harron, survived him. Andy was 75 years old. He was buried next to his son. Elsie married Andy's dear friend George Gray, another Sennett actor, but he died only four weeks after their wedding. Elsie never remarried, and died in October 1990.

Andy Clyde's legacy lasted from the silent era into the television years. Throughout his career, he made many friends and no enemies. Of all the many highlights of his long career, his 79 Columbia comedies are among his best work. Jules White recalled for the author:

> I am proud of the pictures we made. We kept people like Harry Langdon and Buster Keaton employed. Our Stooges pictures got put on TV and never left the air. I couldn't tell you who was the funniest, or the cleverest, or the smartest person we had, but I can tell you the nicest. That would be Andy Clyde.[2]

Notes

I. Before Columbia

1. "Water Wagons," *The Exhibitor's Trade Review*, February 21, 1925.
2. "The Bluffer," *Film Daily*, November, 1930.
3. Cal York, "Cal York's Monthly Broadcast from Hollywood," *Photoplay*, September, 1933.
4. Interview with the author, 1980.
5. Interview with the author, 1983.

II. The Columbia Comedy Shorts

1. "It's the Cat's," *Motion Picture Daily*, October 22, 1934.
2. "In the Dog House," *Motion Picture Herald*, December 8, 1934.
3. "In the Dog House," *Film Daily*, December 5, 1934.
4. "I'm a Father," *Variety*, June 12, 1935.
5. "I'm a Father," *Motion Picture Daily*, June 26, 1935.
6. James Curtis, "James Curtis: L.A. Voices—Jules White," *The Daily Mirror*, August 8, 2012.
7. Ted Okuda, with Ed Watz, *The Columbia Comedy Shorts*, Jefferson, NC: McFarland, 1986.
8. "Old Sawbones," *Motion Picture Daily*, May 5, 1935.
9. "Old Sawbones," *Motion Picture Herald*, May 11, 1935.
10. "A Little from The Lots," *Film Daily*, March 15, 1935.
11. "Alimony Aches," *Variety*, July 24, 1935.
12. "Alimony Aches," *Variety*, July 24, 1935.
13. "It Always Happens," *Variety*, October 23, 1935.
14. "Hot Paprika," *Film Daily*, April 28, 1936.
15. Edward Bernds, *Mr. Bernds Goes To Hollywood*, Metuchen, NJ: Scarecrow Press, 2000.
16. "Share the Wealth," *Film Daily*, May 9, 1936.
17. Bill Cassara, *Vernon Dent: Stooge Heavy*, Albany, GA: BearManor Books, 2015.
18. "The Peppery Salt," *Film Daily*, June 11, 1936.
19. "Mister Smarty," *Motion Picture Herald*, August 1, 1936.
20. "Am I Having Fun," *Motion Picture Daily*, November 11, 1936.
21. "What The Picture Did For Me," *Motion Picture Herald*, May 15, 1937.
22. "Weaver Stars in Two-Reeler," *The Stanford Daily*, May 13, 1937.
23. James Curtis, "James Curtis: L.A. Voices—Jules White," *The Daily Mirror*, August 8, 2012.
24. Steve Randisi, "Lifetime Contract," *Filmfax*.
25. "He Done His Duty," *Motion Picture Daily*, December 9, 1937.
26. "He Done His Duty," *Film Daily*, December 15, 1937.
27. James Curtis, "James Curtis: L.A. Voices—Jules White," *The Daily Mirror*, August 8, 2012.
28. Leonard Maltin, *The Great Movie Shorts*, New York: Crown Publishers, 1972.
29. Ralph Wilk, "A Little From The Lots," *Film Daily*, March 8, 1937.
30. "Swing You Swingers," *Showmen's Trade Review*, April 22, 1939.
31. "Exhibitor Comment," *Motion Picture Herald*, April 22, 1939.
32. "Trouble Finds Andy Clyde," *Showmen's Trade Review*, October 7, 1939.
33. Ted Okuda, with Ed Watz, *The Columbia Comedy Shorts*, Jefferson, NC: McFarland, 1986.
34. Interview with the author, 2017.
35. This same gag also appears in the 1949 Three Stooges comedy *The Ghost Talks*, made while Shemp was a part of that trio.
36. This gag would later be used by Curly

Howard in the 1945 Three Stooges short *Dizzy Detectives*, also directed by Jules White.

37. "What The Picture Did For Me," *Motion Picture World*, March 15, 1941.

38. "Andy Clyde Signed for Hopalongs," *Motion Picture Herald*, April 6, 1940.

39. Ted Okuda, with Ed Watz, *The Columbia Comedy Shorts*, Jefferson, NC: McFarland, 1986.

40. "How Spry I Am," *Variety*, May 6, 1942.

41. "What the Picture Did For Me," *Motion Picture Herald*, October 21, 1942.

42. "Sappy Pappy," *Film Daily*, November 18, 1942.

43. "Sappy Pappy," *Showmen's Trade Review*, December 5, 1942.

44. Scoop Conlon, "The Uncanny Scot," *Hollywood*, June, 1938.

45. "He Was Only Feudin'," *Film Daily*, January 21, 1944.

46. Interview with the author, 1980.

47. "Andy Plays Hookey," at EmilSitka.com.

48. "Two Jills and a Jack," *Film Daily*, May 27, 1947.

49. Interview with the author, 1983.

50. Emil Sitka, "The Fourth Stooge," at www.emilsitka.com.

51. Ted Okuda, with Ed Watz, *The Columbia Comedy Shorts*, Jefferson, NC: McFarland, 1986.

52. *Ibid.*

53. *Ibid.*

54. *Ibid.*

III. Clyde in Feature Films

1. Interview with the author, 1978.

IV. Clyde on Television

1. Andy Clyde feature, *TV Guide*, November 19, 1960.

2. Interview with the author, 1980.

Bibliography

Books

Anthony, Brian, and Andy Edmonds. *Smile When the Raindrops Fall*. Lanham, MD: Scarecrow Press, 1998.

Bernds, Edward. *Mr. Bernds Goes to Hollywood*. Metuchen, NJ: Scarecrow Press, 2000.

Bowles, Stephen E. *The Film Anthologies Index*. Metuchen, NJ: Scarecrow Press, 1994.

Cassara, Bill. *Vernon Dent: Stooge Heavy*. Albany, GA: BearManor Books, 2015.

Doyle, Billy H. *The Ultimate Directory of Silent and Sound Era Performers*. Scarecrow Press, 1999.

Durgnat, Raymond. *The Crazy Mirror: Hollywood Comedy and the American Image*. New York: Horizon Press, 1969.

Forrester, Jeffrey. *The Three Stooges Chronicles*. Chicago: Contemporary, 1984.

Kerr, Walter. *The Silent Clowns*. New York: Alfred A. Knopf, 1975.

Lahue, Karlton C., and Samuel Gill. *Clown Princes and Court Jesters*. South Brunswick, NJ: A.S. Barnes, 1970.

Maltin, Leonard. *The Great Movie Shorts*. New York: Crown Publishers, 1972.

Massa, Steve. *Lame Brains and Lunatics*. Atlanta: BearManor Media, 2013.

Mast, Gerald. *The Comic Mind*. New York: Bobbs-Merrill, 1973.

Okuda, Ted, with Ed Watz. *The Columbia Comedy Shorts*. Jefferson, N.C.: McFarland, 1986.

Roots, James. *The 100 Greatest Silent Film Comedians*. Lanham, MD: Rowman & Littlefield, 2014.

Sennett, Mack. *King of Comedy*. New York: Doubleday, 1954.

Walker, Brent. *Mack Sennett's Fun Factory*. Jefferson, NC: McFarland, 2010.

Articles

Andy Clyde feature, *TV Guide*, November 19, 1960.

"Andy Clyde Signed for Hopalongs," *Motion Picture Herald*, April 6, 1940.

Conlon, Scoop. "The Uncanny Scot." *Hollywood*, June, 1938.

Curtis, James. "James Curtis: L.A. Voices—Jules White." *The Daily, Mirror*, August 8, 2012.

"Columbia's Four Comics." *Variety*, June 19, 1934.

Exhibitor Letter *Motion Picture Herald*, April 22, 1939.

Randisi, Steve. "Lifetime Contract." *Filmfax*, January, 1995.

"Weaver Stars in Two-Reeler." *The Stanford Daily*, May 13, 1937.

Wilk, Ralph "A Little from the Lots." *Film Daily*, March 8, 1937.

York, Cal. "Cal York's Monthly Broadcast from Hollywood." *Photoplay*, September, 1933.

Reviews

"Alimony Aches." *Variety*, July 24, 1935.

"Am I Having Fun." *Motion Picture Daily*, November 11, 1936.

"The Bluffer." *Film Daily*, November, 1930.

"He Done His Duty." *Motion Picture Daily*, December 9, 1937.

"He Done His Duty." *Film Daily*, December 15, 1937.
"He Was Only Feudin'." *Film Daily*, January 21, 1944.
"How Spry I Am." *Variety*, May 6, 1942.
"I'm a Father." *Motion Picture Daily*, June 26, 1935.
"I'm a Father." *Variety*, June 12, 1935.
"In the Dog House." *Film Daily*, December 5, 1934.
"In the Dog House." *Motion Picture Herald*, December 8, 1934.
"It Always Happens." *Variety*, October 23, 1935.
"It's the Cat's." *Motion Picture Daily*, October 22, 1934.
"Mister Smarty." *Motion Picture Herald*, August 1, 1936.
"Old Sawbones." *Motion Picture Daily*, May 5, 1935.
"Old Sawbones." *Motion Picture Herald*, May 11, 1935.
"The Peppery Salt." *Film Daily*, June 11, 1936.
"Sappy Pappy." *Film Daily*, November 18, 1942.
"Sappy Pappy." *Showmen's Trade Review*, December 5, 1942.
"Share the Wealth." *Film Daily*. May 9, 1936.
"Swing You Swingers." *Showmen's Trade Review*, April 22, 1939.
"Trouble Finds Andy Clyde." *Showmen's Trade Review*, October 7, 1939.
"Water Wagons." *The Exhibitor's Trade Review*, February 21, 1925.

Exhibitor Comments

Motion Picture Herald: in their regular feature "What The Picture Did For Me," theater owners commented on how films fared in their theater. These comments are interspersed throughout the text.

Interviews

Lorna Gray (Adrian Booth), 2017
Jon Provost, 2017
Jules White, 1980
Emil Sitka, 1980, 1983
Edward Bernds, 1985
Russell Hayden, 1978

Online

"Emil Sitka: The Fourth Stooge," http://www.emilsitka.com
Internet Movie Database
Wikipedia

Index

Abbott and Costello 99
An Ache in Every Stake 124
Adler, Felix 92, 115, 143, 145, 150, 179, 190
The Adventures of Rin Tin Tin 194
Alimony Aches 27–29, 54, 114
All American Blondes 90–92
All Night Long 122
All Work and No Pay 126–128, 129, 136
Allen, Barbara Jo 124
Am I Having Fun 47–50
Anderson, Clay 175
Andy Clyde Gets Spring Chicken 92–94, 180
Andy Goes Wild 188–190
The Andy Griffith Show 194
Andy Hardy Gets Spring Fever 93
Andy Plays Hooky 160–163
Ankles Away 73–75, 104
Annie Oakley 192
Appleby, Dorothy 105, 178, 180
Arbuckle, Fatty 35

Baby Sitters Jitters 176
Bachelor Daze 132
Back to the Soil 146
Bad Lands 192
The Barker 111
The Barrier 66
Bartlett, Benny 11, 81, 83, 182, 184
Bates, Kathryn 78
The Battle of the Century 23
Beaudine, William 195
Benchley, Robert 86
Bennison, Andrew 11, 14
Bernds, Edward 35, 155, 156, 157, 160, 162, 164, 166, 167, 168, 188
Besser, Joe 1, 10, 171, 176, 184, 190, 191; *see also* Three Stooges
Bevan, Billy 4, 5
Big Business 23
Black, Preston *see* White, Jack
Blake, Gladys 158
Blanc, Mel 147
A Blissful Blunder 11, 105, 177–178
A Blitz on the Fritz 132
Block-Heads 55, 154

Blonde Atom Bomb 175–176
The Blonde Stayed On 156–158
The Bluffer 6–7
A Blunderful Time 173–175
Blythe, Betty 138–139
Bond, Tommy 27, 29, 44, 53–55, 86
Bonney, Gail 182
Boobs in the Woods 100–103, 122, 123
Boom Goes the Groom 84–86
Booth, Adrian *see* Lorna Gray
Born Reckless 14
The Bowery Boys Meet the Monsters 184
Boyd, William 104, 156, 180, 192, 193
Bray, Robert 195
Brooks, Rand 192
Brown, Joe E. 62
Bruckman, Clyde 161, 163, 166
Buckley, Buz 145, 179–180
A Bundle of Bliss 11, 104–107, 177
Burns, Bobby 26

Cash and Carry 152
Catlett, Walter 9, 39
Caught in the Act 36–38
Chaney, Lon 111
Chaplin, Charlie 1, 2, 35, 115
Chase, Charley 20, 22, 29, 55, 63, 64, 66, 67, 68, 69, 71, 73, 74, 84, 96, 88, 104, 111, 112, 114, 124, 169, 170, 190
Cherokee Strip 104, 192
A Chump at Oxford 154
Clayton, John Bell 69
Clayton, Paul 124, 126
Clooney, Rosemary 184
Clyde, John (Andy's father) 3
Clyde, John (Andy's son) 24, 105, 148, 150
Cohn, Harry 9, 29, 62, 188, 191
Compson, Betty 110–111
Conklin Heinie 26, 160
Crime on their Hands 128
Curtis, Dick 84, 85, 86, 90, 173, 174
Curtis, James 20, 67, 73

Dawn, Mary 124–126
A Day with Doodles 62

Dean, Margia 180
Death Valley Days 181, 194
Dent, Vernon 39, 41, 63, 69, 70, 73, 74, 79, 80, 81, 90, 95, 97, 104, 111, 115, 117, 119, 123, 126, 128, 133, 134, 136, 138, 141, 143, 148, 150, 156, 158, 159, 160, 163, 164, 167, 168, 181, 189
DeRita, Joe 2, 54, 133; *see also* Three Stooges
Dickerson, Dudley 111, 114, 117, 118, 119, 155, 169, 170, 187, 190
DiMaggio, Joe 64
Divot Diggers 35
Dix, Mary Lou 42, 173
Dix, Richard 104
The Docks of New York 111
Dodd, Jimmie 108, 109
Dogville Melody 8
Doran, Ann 63, 67, 69, 71, 74, 88, 119, 141
Dora's Dunking Donuts 6-8
Duck Soup 62
A Ducking They Did Go 14
Duggan, Jan 28-29

Edwards, Harry 94, 100, 111, 117, 119, 121, 122, 124, 128, 139, 140, 141, 143, 148, 149, 150, 155, 156, 157, 158, 163, 187
Eight-Ball Andy 167-169
Errol, Leon 9, 16, 39, 55, 114, 152, 172, 178

Farley, Dot 24, 26
Farmer for a Day 116, 136-139
Fields, W.C. 29, 99, 160-161
Fighting Fluid 74
Fine, Larry 9, 78
Fireman Save My Choo Choo 103-104
Flying Saucer Daffy 191
French, Lloyd 122
Fresh Painter 181

Garvin, Anita 23, 86
Gates, Maxine 180
Gay, Betsy 124, 125, 126
Gehrig, Lou 64
Gilbert, Jody 137
Go Chase Yourself 169-170
Godfrey Ruth 178
Gold Is Where You Lose It 145-148
Gracie at the Bat 63-67, 91, 120, 121
Gray, George 50, 54, 111, 112, 124, 195
Gray, Lorna 92, 94, 180
The Great Dictator 115
Grey, John 44, 121, 124, 128
Gribbon, Eddie 26
Griffith, D.W. 1

Half Baked Relations 76
Half Wits Holiday 11
Hamilton, Lloyd 160
Hardy, Oliver 16; *see also* Laurel and Hardy
Hayden, Russell 104, 192
Hayes, Gabby 104, 192
He Cooked His Goose 10

He Done His Duty 53, 58, 67, 68, 69, 130
He Was Only Feudin' 139-141
Healy, Ted 9, 14, 78
Heather and Yon 148-189
The Heckler 64
Herbert, Hugh 18, 117, 118, 141, 158, 170, 176
His Tale is Told 30 141-143
His Weak Moment 8
His Wooden Wedding 74
Home on the Rage 79-81, 98, 104
Hook, Line and Sinker 34
Hooked and Rooked 179-180
Horne, James 17-20, 79, 81
Host to a Ghost 117-119, 187
Hot Icei 128
Hot Paprika 32-35, 41, 52
Housman, Arthur 30, 48, 49
How Spry I Am 124-126, 155
Howard, Curly 9, 78, 146, 148; *see also* Three Stooges
Howard, Esther 30, 32, 50, 53, 56, 100, 12, 103, 104, 119, 122, 123, 129, 130, 131, 143, 145, 150, 152, 159, 160, 177, 186
Howard, Moe 9, 78, 190; *see also* Three Stooges
Howard, Olin 71
Howard, Shemp 1, 2, 10, 64, 76-81, 97-102, 123, 138 148, 150, 166, 169, 190; *see also* Three Stooges
Hurlock, Madeline 5

Ice Cold Cocos 5
Idiots Deluxe 77-79
I'll Never Heil Again 115
I'll Take Vanilla 29, 86
I'm a Father 17-20
In the Dog House 15-17, 28, 114
It Always Happens 30-32, 141, 142
It's the Cats 11-15, 16, 38

Jail Bait 149
Jamison, Bud 8, 21, 27, 30, 32, 36, 39, 44, 47, 50, 54, 56, 63, 67, 69, 70, 71, 75, 76, 78, 86, 97, 100, 102, 108, 115, 117, 126, 130, 141, 143, 145, 148, 158
Jump Chump Jump 71-73

Keaton, Buster 1, 2, 9, 111, 145, 148, 149, 195
Keaton, Harry 41,172
Kelsey, Fred 11, 104, 105, 115, 159, 160, 177, 178
Kennedy, Edgar 16, 23, 26, 55, 114, 152, 172
Kennedy, Tom 115, 117, 176, 177
Kids Will Be Kids 126
Knee Action 53-55, 86, 114

Lamb, Gil 152, 172, 178, 181
Lamont, Charles 24-29, 53, 59, 67
Langdon, Harry 4, 9, 17, 22, 39, 55, 67, 74, 75, 111, 122, 123, 141, 148, 152, 158, 195
Lassie TV series 3, 194, 195

Index

Laurel and Hardy 20, 23, 29, 35, 49, 55, 72, 75, 81, 88, 114, 124, 145, 154, 164
League of Their Own 64
Leavitt, Douglas 138
Leopold, Ethelreda 180
Lewis, Jerry 34, 62
Lipson, Jack "Tiny" 102
Liszt, Margie 174, 177, 180
Little Rascals *see* Our Gang
Lloyd, Harod 145
Lodge Night 60–62, 166
Long, Huey 41
Lord, Del 5, 20, 21, 22, 27, 30, 31, 35, 36–40, 41–43, 63, 71–72, 75–76, 79, 86, 88, 90–92, 94, 100–103, 104–106, 108, 111–112, 117–119, 126–129, 133–136, 141–143, 148, 187
Lovable Trouble 119–121, 136
Love's A-Poppin' 180–181
Lumière, Auguste, and Louis 1
Lynn, Emmett 129, 130, 132, 143, 145, 146, 176, 179

Mack, Betty 68
A Maid Made Mad 133–136
Malmgren, Russell 156
Maltin, Leonard 74
Marinated Mariner 10, 42, 172–175, 176, 275
Marx Brothers 62
McClung, Robert 50, 67, 68
McCollum, Hugh 62, 63, 66, 67, 69, 74, 84, 86, 88, 90, 92, 94, 111, 119, 122, 126, 133, 139, 150, 155, 164, 167, 170, 178
McCoy, Harry 32, 35
McHugh, Matt 108, 122, 123, 138, 166, 169l
McIntyre, Christine 158, 164, 166, 167, 174
McKenzie, Eva 180
McKenzie, Robert 30, 32, 44, 51, 52, 54, 67, 68, 69, 79, 108, 132, 186
Méliès, George 1
Meyers, Zion 8–9
Mickey Mouse Club 109
Mills, Frank 117–18
A Miner Affair 152–155, 185
Mr. Clyde Goes to Broadway 94–97, 114, 168
Mr. Noisy 64
Mister Smarty 44–47, 50, 171
Mr. Smith Goes to Washington 78
Mitchell, Geneva 17, 30, 32, 160
Mitchell, Jackie 64
Moffat, Graham 4
Money Squawks 97–100
Morgan, Gene 83, 74, 79, 81, 104
Muir, Esther 30, 32
Mulford, Clarence 193
Murray, Charles 146
My Little Feller 58–60, 62
My Little Margie 194

A Night at the Opera 62
No Time for Sergeants 195
Normand, Mabel 35

Norton, Jack 141, 143, 148, 150
Not Guilty Enough 76, 77, 80, 98
Now It Can Be Sold 86–88

Oakland, Vivien 15–17, 27–28, 54–55, 84, 94, 111, 114, 128
Oh Say Can You Sue 181–182
Oily to Bed Oily to Rise 14
Okuda, Ted 21, 91, 124, 172, 175, 188, 191
The Old Raid Mule 69–71, 72
Old Sawbones 20–24, 100
On Again Off Again 150
One of the Smiths 69
One Shivery Night 118
One Spooky Night 187–188
Our Gang 1, 29, 35, 54, 55, 72, 86, 91, 97, 99, 100, 126, 152, 184
Our Relations 88

Pardon My Clutch 102
Pardon My Nightshirt 190–191
Pardon My Wrench 181
Pardon Us 35
People's Choice 194
Pepper, Barbara 134
The Peppery Salt 10, 41–44, 172–173
Picking Peaches 74
Pies and Guys 11
Pleasure Treasure 176–177
Porter, Edwin S. 1
Presley, Elvis 184
Prickett, Maudie 169
Provost, Jon 194–195

Railroad Stowaways see *Whispering Whiskers*
Randisi, Steve 67, 71
Ray, Al 11, 14, 36, 38, 41, 47
The Real McCoy (1930) 69
Real McCoys TV series 2, 71, 194
Richmond, Warner 173
Ring and the Belle 111–114, 122
Roach, Hal 20, 23, 29, 63, 68, 86, 114, 124, 154, 164
Rogers, Charley 152, 153, 154, 185
Rooney, Mickey 93
Ruth, Babe 64

Santa's Old Suit 194
Sappy Birthday 121–126, 129
Sappy Pappy 128–129, 134
Saps at Sea 154
Saturday Afternoon 122, 158
Scrambled Brains 176
Scratch Scratch Scratch 186
Sennett, Mack 1, 5–9, 20, 21, 26, 27, 30, 35, 39, 41, 111, 112, 117, 122, 123, 136, 141, 145, 148, 152, 160, 192, 195
Share the Wealth 39, 40, 41
Sherman, Harry 104, 192, 193
Should Married Men Go Home 23
Sidewalks of New York 9

Sidney, George 147
Sitka, Emil 9, 160, 162, 164, 165, 166, 175, 176
Soldier Man 122
The Soul of a Heel 75-76
Soup To Nuts 78
Southern Exposure 69
Spook to Me 155-156
Stanwyck, Barbara 192
Strife of the Party 124
Stuck in the Sticks 53-57, 67, 130
Summerville, Slim 132
Sunk in the Sink 171-172
Sutton, Gertrude 71, 72, 75, 76, 145
Swing You Swingers 11, 92-83, 182-184

Tarron, Elsie (Mrs. Andy Clyde) 8, 104, 105, 139
Tassles in the Air 78
Temple, Shirley 6-8
Thatcher, Leora 44, 47, 50, 58, 63
Them Thar Hills 154
Thicker Than Water 154
Three Arabian Nuts 176
Three Men from Texas 192
Three Stooges 1, 9, 10, 11, 13, 14, 22, 24, 36, 38, 39, 49, 50, 55, 60, 64, 67, 71, 76, 77, 78, 91, 93, 100, 102, 104, 115, 116, 117, 124, 128, 132, 145, 146, 147, 148, 149, 152, 154, 158, 162, 170, 171, 173, 176, 184, 185, 186, 188, 190, 191, 195
Tit for Tat 154
Too Many Highballs 160-161
Tooting Tooters 11, 82, 182-184
Tramp Tramp Tramp (1926) 122, 158
Tramp Tramp Tramp (1935) 24-27
Triple Crossed 10
Trouble Finds Andy Clyde 88-90, 173, 174
Turner, Joe 184
Turpin, Ben 4, 5, 104
Two April Fools 185
Two Jills and a Jack 163-164, 181
Two Local Yokels 150-151
Tyrrell, John 81, 184

Ullman, Ellwood 53, 63, 90, 91, 92, 94, 108, 117, 164, 167, 176, 187
Urecal, Minerva 175

Vague, Vera *see* Barbara Jo Allen
Vallon, Kay 180

The Watchman Takes a Wife 108-111
Water Wagons 5
Watson, Delmar 15-16
Watz, Edward 21, 91, 124, 172, 175, 188, 191
Way Out West 81, 154
Weaver, Doodles 58-61, 62, 166, 175
Wessel, Dick 161, 165, 166, 169, 189
Whispering Whiskers 5
White, Jack 17, 20, 32, 35, 39, 40, 41, 44, 45, 47, 50, 56, 60, 124, 129, 141, 171, 176, 177, 179, 180, 181, 182, 185, 186, 187, 188
White, Jules 1, 9, 11, 12, 14, 15, 17, 20, 21, 24, 27, 29, 30, 32, 35, 36, 38, 39, 41, 44, 47, 50, 52, 53, 55, 58, 59, 60, 63, 66, 67, 71, 72, 73, 74, 75, 76, 78, 79, 81, 82, 83, 84, 88, 89, 91, 92, 93, 94, 95, 97, 98, 99, 100, 103, 104, 105, 108, 111, 115, 116, 124, 126, 128, 129, 132, 136, 143, 145, 146, 147, 148, 150, 152, 159, 160, 163, 164, 166, 169, 170, 171, 172, 173, 175, 176, 177, 178, 179, 180, 181, 182, 184, 185, 186, 187, 188, 190, 191, 194, 195
Wilson, Whip 193
Wolf in Thief's Clothing 129-233, 245
Woman Haters 1, 14
Wood, Britt 192
Woodbury, Joan 61, 62, 175

Yankee Doodle Andy 115-117
Yes We Have No Bonanza 146
The Yoke's On Me 132
You Can't Fool a Fool 159-160
You Nazty Spy 115
You Were Never Uglier 143, 145, 179
You're Darn Tootin' 23

www.ingramcontent.com/pod-product-compliance
Ingram Content Group UK Ltd.
Pitfield, Milton Keynes, MK11 3LW, UK
UKHW042004140426
5217IPUK00015B/978